BULLS, BEARS, AND BRAINS

BULLS, BEARS, AND BRAINS

Investing with the Best and Brightest
of the Financial Internet

Adam Leitzes
Joshua Solan

John Wiley & Sons, Inc.

Published by John Wiley & Sons, Inc.
Published simultaneously in Canada.

This publication is designed to provide accurate and authoritative information in regard to the subject matter covered. It is sold with the understanding that the publisher is not engaged in rendering professional services. If professional advice or other expert assistance is required, the services of a competent professional person should be sought.

Library of Congress Cataloging-in-Publication Data

Leitzes, Adam.
    Bulls, bears, and brains : investing with the best and brightest of the financial
  Internet / by Adam Leitzes & Joshua Solan.
      p. cm.
    Includes index.
    ISBN 0-471-44294-1 (cloth : alk. paper)
      1. Investments—Computer network resources. 2. Internet. 3. Electronic trading of
  securities. I. Solan, Joshua. II. Title.

  HG4515.95 .L45 2001
  332.6'0285'4678—dc21

                                   2001046614

Printed in the United States of America

10 9 8 7 6 5 4 3 2 1

To our mothers,
for 21 years of love.

ACKNOWLEDGMENTS

Writing a book is no easy task. Writing a book at the age of 20 while maintaining a healthy college lifestyle is an even greater challenge. Without the support of dozens of individuals and organizations, we would hardly have gotten off the ground in the process, let alone completed the final manuscript. First and foremost, we would like to thank the University of Pennsylvania, and in particular the Wharton School and the School of Engineering and Applied Science. We appreciate the University of Pennsylvania's eagerness to extend learning beyond the classroom by encouraging students to tackle entrepreneurial and creative projects. William F. Hamilton, director of the Jerome Fisher Program in Management and Technology, served as our academic advisor over the course of 18 months and helped us balance our commitments as students and authors. Professors Joao F. Gomes and John D. Keenan offered helpful advice and encouragement, and Michael Baltes and Nancy Shils went out of their way to put us in touch with important university resources.

Family members were critical editors, contributors, and supporters from day one of this book's life. Our mothers, Judy Leitzes and Merrill Solan, added their literary flair to the manuscript, and our fathers, Michael Leitzes and Andrew Solan, contributed valuable views from the individual-investor perspective. Not a single day passed during the planning, writing, and editing of this book that our parents were not consulted on a variety of issues. For their lifelong support and love, we owe them an enormous amount of gratitude. Special thanks must go to Martin Leitzes, who opened up many doors and gave at least one of this book's authors his first true glimpse of Wall Street and investing. Nearly every member of our extended families played a role in the creation of this book, and we would like to acknowledge Myles Silton, Jennifer Leitzes, Jon Hoeber, Jackie Leitzes, Pauline Leitzes, Harvey Silton, Leah Silton, Amy Solan, and Alex Leitzes.

Thanks to all of our closest friends and acquaintances at school for enduring endless months of discussions about all things Internet and investing. We are indebted to Kim Nguyen and Jen Burgess for putting up with our stock market obsessions and for the many hours they devoted to reading and revising. Hats off to John De Palma for sharing contrarian wisdom far beyond his college age. The following people warrant our deepest appreciation for their candid outside opinions and support: Steve Samuel, Howard Kritzer, Scott Pollack, Samir Dhruva, Dan Mahoney, Luke Fronefield, and George Nachtrieb.

Although we've been attending school since age 5 and have yet to complete our academic duties, we are grateful for a number of enlightening work experiences and invaluable mentors. David Bellet and Geoff Block of Crown Advisors have displayed a passion for investing that not only helped to inspire this book but also shaped our desire to attend the Wharton School and pursue careers in business. We have benefited greatly from the guidance and encouragement of Matthew Schifrin and everyone else at Forbes. Buzzy Geduld and the traders at Herzog Heine Geduld provided a priceless picture of the mechanics of the stock market. The entire team at Broadview International gave a valuable and informative inside look at the world of finance and investment banking. Thanks also to Adam Winnick, Andrew Murray, Brendan McDermott, and the rest of the ITU Ventures team for their support during the final months of editing.

We would like to express our sincere appreciation to Joan O'Neil, Debra Englander, and Greg Friedman of John Wiley & Sons for believing in this project and for supporting two first-time authors each step along the way. Paul McCurdy of Graphic Composition, Inc., was extraordinarily accommodating and helpful throughout the copyediting process. Last, but most certainly not least, a great thanks to our agent Jim Fitzgerald of the Carol Mann Agency, who taught us the book publishing ropes and offered valuable advice at every juncture.

Finally, this book would not have been possible without the cooperation of the investors, traders, strategists, and visionaries who agreed to be interviewed. Our understanding of financial markets was expanded many times over as a result of hours of fascinating conversations with these individuals. Their insights will remain with us for years to come, and we hope this book will allow others to share in their extraordinary knowledge and expertise.

CONTENTS

"There is no formula for this. It's all about risk taking and
judgment and being right. You hear people say stupid things like,
'No rewards without risk.' That makes you think, 'Well, if I want
rewards, I just have to go out and take as much risk as I possibly
can. That means I'll get rewards.' It may not be false, but it's
certainly not true. The only rewards you're going to get in this
business are by being right."

"I'm probably the only short seller who stays away from the
Nasdaq. People look at the Nasdaq and say, 'That's really
overpriced.' And they're right. But then again, knowing that the
Nasdaq is overpriced and being able to sell short on it are two
different things, as a lot of people learned in 1999."

"Corporations were invented in the twelfth century, and up until
the 1930s for-profit businesses were never successful as widely
held public corporations; insiders always stole the money. It was
only with the adoption of accounting standards—the Securities
and Exchange Acts of 1933, 1934, and 1940—that we got the
existing system of corporate governance. It worked for about 20
years, from 1945 to 1965, after which management quickly
learned how to co-opt the boards."

"If there is one single piece of advice that I could give to every investor in the world—if they only got one message from me—it's to have a sell rule. People ask Warren Buffett, 'When do you sell stock?' And he says, 'Never.' You know what that is? That is the arrogance of the rich. The arrogance of the rich is this notion that you can tell somebody who's finally saved up $5,000—and they don't want to get 4 percent on a money market—to buy and hold. That is just as extreme as any day-trading philosophy."

"I ask, 'Am I going to be at an informational loss? Am I starting off with a couple of strikes against me?' There's always somebody that's selling me that stock; they could have good reasons for selling me the stock—maybe they know more than I do. After you've been in the business as long as I have, you build up a whole bunch of prejudices that help you filter out a lot of information so you can focus on what's important."

"The e-commerce thing lasted a year. The Linux thing lasted three months. Now, three or four days is a sustained rally in one of these sectors. It's hot money looking for a place to go, and in a bear market, you get huge time compressions in these rallies. Nobody wants to hold a hot potato—but everyone is looking for it."

"Most people only know how to make money when the rising tide is raising all boats. In that case, you don't have to know anything—you buy every dip, and then you pray. That's what I call the ostrich approach. You buy a stock today, you take a nap, and you hope everything is okay when you wake up—it takes no skill. But when that market environment stops, when the drummer stops beating, when the sun dies down, what are you going to do?"

"A community spread around the world has got to be the best possible collective research team, definitely better than Salomon Smith Barney, Merrill Lynch, or Morgan Stanley—people stuck in a New York office. People on discussion boards are all around the world, researching new ideas, working in new industries, with their fingers on the pulses of hundreds of different emerging companies."

18. Beauty and the Street: Karin Housley   253

"Money is very important to women, but it's not number one on
our list. I think that we can put it all in perspective much more
easily than men can. When the stock market has a down day, we
just say, 'You know what, I'm going to go to the park with the
kids. Screw the market.' But guys, they go to sleep with it."

19. Wharton Wizard: Jeremy Siegel   265

"Very few individuals have had very good investment
performance that cannot be attributed in large part to luck.
Unfortunately, there is also a psychological propensity in that the
average individual sees somebody win three, four, five times in a
row and believes he's a winner. Go to the craps table in any
casino. Once somebody starts winning four, five, six times,
everyone thinks, 'Boy, this guy's a winner!' Well, you know, the
probability that he's going to lose on the next roll is no different
now than it was on the very first roll he made."

20. The Mathematician Meets the Markets: Suri Duddella   275

"Educated and savvy investors should at least use basic
indicators—not blindly go and buy Intels and Ciscos because
they are the best companies. If you know that this company has a
negative momentum built in and the stock is going to fall, you
shouldn't go and buy it just because it's cheap."

21. King of the Market Meritocracy: Ken Kam   287

"Most people's jobs offer them much more relevant investment
information on a day-to-day basis than an analyst's job does. An
analyst is able to talk to top management, but top management
is always going to give an optimistic spin. The people who really
know what is going on are the sales reps, the people who take
orders, the people scheduling the production floor."

BULLS, BEARS,
AND BRAINS

INTRODUCTION

With all the talk of bits, bytes, and bandwidth, we often forget that the Internet is, at its core, a network of interconnected people. Behind the screen, at the other end of thousands of miles of fiber-optic cable and telephone wire, in another state or in another country, there are actual human beings—human beings with thoughts, stories, ideas, philosophies, skills, and expertise.

Some of those human beings are incredibly talented investors. Some of them are economics experts. Some of them are technical analysis wizards. Some of them are super-successful, trigger-happy day traders. Some of them are multimillionaire long-term investors. And many of them are willing to lend a helping hand in the complex game of investing.

Before we delve any further, let's get a few things straight. This is not a book about investing *on* the Internet. This is not a book about investing *in* the Internet. This is a book about investing *with* the Internet and capitalizing on an investment approach that was not possible prior to the Internet.

This book is an interactive journey that introduces you to some of the world's most talented and successful investors and then shows you how to *connect with them* and *invest with them* on an ongoing basis. We think that the investing tool kit revealed in this book will be the key to prospering in the hypercompetitive financial markets of the next decade and beyond. A simple fact: Two heads are better than one. Unless you disagree, we suggest you read on.

Bear with us as we take a short detour from financial markets for a moment and consider the world of sports. "I want to be like Mike" is the phrase that Gatorade used in its sports-drink marketing campaign featuring basketball superstar Michael Jordan. The obvious implication of this advertising slogan is that consumers could match Jordan's level of skill by indulging in nutritious gulps of Gatorade's fluorescent juice drinks. Even though the slogan became an international hit, we doubt that anyone improved his or her athletic ability as a result of Gatorade consumption.

The truth is that it's impossible to "be like Mike." You can read an article about Michael Jordan in a magazine or newspaper, but that won't improve your layup. You can gawk at a poster of the basketball legend,

1

but that won't increase your chances of being drafted into the NBA. You can read any of the dozens of books written about Jordan's life, but don't expect the information to enhance your free-throw percentage.

So, you can't miraculously "be like Mike" by reading about Jordan, watching him play, or drinking Gatorade. But what if you could convince Michael Jordan to join your basketball team? With Jordan on your side, it's very likely that your team's performance would be well above average.

Now consider the same scenario in the investment world. You read a newspaper article about Warren Buffett, billionaire investor extraordinaire. Aside from its entertainment value, what does the article do for you? How does it improve your investment performance? Unless you're compelled to invest in Buffett's Berkshire Hathaway, the article is fairly useless. What you really want is Warren Buffett on your investment team.

Until now, there hasn't been a way to get the Michael Jordans of the investment world on your team. Financial superstars have never had any incentive to lend a helping hand. More simply, they've never had the means of connecting with the investing public on a continual basis. The only viable alternative has been to hand over your money to fund managers or other Wall Street professionals, thereby losing all investment autonomy. The Internet changes all that. This book changes all that.

We are not unabashed fans of the Internet. Despite all the hoopla, the Internet doesn't significantly change the investing game. With the Internet, you can make a stock trade at Schwab.com. Big deal! Prior to the Internet, you could walk into your local Schwab bricks-and-mortar office and make a trade or give your broker a call on the phone. With the web, you can perform fundamental research at Yahoo! Finance or Quicken.com. So what? For decades investors have been poring over fundamental research from services such as Value Line and Bloomberg. Online services let you analyze charts and assess financial metrics. Nothing new. Newspapers and financial rags have been providing the same information since the dawn of the stock market.

Although the Internet facilitates many investing tasks, simplicity alone will not generate superior investment returns. Obtaining an information edge is the key to beating the market. What information advantage does the Internet bring to the investing table that was never available before? Community. Interaction. Discussion. Networking.

The Internet provides top investors and traders with a low-cost method of distributing their investment ideas and strategies. How would you like to receive daily commentary from an ex–Goldman Sachs trader who worked under Nobel laureate Fischer Black and has registered annual gains in excess of 100 percent in the past several years? How would you like to access economic commentary and financial analysis from one of the most influential people on Wall Street? How would you like to chat daily with the author of several books on day trading or the manager of a successful hedge fund? How would you like to peek into the portfolio of a successful fund manager who mimics Warren Buffett's investment style?

You will learn how to do all of this and more within the pages of this book. You will be introduced to 20 successful investors, all of whom share their tips, picks, and tricks on the Internet. You will have a chance to read illuminating interviews with these individuals and learn about their investment strategies, successes, failures, and philosophies. Most important, you will discover how to connect with these individuals and invest *with* them on a go-forward basis via the Internet.

Get ready to play ball. More than a few Michael Jordans are about to join your investing team.

Chapter 1

BLOOD AND GUTS
MEET BITS AND BYTES

Bulls, Bears, and Everything In Between

The Internet is home to expert investors of all kinds—die-hard buy-and-hold Buffettologists, hyperactive day traders, slightly calmer momentum players, number-crunching technical analysts, passionate stock fundamentalists, cynical short-sale artists, discerning options traders, scholarly academics, and broad-minded economists. There are bulls, bears, and everything in between.

We have not discriminated against any types of financial-markets participants in this book. In the following pages you will read interviews with investors who approach the market with widely differing strategies. On the surface, some of the various moneymaking methods discussed in this book may appear to be in conflict with each other. As you progress through the book and come to understand fully the tenets of the individuals whom we profile, however, the lines between investing styles will begin to blur. Technical analysis will become a necessary complement to fundamental research. Options will become tools for understanding the price movements of equities. Short selling will become as valid a strategy as going long. The day-trading mindset will become powerful as an approach to uncovering long-term investments. Investing will turn from black and white into a complex portrait that blends wide-ranging strokes of various investing strategies.

There are many valid methods of making sizable sums of money in the world's financial markets. There are fabulously wealthy day traders, and there are absurdly rich long-term investors. But the best of the best are financial chameleons, combining all methods into a dynamic wealth-generating strategy. As one of the investors in this book explains, "There are no rules when it comes to investing because the rules change all the time."

The implication of this statement is simply that you must be prepared for the unexpected. Individual investors have been led to believe that buy-and-hold investing is the safest and surest bet. But what would have happened to buy-and-hold investors who decided to stash money away in "innovative" and "ground-breaking" technology companies back in 1999 or 2000? Only time will tell for certain, but our best guess is that these investors would have been crushed in the market downturn. Even if some of those stocks do rebound from their burst-bubble levels, can most investors afford to wait out an extended bear market? Indeed, blindly buying and holding is a luxury that only the superrich can afford.

This is not to say that we are advocates of neurotic short-term trading. The point is that there is no simple answer. Day traders should not dismiss long-term investors as ostriches with their heads in the sand. Long-term investors shouldn't label day traders as commission-crazy volatility inducers. There is a valuable lesson to learn within every methodology, and this book will introduce you to investors who beat the market with a wide array of tactics.

Consider technical analysis, one of the many strategies discussed in *Bulls, Bears, and Brains*. This book is by no means a study in technical indicators or historical data analysis. In fact, some of those profiled herein pooh-pooh technicians as practitioners of market voodoo. Despite that, words such as *resistance* and *trend lines* are bound to come up in conversation with certain successful investors. There is no reason to ignore technical analysis as well as its entire arsenal of quantitative and graphical tools simply to claim a devout allegiance to fundamentals. Even if technical analysis is utter mumbo jumbo, the fact that it provides investors with unambiguous alerts, signals, and targets means that those who follow even a small portion of technical tactics will be more disciplined in their transaction approach. For example, technical analysis might provide an investor with a specific sell price, freeing him from endless second-guessing and constant worries about when to pull the trigger. Understanding the past price movements of securities can help put future price movements in perspective, and this perspective gives the technical investor the ability to execute decisions with more precision and confidence. Indeed, professionals on Wall Street are almost unanimously proficient in some form of technical analysis. No one in this book claims that technical analysis can predict the future. It is merely one approach that may help fill in many of the gray areas in the risky game of investing.

Being a "fundamental technician" might be one key to profitability in an increasingly volatile market, but profitable "oxymoronic" investment ideals and ideas don't stop there. For example, in your quest to reach the pinnacle of investment understanding, you should consider the possibilities of being a "long short seller" or a "buy-and-hold day trader." Why would any investors resign themselves to profiting merely from the upside of the market? Even if you have been investing for only a few years, you have undoubtedly seen how quickly the market can turn from "sky's the limit" to "batten down the hatches." In a market that is going down the tubes, it is much easier to profit from short selling than it is to find promising buying opportunities. By the same token, as investors take financial matters into their own hands, trading styles are converging rapidly. Most so-called day traders have considerable medium-term, if not long-term, positions to augment their daily trading activity, and traditional buy-and-hold advocates are now recognizing additional profits—not to mention sheer pleasure and education—by setting aside a portion of their assets for short-term opportunities. Little by little, these apparent contradictions are beginning to roll off the tongue as logical complements. Indeed, over the next few years investors will be forced to acquire a broader financial skill set in order to survive.

Remember, the key to winning the investing game is not to be right about your own thinking. The key is to be right when it comes to knowing what *other* investors are thinking. It doesn't matter how you personally interpret a piece of data; it only matters how correctly you predict how other market participants will interpret the information. *Bulls, Bears, and Brains* will help you beat the mind games of the market.

Most books profess to teach you a specific method of investing, with defined rules, theories, and practices. By the time those books appear on store shelves, the methods described within are outdated, and there isn't anyone around to tip you off to the new rules of the game. You don't want to rely on a one-trick pony. *Bulls, Bears, and Brains* is a book about people who can join your investing team, and the strength of their involvement is that they (and you, too) can adapt their investment strategies as the rules of the game change.

We like to think of this book as an investing bible for the early twenty-first century. Not only do the investors profiled in this book utilize cutting-edge technologies to take Wall Street to the next level, but they also represent the mélange of participants that have come to control the modern-day financial markets. If you read this book from front to back, you will have a respectable understanding of dozens of investment strategies, and you can select those that you will take on as your own. You certainly won't know everything, and that's precisely the point.

With this book as your tour guide on an interactive investment journey, you will get to know 20 impressive individuals who will divulge the secrets of their success. Then, with this invaluable Rolodex in hand, you must snuggle up to your computer and connect with these individuals on a regular basis. You must get inside their heads and merge their strategies with your own. You must leverage their talents to enhance your own level of performance. That is the whole idea behind teamwork, and it is the crux of this book.

Information Commoditization

In December 1999 a Minnesota man paid $210,000 at auction for Warren Buffett's 20-year-old wallet. True, it was a wallet with a fairly storied past, having traveled on the backside of a billionaire, but that was not the bidder's motivation for doling out all that cash. Inside the wallet was a golden egg: a stock pick from none other than the Oracle of Omaha himself. Each of 30 additional individuals donated $1,000 to charity at the behest of the auction winner in order to learn the two-letter ticker symbol of the stock pick, which happened to be real estate investment trust (REIT) First Industrial Realty. On top of all that, after the *Wall Street Journal* published the stock pick in a printed article, the Morgan Stanley REIT Index registered its largest gain in over a year.

Ah, the power of information! For $210,000 one individual was able to recruit Warren Buffett temporarily to his investing team. But why pay so much moola for a single stock pick? Can't people come up with their own ideas? The troubling answer is that a good stock is darn hard to find. The only way to rake in above-average profits is to harness information that is not already priced into the dollar value of a stock. But obtaining an information edge is harder than ever in this wired world where every bar is tuned in to CNBC and every other web site is a financial news portal. Yes, blame your troubles on the Internet. Information travels so quickly and in such massive quantities across the Internet ether that everyone seems to know everything all the time. It's not information anymore; it's entertainment.

Although the Internet has in this sense leveled the playing field for investors, it can also give them an information edge. Don't regard the Internet as merely a tool for distributing existing data more rapidly. Instead, capitalize on the Internet's ability to create new ideas and information. That's what everybody is pining for, right? A new idea. An undiscovered gem. A diamond in the rough. A fresh financial opportunity.

For the majority, the Internet is not about new ideas. The Internet and computers in general are very good at providing detailed data relating to past events and existing information. If General Electric is a stock in your portfolio and you want to perform some due diligence, you can gather reams of information about the company via the Internet. That's all well and good, but it's certainly not diamond-in-the-rough material. The subtle difference is that you must know what you are looking for when you type "GE" into the ticker search.

So where do investors unearth the next big thing? Traditionally, investors might stumble across an interesting investment concept in a financial newspaper or magazine. But the obvious problem is that everyone else is finding his or her ideas in the same place, which renders the information useless. The truly valuable information and ideas can be plucked from the minds of the collective online investment community, where, shining through amidst pages of hype and hyperlinks, the top financial minds come out to play. This book is all about bucking the trend of information commoditization; it's a guide to the Internet's investor-to-investor communication playground where you can join the fun and make investments to secure your financial future.

Don't jump to the conclusion that information suddenly turns from garbage to gold once it's converted into bits and bytes. More than 14 million messages have been posted on the leading investment message board, Silicon Investor, and five million on competitor Raging Bull; there are thousands of financial web sites; and there is constant discussion in hundreds of online chat rooms. We'd be generous if we said that any less than 99 percent of all that content—that mass (and mess) of information—were garbage. Hype. Scams. Spams. Useless posts. Wasted time.

Despite the gargantuan amount of blather, there is a precious micropercentage of information that is arguably more useful than any other investment resource you can obtain, online or offline. This book leads you to the virtual doorstep of the most valuable information available on the Internet. Not only that, this book provides you with the background and theories that allow you to interpret the information in the right context. Take Bill Ginsberg, for example. Consider yourself lucky to have ever heard that name at all, because most people know Ginsberg only as "Shortboy." Ginsberg runs Shortboy.com, a bare-bones investment-advice web site with a stick-figure mascot and an enviable track record of beating the market consistently from the short side. As the market blazed ahead in the late 1990s, Ginsberg trounced the averages by betting in the opposite direction. "Like Mike Tyson said—he's the baddest man on the planet," boasts Ginsberg in our interview. "I feel that I'm the best short seller on the planet." Ginsberg may very well be one of the best short sellers on Wall Street; luckily for all of us, he's willing to prove it in an open forum on the Internet by providing terse, daily commentary on the market and by suggesting regular short-sale candidates.

If you stumbled across a guy named Shortboy pitching investment ideas on a rainbow-colored web site, chances are you would click your browser's "Back" button without thinking twice. We could not blame you for such a visceral response. But once you read our interview with Bill Ginsberg, we bet you will be itching to log on the Internet to get to know this colorful character. Our profile of Ginsberg and his Shortboy. com web site will provide you with an understanding of how Ginsberg attacks the market and racks up stellar gains year after year. You will hear about his transformation from math whiz to business school drop-out to Wall Street floor trader to millionaire short seller. You will begin to see how tapping into the network of networked investors can expose a wealth of investment opportunities.

That's the experience we hope you will have over and over again as you read the interviews in this book. Plenty of investment books contain interviews with market gurus, fund managers, and famed traders. But all of these books suffer from the Michael Jordan syndrome. You're not going to "be like Mike" from reading an interview with the slam-dunk celebrity. Interviews with investment pros are entertaining, but the value proposition doesn't extend much further than a few hours of enjoyable reading. Not that we're discounting the significance of entertainment. On the contrary, we structured this book as a set of candid interviews precisely because we felt it would be the most appropriate and enjoyable way to introduce the world to our *Bulls, Bears, and Brains.* But where other investment books end, this book only begins. An introduction to a whole new slate of investing allies, *Bulls, Bears, and Brains* will become a trusted and well-worn addition to your office desk or computer table.

That Was Then, but When Is Now?

Although we believe that the content in this book is timeless, it never hurts to put things into perspective. The bulk of the interviews contained in this book were conducted from January 2001 through May 2001. Consider the charts from January 2000 to May 2001, of the Standard & Poor's (S&P) 500 index (Figure 1.1) and the Nasdaq composite (Figure 1.2).

One chart is unpleasant, and the other is downright nasty. The first half of 2001 was not a fun time for equity investors—especially if you were keeping up with the news. Tales of dot-com deaths were all the rage,

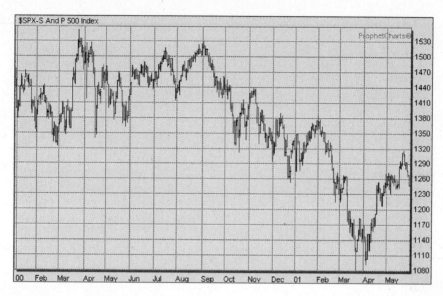

Figure 1.1 www.ProphetFinance.com
Source: Prophet Financial Systems, Inc.

and the financial media spewed bad news around the clock. Pundits were mixed about whether the economy was teetering on the edge of recession or whether it was poised to rebound upwards. Tech was the bogeyman, and "IPO" was a dirty word. There is no question that stocks took a sobering nosedive in 2000, and the market continued its downtrend throughout 2001. But you'll notice something peculiar about the tone of the investors profiled in this book. Not one of them is particularly pessimistic or sour. They are all upbeat, attentive, excited, and—most important—consistently making plenty of money.

This is even more surprising when you consider that many of these individuals rose to prominence during the go-go days of the late 1990s. But these investors are not one-night stands. Even as stocks were sky-rocketing in 1998 and 1999, these investors were attacking the market with a disciplined approached that in most cases had been honed from years of prior practice. Yes, the golden months of the Nasdaq bubble were an anomalous time when investors seemed to be printing nearly free money on a daily basis. It won't be *that* easy for a long, long time to come. But that's okay. When others are finding it hard to eke out a dime, it means that there are more substantial profits to be reaped by the few who can master the less palpable markets.

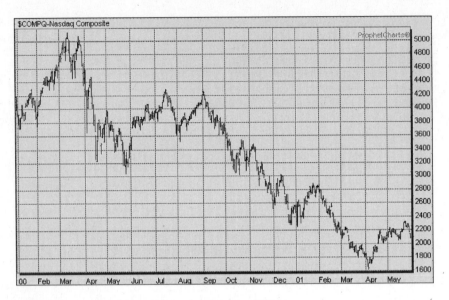

Figure 1.2   Nasdaq composite, January 2000–May 2001
Source: Prophet Financial Systems, Inc. (www.ProphetFinance.com).

A Free Lunch on Wall Street?

At the conclusion of each interview in this book, we inquired about the investor's motivations for sharing his or her insights with the rest of the world. The answer is more obvious in some cases than in others. A number of individuals profiled in this book charge a fee for access to their services and commentary, and you get what you pay for. The for-fee services that we profile in these pages are unquestionably of the highest quality, and they are well worth the expense. In addition, plenty of free information is always available, and temporary free trials are typically offered for any portions of the site that require payment. But the majority of the investors interviewed dole out investment advice free of charge. Most of these folks simply love to teach, to talk, and to think. Some of them really relish the attention; these investors use the Internet as a sounding board, sharing ideas with the world and receiving volumes of feedback in return for their outspoken opinions. It's a symbiotic system that is made possible by the Internet.

What none of these investors profit from is hype, scams, or fraud.

Not one is out there sharing information in hopes that desperate speculators will blindly follow his or her word and bid up the prices of particular securities. Several who deal directly with making stock picks
don't even maintain active personal portfolios—they don't want there
to be any chance for real or apparent conflicts of interest. A considerable
portion of this book's value lies in helping you to identify trustworthy
mentors. Plenty of investment sites that claim to offer profitable advice
are operated with questionable integrity. Slews of sites publish stock
picks in return for cash payments or even stock options from the same
companies that they recommend. If you venture off on your own to find
untapped online information, make sure you read the fine print carefully.

This book solves many of the problems associated with investor-to-
investor communication and online financial communities. As you
read each interview, you'll understand the motivations behind each individual's Internet endeavors. If you're willing to feed a few financial
egos, you may even get a tasty and profitable free lunch on Wall Street.

Beating Wall Street, Literally

Many of the investors profiled in this book have substantial peeves with
conventional financial markets and like to beat up on Wall Street frequently and feverishly. Their concerns stem from an industry profit
structure in which investment-banking fees bring home the bacon and
so-called "research" acts merely as a loss leader for major financial institutions. Banks don't make money issuing "strong buy" and "accumulate" recommendations; they rake in the dough by financing deals and
trading securities. The research exists merely to please the companies
that they finance and to urge their clients to trade.

If research is not a profit center for these institutions, you can expect that the motivations for its production may not be in tune with
your reasons for listening. When was the last time a major brokerage
house issued a "Sell" recommendation? The ratio of "Sell" recommendations to "Buy" recommendations is miniscule. Investment banks'
coffers are drained when the markets turn sour and financing deals dry
up, so you can bet that they'll attempt to buoy the market for as long as
possible by squeezing every last drop of naive bullishness from any investor who will lend an ear. The bottom line is that your interests and
banks' interests are not aligned.

The individuals profiled in this book prosper only when you pros-

per; they provide impartial analysis. That's a profoundly important difference between these folks and the talking heads you see on television
every day. We don't hate Wall Street; most of our business-school pals are
prepping themselves for prosperous careers in investment banking, and
they're certainly not evil people. But financial institutions don't make
money from issuing good advice and picking good stocks—it's a simple
fact with dramatic ramifications.

Peter Still Hasn't Been Lynched

Nearly everyone is familiar with ex-Fidelity fund manager Peter Lynch
and his "buy what you know" approach to investing. The basic gist of
Lynch's proposition is that individuals hardly realize the abundant
valuable investment information that is all around them in their everyday lives. Doctors should have a leg up on understanding the medical,
health care, and biotech fields. Engineers should be able to identify the
most promising technology companies. Shopping addicts should be
able to pick out the most popular stores and lucrative retail investments.

In many ways, Lynch is the granddaddy of the individual investor
revolution. His philosophies still ring true today, and many of the investors profiled in this book promote his tenets. We're fond of the "buy
what you know" strategy, but we believe that the corollary—"buy *who*
you know"—can make the approach even more effective. "Buy what
you know" is about capitalizing on personal expertise, insights, and information. The Internet and this book make it possible to connect with
experts who can show you how to buy what *they* know. By participating
in online forums and communities, you'll experience an expansion in
your intellectual sphere of competency. You'll share your insight with
other investors so that they can learn to buy what you know, and they'll
share information interpreted through a different expert lens so that you
can enhance your ability to buy what they know.

Interestingly, traditional Wall Street doesn't play the "buy what you
know" game. Money managers are typically not recruited from industry; rising through the ranks from junior analyst to fund manager, they
are trained and polished from inside Wall Street itself. They are "very
good observers," as one of our experts puts it, but they typically do not
have actual domain experience. The investors profiled in this book have
a wide range of backgrounds, some financial, some far from it. We will
not claim that there are any superior routes to investment success, but

make certain not to write people off simply because they don't have Harvard MBAs.

"It seemed to me that most of what I learned at Wharton, which was supposed to help you succeed in the investment business, could only help you fail," wrote Wharton alumnus Peter Lynch in his do-it-yourself manifesto, *One Up on Wall Street*. We're Wharton students ourselves, but we made it a point to pick up an engineering degree along the way, too, just to ensure that we don't get financial tunnel vision. This book is about broadening your horizons, connecting with other minds, and enhancing your investment prowess. We hope that Peter Lynch would be proud.

Enter the Electronic Jungle

In an entertaining Morgan Stanley Dean Witter Online commercial, a man sits in a dark room by a computer, his eyes glued to an Internet stock chat room. "VBNM," writes an anonymous chat room member, seemingly offering a hot stock tip. "Are you sure?" asks the man, suddenly excited at the prospect of great riches. "VBNM. VBNM. VBNM. VBNM," shouts the entity on the other end of the computer line. The commercial now switches to another setting: a bustling office party, where a particularly large lady's rear end is bouncing up and down on her keyboard, inadvertently typing out the letters VBNM, VBNM, VBNM. The commercial ends with an amusing platitude: "Know your source."

Count on good old Morgan Stanley to scare individual investors away from the Internet and into the offices of their financial advisers. Sadly, Morgan Stanley's scare tactics are partially justified. Traversing the Internet's communal underworld can be a journey into the dark side, a trek through the electronic jungle. According to David Gardner, cofounder of The Motley Fool and one of the investors profiled in this book, you could fill four books with the 10,000 messages posted to The Motley Fool message boards on a daily basis. There are literally millions of messages sitting on the boards of Raging Bull and Silicon Investor, two additional leading financial community sites.

In our opinion, the colossal quantity of content on these boards represents a problem that is far more daunting than stock fraud stemming from these communities. Sure, seedy pump-and-dump schemes take place on the Net on a regular basis. Mostly, though, these scamsters stick to dirt-cheap, low volume penny stocks that are responsive to manipulation. Usually, these scams are blatantly too good to be true. If you fall for a get-rich-quick scheme on the Internet, you probably have yourself to blame. You also need to keep yourself educated by regularly visiting the Securities and Exchange Commission's web site (www.sec.gov) for updates on the latest known scams. Several web sites are dedicated to alerting investors to fraud; we mention two such sites in Chapter 3.

Ignoring scams for the moment, consider the difficulty of wading through millions of messages in search of valuable, authentic, and relevant information. Browsing through message boards is like watching a three-ring circus of wackos, irate shareholders, and hypesters, with an occasional impressive act performed by a talented, anonymous stock guru. The signal-to-noise ratio is dismal, which makes jumping into the financial discussion game incredibly difficult. The same goes for most Internet chat rooms, as exemplified by Morgan Stanley's comical commercial.

The trick to turning this worthless geyser of prattle into beneficial investment enhancements is to identify the pockets of competency within these communities. Intelligent minds seem to gravitate toward each other even in the virtual setting of the Internet. They're out there, somewhere—you just need to find them. *Bulls, Bears, and Brains* identifies 20 shining stars on the Internet. But if you want to broaden the possibilities and explore even further on your own, you simply have to be willing to take the time to wade through thousands of boards, threads, and messages until you find a promising dialogue. Once you stumble upon apparent intelligence, bookmark the link and visit the board frequently for several days before you jump into the discussion.

Look for less populated boards or boards that cater to specific investment niches. At LuskinReport.com you can join a clever crowd of message-board posters and discuss expansive investing themes and trends. Another web site, eRaider.com, hosts message boards for stock investors who want to rally with other investors and force changes at public companies through shareholder activism. Le Metropole Café at www.lemetropolecafe.com is a unique, bare-bones site where investors can learn from economics experts and mingle with other investors, especially those who are interested in gold and other commodities. Designed for experienced investors, ClearStation.com is a unique community site that integrates technical and fundamental analysis tools with a communal stock recommendation and analysis platform.

After acquainting yourself with several online forums, you'll probably realize that taking part in these exchanges is less about finding hot stock tips and more about forcing yourself to think critically by taking part in an animated community. If you are taking financial matters into your own hands, chances are that you get some level of enjoyment out of the investing process; otherwise, you would hand your money over to a mutual fund manager or financial adviser and steer clear of the details. Financial communities take the investing game to a whole new level, introducing you to bright folks from all around the globe and enhancing your ability to identify new trends and opportunities before the rest of the world takes notice. The 20 investors profiled in this book are indisputably among the most talented financial minds on the Internet, and once you become addicted to the networking game, you will no doubt be able to uncover others who can join your investing team to great success.

About This Book

Bulls, Bears, and Brains is structured so that interviews toward the beginning of the book contain information and explanations that may be relevant in later interviews. That being said, the book is very flexible; you will enjoy a complete reading from front to back, but you can also jump to specific interviews and return to read the others later. We urge you not to skip an interview simply because the individual doesn't appear at first glance to be consistent with your traditional market approach. Remember, there are kernels of knowledge to be gleaned from every investing style and from every investor in this book.

The glossary at the end of the book is provided by Campbell R. Harvey's Hypertextual Finance Glossary, a 7,200-word financial dictionary available in hyperlinked form at www.duke.edu/~charvey. Harvey is the J. Paul Sticht Professor of International Business at Duke University's Fuqua School of Business. In keeping with the theme of this book, Harvey is an acclaimed expert who uses the Internet to educate the investing public. We're grateful for his willingness to provide us with a snippet of his glossary's massive content.

Finally, make good use of the charts and figures within each interview. We do not intend for this book to be a how-to guide in technical analysis or any other type of investment approach. There are times when investors discuss complex strategies of investing, and we have chosen not to dwell on these topics with advanced graphs and charts. There are many satisfactory guides to fundamental analysis, technical analysis, options investing, behavioral finance, and many other market methods. *Bulls, Bears, and Brains* provides a taste of many strategies and shows how you can learn more by involving yourself with experts online. Most of the illustrative charts are provided by Prophet Financial

Systems, an innovative company that excels in combining the powers of technology with investing. Prophet Financial Systems' products and services can be accessed at www.ProphetFinance.com.

The advice offered in the pages of this book can help you become one of those investors who wins when the going gets tough in the zero-sum financial game. As the rules of the game change dynamically, you will be able to see how 20 proven investors react.

Chapter 2

WHO WE ARE AND WHY IT MATTERS

Rather than leave our biographies to the jacket cover without discussing the specifics of our backgrounds and experience, we think it is important for you to understand the biases that may have guided our choice of interviewees and shaped our line of questioning as interviewers. We were both born in 1980, which means that we couldn't even celebrate our book-publishing contract with a drink—not legally, anyhow. We wrote the majority of this book during our junior year at the University of Pennsylvania, where we are enrolled in the Jerome Fisher Program in Management and Technology, pursuing degrees in finance from the Wharton School and in systems engineering from the School of Engineering and Applied Science.

Aside from our academic pursuits at the crossroads of business and technology, we have spent the past several years devoted to the online financial space. We've developed Internet information strategies for several top firms on Wall Street, helping traders, money managers, and analysts unleash the investment power of the Internet. As contributing writers since 1999 for Forbes's *Best of the Web* print guide to the financial Internet, we have covered the entire e-brokerage space, hyperactive trading resources, venture investing services, technical analysis tools, several business-to-business industries, peer-to-peer computing, and other Internet technologies. During 1999 and 2000 we wrote a biweekly column for Forbes.com that explored strategies for obtaining an information advantage by utilizing online resources.

In 2001 we decided to bring everything together by writing *Bulls, Bears, and Brains.* Knowing that investor-to-investor communication and financial communities were the Internet's most unique contributions to the investing game, we decided that compiling a book of interviews with the smartest, most successful investors on the Internet was the most compelling way to introduce these resources to the world at large. From day one of the writing process, we already had a dozen names in mind of folks we wanted to profile, and we spent several months searching for an additional half-dozen online superstars. Our primary desire was to fill the book with best-of-breed investors representing a wide variety of disciplines. We believe we succeeded in identifying the crème de la crème—investors so talented and so successful that you will be surprised at how willing they are to share their strategies and help others learn the investing craft.

On January 15, 2001, we were pleasantly surprised to find our names mentioned in the *Wall Street Journal* in an article profiling young business authors. Two other authors highlighted in the article were, oddly enough, both University of Pennsylvania students who had each written "by teens, for teens" investment books. The article questioned whether teenagers could offer valuable investment advice and turned to Vanguard Group founder John C. Bogle for some answers. "I honestly wouldn't take advice from a teenager about how to beat the market," Bogle commented in the *Journal*.

We couldn't agree more with Bogle. We wouldn't place the health of our financial future in the hands of a teenager or college undergrad. In fact, we are reluctant to trust most adults with the task of proffering investment advice. Thankfully, this book has nothing to do with us greenhorn authors advising anyone on methods to master the market. We would never be so bold as to think that three years of an undergraduate business education would provide us with sufficient insight to crack the market's code. But we *will* go out on a limb and say that we've spent enough years glued to our computer screens to offer valuable tips on using technology to its fullest extent. We *will* suggest that even John C. Bogle himself might be intrigued by the individuals profiled in this book and the one-of-a-kind analyses that they have to offer.

We hope you will find that the questions we asked our interviewees are the same questions you would ask if you had a few hours to chat with an investing all-star. But the fact is that you will have many more than a few hours to get to know each and every individual profiled in this book. That's the interactive beauty of *Bulls, Bears, and Brains:* Once we whet your appetite with inspiring success stories, you'll want to run to your computer and begin networking with the best and brightest of the financial Internet.

Chapter 3

THE BEST OF THE BEST
OF THE NET

We opened our introduction by insisting that *Bulls, Bears, and Brains* wasn't about investing *on* the Internet. To be sure, we don't want to turn this text into a tutorial on how to point, click, and navigate the World Wide Web. Numerous other authors have tackled that topic, and if you need basic instructions for doing things such as typing an Internet address or even entering stock orders online, we recommend that you go buy one of their guides in addition to this text. Contrary to what some might tell you, however, we think that even a dummy can explore the web on his own. There's nothing too complicated about using any e-broker or navigating the sites discussed in this book—or anywhere on the web for that matter. One rule of thumb for Internet beginners: If you're exploring a web site and you get lost or confused, just close your browser, reopen it, and go to a different site. If an online financial services or data provider hasn't provided ample instructions, it doesn't deserve your business.

Because our first paid writing engagement was for Forbes' *Best of the Web* guide, however, ranking and rating web sites is an area where we have developed considerable expertise. In this section we have decided to provide just a small taste of our favorite financial Internet destinations. This smorgasboard of sites will more than get you started investing online, finding basic financial data, and investigating all types of market analysis. Though 99.9 percent of this book is about identifying profitable money-making resources, communities, and individuals on the Internet, we will digress for a moment to go over the basics. It is difficult to start constructing a profitable portfolio without a good set of tools. The sites listed here provide those tools; each is master of its respective domain.

Online broker: **Charles Schwab** (www.schwab.com). Talk all you want about eight-buck, deep-discount, bare-bones trades, but we prefer

$29.95 per trade with Schwab's commitment to personal service and top-notch online tools.

Direct access broker (nonbrowser-based tool for active investors): **CyberTrader** (www.cybertrader.com). CyberTrader is owned and operated by Schwab as well. No, we're not shills for the brokerage powerhouse. The firm has been the consistent technology innovator on Wall Street, and that commitment shows in all of its services.

Financial statements and Securities and Exchange Commission (SEC) filings: **U.S. SEC EDGAR database** (www.sec.gov) and **10-K Wizard** (www.10kwizard.com). The SEC's home page is a quick, no-frills approach to accessing a company's financial data. Of course, unless you're a corporate accountant, it's hard to get creative with an income statement; 10-K Wizard tries to be a bit fancy by supplying real-time filings and full-text searches within the documents.

Investor watch dogs (protecting individual investors against fraud): **SecuritiesSleuth** (www.securitiessleuth.com) and **Investor Protection Trust** (www.investorprotection.org). This is just one of those issues to which responsible investors and responsible books must pay attention. The warnings and stories posted on the SecuritiesSleuth site cover online investment scams as well as potential cases of corporate fraud. Investor Protection Trust's web site provides links to various education- and fraud-related information on the web. If you use the Internet and investor-to-investor communication resources wisely, online scams won't be a problem, but it still can't hurt to have these two sites among your browser's bookmarks.

Financial portal: **Yahoo! Finance** (finance.yahoo.com). There is no easier way to obtain a (delayed) stock quote or find news on a specific security. For $9.95 per month, Yahoo! will replace the time-delayed quotes with real-time data.

Basic stock charts and technical analysis: **Prophet Financial Systems** (www.ProphetFinance.com). This site offers simple-to-use, powerful charting tools directly from your web browser in all investment time frames. If you've had no experience with technical analysis, this site will give you in-depth instruction on how to construct charts much like those throughout this book (well, *exactly* like those throughout the book—in case we haven't recognized them enough yet, they were nice enough to provide the charts in *Bulls, Bears, and Brains*) and to utilize the indicators discussed in some of our interviews.

Not-so-basic stock charts and technical analysis: **TradeStation** (www.tradestation.com). For $299.95 per month, TradeStation is the software that technicians dream of at night. Maybe one day.

Daily news and opinions: The **Wall Street Journal** (www.wsj.com) and **Briefing.com** (www.briefing.com). Sure, the *Wall Street Journal* is one of the few newspapers to charge for their online content, but what are you going to do? It's worth it. Briefing.com also charges for various levels of service and provides real-time news analysis, rumors, and market commentary. Its content is short, sweet, and punchy—we like that.

Fundamental company information: **MarketGuide** (www.market-guide.com). Offering detailed business descriptions, this is a good place to start to learn about what a company actually does, which can be important these days.

Options quotes and information: **Chicago Board Options Exchange** (www.cboe.com). This book doesn't focus extensively on options investing, but the CBOE is a great resource for basic quotes and extended education.

Links to these sites and more are available at the homepage of *Bulls, Bears, and Brains* at www.MarketBuster.com. More about that now.

Chapter 4

THIS IS ONLY THE BEGINNING

What? Twenty investing allies aren't enough for you? You want more? Although we fully expect the investors profiled in this book to remain profitable and relevant for many years to come, it never hurts to remain on the prowl for the financially gifted. To ensure that you can responsibly make "relationship investing" a centerpiece of your financial strategy, we want to provide you with a dynamic tool that you can turn to once you finish reading this book.

For updates on our *Bulls, Bears, and Brains* and for information on additional networked superstars, point your web browser to www. MarketBuster.com. On the web site, we provide instructions for nominating other *Bulls, Bears, and Brains* who are worthy of attention and respect. We profile noteworthy online investors on a regular basis and make it our mission to point you toward resources that offer an information edge. With MarketBuster.com, the information in this book will truly withstand the test of time.

Chapter 5

INVESTING OUT LOUD
Don Luskin

Internet Alias	Investment Style
Don Luskin	All time horizons
Year of Birth	**Location**
1954	San Francisco, CA
Education	
Dropped out of Yale University after one year to pursue career	
Web Site (Free)	
The Luskin Report: www.luskinreport.com	

We knew that Don Luskin was not your typical investor when he posed the questions, "What are we going to do when you can simply take a pill and turn death off in your body? What are the economics of that world going to be?" Although many of our conversations with individuals in this book were intellectually demanding and philosophically stimulating, none required more contemplation and reflection than our dialogue with Luskin, founder and head guru of The Luskin Report (see Figure 5.1). Luskin is not merely spinning science fiction tales with his peculiar questions about the bounds of existence; he is serving up his own incisive analysis of the biotech industry and identifying big-picture themes that could literally change the world. Thirty years ago, the notion of a computer on every desktop and in every home was considered outlandish. Twenty years ago, the concept of an electronic network that could span the globe and ignite an information explosion was rejected as entirely off the wall. Yet both of these fantastic visions became sweeping realities, and investors who were quick to recognize these

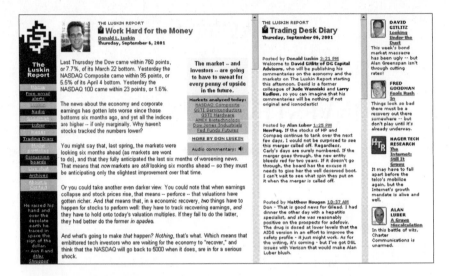

Figure 5.1   www.LuskinReport.com
Source: The Luskin Report.

trends were rewarded handsomely. The lesson: Don't dismiss Don Luskin as a loony. He's a brilliant investor who is merely guilty of thinking *way* outside the box.

Luskin's creative thinking and execution have brought him great success on Wall Street. His curriculum vitae includes stints as the CEO of Barclays Global Mutual Funds, vice chairman of Barclays Global Investors, vice chairman of Wells Fargo Nikko Investment Advisors, and senior vice president of Jefferies & Co. At Jefferies, he essentially started the world's first electronic communications network (ECN) and founded the firm's Investment Technology Group, now its own billion-dollar company. The common link among many of Luskin's early experiences is the integral role that technology played in assisting his financial endeavors. "I've always been interested in the way that technology impacts the investment process," explains Luskin. "That can have to do with the way it impacts the decision making process—what securities to hold or how to control risk. It can have to do with the trading process. It can have to do with applying technology to the customer-relation process. In 25 years, I've been at ground zero for a bunch of fundamental technology developments."

In 1999 Luskin took a big step even for a veteran visionary. He launched an Internet start-up called MetaMarkets.com with the intent of turning the mutual fund industry on its head. MetaMarkets.com was home to the world's first family of interactive mutual funds, the *OpenFund* and the *IPO and New Era Fund*. With complete transparency, Luskin and his team of traders and strategists disclosed every single purchase and sale of securities in real time. There were no mysterious, invisible money managers at this radical mutual fund company—a webcam even streamed live pictures of the trading desk to the MetaMarkets.com web site.

Besides its voyeuristic value, we asked Luskin to describe the benefits of a transparent mutual fund. "From a business perspective, it's a way of offering customers a choice that they didn't have before," argues Luskin. "There is a market completeness argument that in a world of secretive, disempowering, isolating, distant products with purely economic value, you create an option for a certain segment of the market that wants experiential value attached to its investments."

Experiential value at MetaMarkets.com was derived not only from full disclosure of fund activities but also through a vibrant Internet community that mingled on the site's message boards. During our interview Luskin told us, "The hallmark of the Internet is that it's interactive. The greatest value is when it allows you to interact with people that previously had been isolated." In an effort to make Meta-Markets.com even more revolutionary, Luskin enlisted a group of famous visionaries and intellectuals to interact with MetaMarkets.com members on the message boards. Members of the think tank included Nicholas Negroponte from the MIT Media Lab, Nolan Bushnell of Atari and Chuck E. Cheese Pizza, ex-chairman of National Semiconductor Corporation Peter Sprague, and many others. Along with his think tank, Luskin defined four metathemes that formed the basis of MetaMarkets.com's investment strategy: infogenesis, biocosm, corporate tribalism, and innovate or die.

Perhaps it was an idea ahead of its time, or perhaps it was an idea stuck in a bear market, but MetaMarkets.com regrettably closed its doors on August 17, 2001. When MetaMarkets.com launched its first fund on August 31, 1999, the Nasdaq composite sat at 2,739, after having fallen from a high of over 3,900. Over a tumultuous two years, the technology-laden Nasdaq continued to fall over 30 percent; on the day MetaMarkets.com threw in the towel, the index stood at 1,867. Instead of focusing their efforts on registering abundant gains, Meta-Markets.com's fund managers were forced to devote their time to paring losses in a brutal market environment. As Luskin explains, "The mutual fund business is like auto manufacturing—it's a scale business." Despite several thousand fund investors, MetaMarkets.com could not scale to a sustainable model in the midst of a bear market.

Our original interview with Luskin took place in early 2001, when

MetaMarkets.com was still fighting to survive. Although we could have removed all mention of MetaMarkets.com from the interview following the closure of the company, we believe there are important lessons to learn from Luskin's noble mission to change the staid financial industry. Indeed, MetaMarkets.com continues to have a profound effect on the mutual fund industry by prompting executives and regulators to make the fund management process more transparent. "This is a very broad spectrum, where you have on the one end pretty much the whole industry, in complete secrecy, and us at the other end of the spectrum," noted Luskin about the vast space between the transparency of Meta-Markets.com and the closed-door policy of the traditional fund industry. "You see tiny moves from the mutual fund industry in our direction, and because we've opened up so much space between them and us, they seem like tiny moves. But if you're in the mutual fund industry and you go from sending people paper documents showing positions every six months to putting that on the web every six months, already you've made a huge leap. Now you don't have to wait two months to see the price, print it, and mail it. Now, at least every six months, it's current. These are very timid steps compared to the radical leap we've made, but that's fine. Every day you hear of some mutual fund that's taking one of these timid steps, and they eventually will compound it to a completed journey."

The good news is that Luskin is still very much a voice on the web. As Luskin and his MetaMarkets.com cofounder Dave Nadig wrote in a farewell letter on the day of the site's closing, "Every ending is a beginning. While this site may fade, our interest in the markets won't. Nor can the muse that brings us to the keyboard each morning be easily muted." These days, Luskin and several of his clever cronies can be found offering daily market analysis at The Luskin Report. The mission of this new site is to provide investors with "iconoclastic and actionable real-time commentary on markets, economics, and politics." Although the mutual funds are gone, the spirit and utility of MetaMarkets.com is still alive and well at The Luskin Report. The site even maintains a trio of model portfolios that track a broad range of companies. In addition, the new site boasts lively message boards and a real-time chat room to ensure that interactivity reigns supreme.

Luskin's candid comments and unique analysis are guaranteed to lead investors to many novel investment ideas. He tosses conventional investing timeframes out the window and refuses to differentiate short-term trading from long-term investing. At the heart of every investment Luskin makes, however, is a prophetic focus on the future. "It's hard to make money on things that aren't changing," he muses. Put on your thinking cap and join Don Luskin as he tackles the market with a refreshing dose of honesty and intellect.

Of all the experiences you've had on Wall Street, which have shaped your current philosophies and strategies most strongly?

There have been quite a few. I've always been interested in the way that technology impacts the investment process. That can have to do with the way it impacts the decision making process—what securities to hold or how to control risk. It can have to do with the trading process. It can have to do with applying technology to the customer-relation process. In 25 years, I've been at ground zero for a bunch of fundamental technology developments. For example, in the late seventies I was one of the first option traders to be on the floor of an options exchange with real-time access to options valuation formulas capable of evaluating complex positions. Now everybody's got wireless devices that do that; but then, it was like being the one-eyed man in the land of the blind. Truly, it was a license to print money for a while—to have scientific real-time tools standing in a crowd of people who are basically doing it by licking their finger and holding it up to the wind. That was my first taste of a technology advantage in investing. The next version of it was when I was at Jefferies, and I created the POSIT Crossing Network, which was really the first ECN, or electronic communications network. That was the first application of distributed networking to allow customers to transact entire portfolios with each other without using traditional exchange mechanisms, which limit you to trading individual stocks. This is all pre-Internet; it would be much simpler to do today, but the principles would be the same. That product has now been spun off into a separate public company and trades 50 to 100 million shares per day.

During my years at Wells Fargo and Barclays, I was involved in the application of technology to the portfolio construction process, where the challenge was, how do you beat market? You answered that question by starting from the mindset of an index fund—by figuring out how to at least match the market, which most people can't do. It turns out that if you set yourself to the challenge of matching the market exactly, where you will not permit yourself even a basis point of variation over an entire year, you get deep inside the microstructure of markets and start treating it as a process management problem, rather than a traditionally framed investment problem. Once you create technology tools in order to implement perfect indexing, you can now extend them to beat the index.

If there was a single day when people realized just how powerful the influence of technology in markets was, it would have been October 19, 1987. You saw the conversions of a lot of different portfolio-management and trading technologies that for a brief time basically overwhelmed the world and so completely virtualized the investment process as to pretty much reduce it to nothing for about 48 hours. And it came back to life promptly when the technology was withdrawn. [Many people blame the widespread use of computerized program trading for accelerating the stock market crash of October 19, 1987, also known as Black Monday, when the S&P 500 lost over 21% of its value in a single day.]

Do you believe that technology has taken over Wall Street to the extent that there is too much knowledge, too much information? You said you had an edge on the options floor, but it seems like everyone has an edge now.

If everyone has an edge, no one has an edge. It has to be a differential advantage, an asymmetrical condition. MetaMarkets is about using the Internet to convey information that is normally hidden or too expensive to convey to investors. There has never been a way for investors to communicate with their mutual fund managers, a way for investors to understand what the mutual fund managers are doing and what they're holding. The Internet dramatically lowers the cost of doing all that. The only question is whether you want to do that, whereas five years ago the question was whether you could afford to do it. Is there too much technology? I don't know. Should lumberjacks use chain saws? I suppose they can hurt themselves, but I'm sure using the old-fashioned ax, there was the occasional lumberjack who cut his foot off. I think one is much better off having power tools. There are exceptions. The world would probably be better off without nuclear weapons, but, short of that, I think technology is pretty much always good.

Take us through your investing strategies and philosophies. What criteria must securities meet before you will consider taking action?

The current fund management process—investment decision-making process—here at MetaMarkets is an extremely traditional process. It's just good, old-fashioned, judgment-driven active management, where you get a bunch of smart people in a room and decide what you want to buy. The application of technology here is about communicating that to a customer audience. I can tell you how we manage money, but except for the particulars, it won't be any different than if you called a money manager from 30 years ago. There's no computer doing the decision making here. There are no quantitative rules. There's no artificial intelligence. There's nothing sexy about that part of what we're doing. There are two value propositions here—a conventional one, an active management process, overlaid on an extremely unconventional process of how we communicate with people about the management of their money. Not only do we give them a tremendous amount of information about what we're doing in real time, but we open ourselves up to hearing their opinions as well.

Before we get to that second value proposition, give us a taste of the conventional active management part. What is your take on the investment process? Take us through some recent trades and give us your reasons for transacting.

We are very thematically driven in that we are generally not into the old-fashioned Graham and Dodd approach of deeply understanding companies' balance sheets and income statements, trying to guess what their earnings are going to be. We figure that vein of gold has been so thoroughly mined by others that there's no edge in it. Where you get the edge is in the interstices above and below that traditional mode of analysis. The space above, which I believe we can successfully occupy, is the thematic space, devoting our time not to the nitpicky little particulars of a company's financials, but instead trying to understand the larger meta-space in which the business operates, understanding the great thematic drivers that are going to be the tides that carry the boats in and out, without obsessing about exactly how each little boat is constructed. That makes us a big-picture, top-down, theme-driven investor. We are interested in understanding elements of the way politics, society, law, regulation, and technology development interact at an abstract level to create opportunities for companies. We've got Nicholas Negroponte in our think tank. In the mid-1980s he was at his Media Lab at MIT, posing to students an academic question: What would the world look like if you had infinite free bandwidth? What would happen if bandwidth were becoming exponentially more cost-effective every year, the way processing power does according to Moore's law? This was an academic exercise in the mid-1980s, but it is now very much a real-world situation. We're going through these agonizing boom and bust cycles because on the one hand, the technology that makes bandwidth effectively infinite and free is now bursting on the scene. But at the same time, it challenges companies to make any money. That all interacts with the regulatory environment, where all this infinite and free bandwidth has no way of getting to your house. If you understand those big-picture issues better than the next guy, that gives you a huge advantage in understanding where companies like Cisco or Global Crossing or Applied Micro Circuits are going to end up.

MetaMarkets.com discusses four metathemes—trends that will drive a new paradigm. How did you come up with those four? Where can an investor look to discover how the world is going to change in the next 10 years?

You just have to have a curious mind. I'm simply interested in those things. In biotechnology, I'm not interested in medicine or healthcare or biology; I'm interested in the legal and ethical issues. That happened to be my personal entrée into that world. It also happens that those turn out to be extremely important issues when investing in biotech stocks. Biotech stocks deal with very personal issues of life, death, and human identity—questions of human cloning, profound ethical issues, where you start having to ask yourself, "What would happen if one of these companies actually came up with a cure for death?" Death is just a pre-programmed genetic disease. The day will come, probably in the next 20 years, where if we want to deal with the economic issues of it, we can just go in and turn death off. And that is today like it was for Nicholas Negroponte 15 years ago to ask about infinite free bandwidth. What are we going to do when you can simply take a pill and turn death off in your body? What are we going to do when all these people are just always around? What's the world going to look like when you can turn aging off? What are the economics of that world going to be? That's going to be a hell of a deal for the social security system. I guess we better get space flights going pretty quick. Those things are interesting to me. I like reading science fiction, and the best science fiction is based on science; the fiction component becomes a prediction. If you take these things and extend them in your mind, you can find some really neat investing opportunities.

To bring it down to earth, there's a division within biotech research: embryonic stem cells, which are a particular kind of living cell that you find in the tissue of embryos. These stem cells have the property of being very easily transformed into whatever you need them to be. They are seen as the raw materials for crafting biologic agents that would go in and cure degenerative diseases. Parkinson's disease is a major target of stem cell research. There are three or four companies that are involved with this, and the one that's the most famous and that has the most money is called Geron [see Figure 5.2]. A month ago, an AP wire story came out about some experimental work that's being done at the Uni-

Figure 5.2 Geron (Nasdaq: GERN), November 2000–May 2001
Source: Prophet Financial Systems, Inc. (www.ProphetFinance.com).

versity of Colorado using stem cells in an experiment to try to cure Parkinson's. The story was just absolutely grizzly. It had to do with drilling holes in patient's skulls and stuffing stem cells from aborted fetuses into the holes, and a whole bunch of people had violent convulsions; you can visualize them convulsing in their hospital beds, and the stuff pouring out of the holes in their skulls. When that story broke, we said, "You've just got to short Geron." Now, does Geron actually have anything to do with that experiment? Is that the technology that Geron is working on? It turns out the answer is no. Geron didn't have anything to do with that. Even though it was reported by the AP as being a stem cell experiment, it turned out to be a brain cell experiment. That not only has nothing to do with Geron, but actually has nothing to do with stem cells or aborted fetuses. It ended up getting corrected the next day; but, of course, the retraction in the newspaper is never as big as the headline. The original version got picked up on the front page of the *New York Times.*

We have a Republican administration that is eager to step all over anything that remotely touches the abortion issue, so whether Geron deserves to get hit because of the story or not doesn't matter. It will. So, we shorted at $15 1/8. We covered the short three or four days later as the publicity crested. I think it was $13, but it's gone all the way down to $9. We actually took a long position in Geron last Friday in the $10s. The reason is that we noticed that a bill sponsored by Senator Arlen Spector, who is pro-choice, has been introduced in the Senate to block attempts by the Bush administration to forbid federal funding of stem cell research. This bill had broad bipartisan support. It's cosponsored by Hillary Clinton and Strom Thurmond. And here's a time when Bush really needs to get every vote he can to get his tax cut passed, to get his budget passed, and to get his base-of-defense deal passed. When you come right down to it, George Bush isn't really worried about stem cells, especially when there's a bill on the floor that's got both Strom Thurmond and Hillary Clinton supporting it.

So, you understand what these companies do, then you wait for these news catalysts, and you take advantage of them. Is that investing, or is that trading? I don't know. I'm not sure I know the difference between those words. I know the way people use those words, but I'm not sure why it's "trading" if you expect it to come to fruition and yield profits for you over a short period of time, whereas if you have some ideas that you think will play out over a longer period of time, then all of a sudden it moves to a different page in the dictionary, and you call it "investing." It seems like it involves all the same mental processes and the same risk-taking processes. It just plays out over a different time frame.

Why not just buy Geron and hold it for five years?

You could do that. I could get into a debate with you about whether that involves more or less risk. You could argue that buying something and saying in advance that regardless of what happens you're going to stop reading the newspaper and hold it for five years is actually a dangerously imprudent process—even though it's what all the textbooks recommend as the essence of safe investing. Whereas, if you follow this thing closely, and you get to understand every nuance of what moves these stocks, all of a sudden you're a speculator. I don't think that's playing fair.

To bring this back to the point I was trying to make before, I was saying that there's a space above and a space below traditional modes of analysis. The space above is understanding these themes. You could call that the long-term space. The space below is understanding how the market works as a game. Think about Wall Street analysts who get so much publicity: If you want to think about the content of what they're saying as truth, then that's one activity, and you can invest based on that.

On the other hand, you can think of them as being players at a poker table who are putting out signals, turning cards over; and just as in poker, you have to deal with the multiple realities of the actual cards hidden and revealed and the more dominant reality of how the other players are going to react to that, what their betting strategies are, what they think the reality of the hidden cards is. It doesn't matter what the hidden cards really are until the very last showdown. And in the market, the very last showdown never happens.

Think of the market as a big information-processing mechanism; figure out how it works, and relieve yourself of all this claptrap of having to really understand companies and invest in what you know—as though there's something noble about marrying a company for life. Economists of no less prestige than John Maynard Keynes, who made a fortune as a speculator, described it just this way. He said that the market was a beauty contest, where the idea isn't to pick the prettiest girl, but to pick the girl that all the other judges think is the prettiest. And you're doing that in an iterative environment where all the other judges know that that's the true nature of the game. Their communications to each other are aimed at optimizing their own chances of discovering and influencing what others will do, without revealing what they will truly do themselves. It's a very complex, multilayered game, and most of the advice that's given to people about how to play it is just shockingly oversimplified and really designed to keep them passive and stupid and to leave these more interesting games to the pros.

You talked a lot about biotechnology as an area for investors to watch. Tell us about your other investing metathemes and ideas. What is "innovate or die"?

We created "innovate or die" primarily as a catchall category to allow us to look at companies that have innovation as their comparative advantage or signature competence. An example would be companies like the independent power producers—the kind of transformations they're having to go through to deal with the California energy crisis, which is a weird confluence of regulatory problems, economic problems, physical scarcity problems, delivery problems, and environmental problems. That's a case where the ordinary rules of business don't apply anymore, where you're basically in a world of constant white-water rapids—a wholly new environment that is extremely unpredictable and chaotic at every turn. Calpine Corporation [see Figure 5.3] has played that situation like a violin; at any turn they could have completely blown themselves up. I would characterize that as "innovate or die." It's innovation

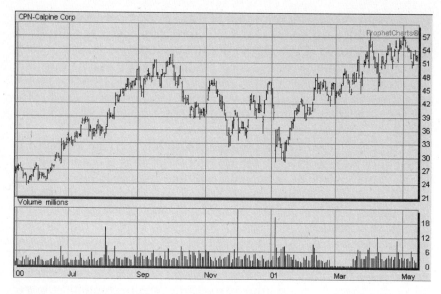

Figure 5.3　Calpine (NYSE: CPN), May 2000–May 2001
Source: Prophet Financial Systems, Inc. (www.ProphetFinance.com).

in terms of a business process and political process—adaptability to a changing, chaotic environment.

What about "corporate tribalism"?

If MetaMarkets were a public company, we would put it in that category. In a world where most important transformations are being catalyzed by a revolution in communication, the content of communication is relationship. These are companies that can transform their relationships with their audiences—in the case of General Electric, transforming its relationship with workers, and in the case of Dell Computer, transforming its relationship with customers. Instead of an isolated world, where people are independent, atomistic, lonely, existential entities, you have a McLuhanesque global village where people are united in tribal bonds that knit them together in inextricable common interests. You have the potential to implement very powerful business models. In the one case, you have a world of pervasive transaction costs, where you're constantly overcoming trust barriers; and in the other case, you have a world with very low transaction costs, where you're operating under very high levels of trust. "Corporate tribalism" is a cute way of saying that.

You follow an aggressive investment approach with the potential for big swings up and down. Many people have obviously become wary of such risk-oriented strategies. Given the lessons learned in the past few years, what investment strategy or outlook would you recommend to the average investor?

There's no such thing as an average investor. That's one question to which every mutual fund manager in America would give you some bullshit answer—except me.

But there are many individuals who only recently involved themselves in the stock market and haven't been around to learn from history. Do you think a new thought process is necessary to prosper in the next 10 years of investing?

There always is. There's that saying that the four most expensive words on Wall Street are "This time it's different." They say, "You have to learn from history because—believe me—I've been there. I've seen it, and it's always the same cycles, the same patterns." That's true, but it's also true that every single day is different. There's always some bizarre surprise. The reality is that the market is not tractable with respect to these little homilies and clichés. It is a very tough business that engages the minds of the smartest, most highly incentivized people in the world. If you absolutely must have a homily or a cliché about the market, it would be, If you sit down at a poker table, and you can't tell who the sucker is at the table, it's you. And that's probably what the average investor ought to be asking himself. What the hell are you doing in this game? This is a very, very tough game.

If you're an investor who's decided you can't play the game, should you put your money in an actively managed fund, an index fund . . .

There are so many different games. You could say, "Should you be managing your own account at Charles Schwab?" That's the deepest version of playing the game yourself. Or should you be going to a money manager? Then you've got to play a different game. You've got to play the game of picking the money manager. Or should you pick an index fund? I suppose the ultimate answer about not playing games is holding index funds, but even then you're going to have to make choices about which index, foreign or domestic, large cap or small cap, stocks or bonds. It all boils down to having to make a set of risky decisions about your future, where you're basically trapped between pincers. On the one hand, you can take too much investment risk and not have enough to meet your goals because you lost money along the way, or you can take too little investment risk and not have the money to meet your goals—not because you lost money, but because you didn't make any.

There is no formula for this. It's all about risk taking and judgment and being right. You hear people say stupid things like, "No rewards without risk." That makes you think, "Well, if I want rewards, I just have to go out and take as much risk as I possibly can. That means I'll get rewards." It may not be false, but it's certainly not true. The only rewards you're going to get in this business are by being right. What makes you think you're going to be right? If you can't answer that question, then you probably need to boil this thing down to the point where you have made as few decisions as possible. Because if at every decision point you believe you will probably get the wrong answer, you should probably make as few decisions as you can.

Do you follow that tenet yourself?

No, of course not. I dedicated my life to playing this game as a profession. To do that, I'm willing to say that I think I can be right. You asked me about the average investor . . .

Well, it takes considerable insight to construct the investment reality that you just proposed . . .

True. Don't forget: Most of the professionals in this business don't take any risk at all. They just make money off your risk. They just extract transaction fees from the process.

What are some of the most exciting companies on your radar screen?

The most exciting companies are probably biotech companies. Some of my favorites are Protein Design Labs, Human Genome Sciences, Abgenix, Geron, and Vertex Pharmaceuticals. You can draw a series of extremely interesting contrasts between biotech stocks and Internet stocks. They start out having superficial similarities—mostly that they don't make any money. Most people want to stop there and say, "Oh my God, didn't you learn anything from the last cycle? You ought to be investing in companies that make money." But there are differences: Biotech companies know how they're going to make money. Internet companies never knew. It was always just "somehow": We'll get market share; we'll sell advertising; we'll have customer relationships. Nobody really knew what they were ever going to do to make any money. If you're a biotech company, you know how you're going to make money. You're going to find a cure for cancer, and you're going to sell it to all these poor victims for the highest price you can possibly extort from them. That is a wonderful, age-old strategy for making

Figure 5.4   Millennium Pharmaceuticals (Nasdaq: MLNM), May 1999–May 2001
Source: Prophet Financial Systems, Inc. (www.ProphetFinance.com).

money—produce something valuable and scarce and charge top dollar for it.

These companies, like the Internet companies, are standing at the threshold of a completely profound, transformative technology revolution that's going to enable them to do all this stuff—with the good news that once they've done it, they'll be able to make money. Add to that the fact that these companies, at least the ones I've mentioned, all have huge war chests. One I didn't mention is Millennium Pharmaceuticals [see Figure 5.4]. It has over a billion dollars in cash. That's because it learned that when the window is open, sell stock, raise money, and put it in the bank. You're not going to have a situation where these companies are operating on a shoe string, hoping that some funding event is going to happen to keep them going. Somehow, someday, they'll make money. These are companies that can last 20 years just on the cash they've got in the bank right now. And believe me, by the time 20 years have gone by, there'll be a cure for cancer, for aging, and for death, and these are going to be the most valuable companies in the world. Here's the amazing statistic: Take Pfizer and Merck, two big pharmaceutical companies. If you take their combined market cap, you could buy every single biotech company in the entire world and have a couple of billion dollars left over. What about that is keeping you from opening your checkbook? I think that's the most exciting sector, and I've named these individual stocks, but it doesn't really matter which stocks. I think you just want to be in the sector.

You've been a visionary when it comes to technology and Wall Street. Where do you see Wall Street headed over the next 10 years?

There needs to be a better way for individuals to become diversified into new companies and new ideas before they reach the public stage. There needs to be a good mechanism for public venture capital. There have been some attempts, but they've been poorly timed and poorly structured. The reason that it's so difficult is because the very best opportunities are basically completely monopolized by two or three private firms that have every incentive to keep it that way, and the attempts to make public versions of the same thing invariably get the crumbs from their table. I don't know how to get around that until a guy like John Doer at Kleiner Perkins has a near-death experience, wakes up, and gets the religion of John Bogle and tries to figure out a way to Vanguardize his fiefdom.

Also, there's a web start-up by a Stanford professor, Bill Sharpe, called Financial Engine (www.financialengine.com). That's the first experimental attempt to put at the disposal of the individual the same type of analytical tools that the institutional investor has. Where that has fallen down is in the interface. They have not succeeded in simultaneously dumbing it down so a nonprofessional can understand it, while at the same time leaving any value in it. There's a weak spot there that's going to take some true genius to figure out. It won't be an investment genius; it'll be a communications genius. When that person comes along, he's going to change the world.

Chapter 6

SMARTER THAN THE AVERAGE BEAR
Bill Ginsberg

Internet Alias	Investment Style
Shortboy	Short-term

Year of Birth	Location
1964	New York, NY

Education	
Math and economics, Wesleyan University; dropped out of Columbia Business School	

Web Site (Pay)	
Shortboy.com: www.shortboy.com	

Bill Ginsberg is careful not to be too pessimistic. He doesn't want to be labeled the bad guy. When the market tanks, he forces himself to keep a straight face. When his stocks plummet, he just twiddles his thumbs. But deep down inside, Ginsberg is grinning. With the nickname "Shortboy," Ginsberg sometimes finds it difficult to convince people that he's only trying to make a living. "I don't want to be known as someone trying to push down prices," he explains. "I've just crafted a skill that enables me to profit off of some good companies." Ginsberg's skill, of course, is shorting—profiting from the downside of the market.

To put it simply, when individuals short stocks, they borrow securities from a third party and then sell them on the open market. Eventually, those shares must be returned to their owner. If the price of the security has fallen, then the short seller can buy back the stock (known as covering) at a cheaper price, return the borrowed shares, and pocket the

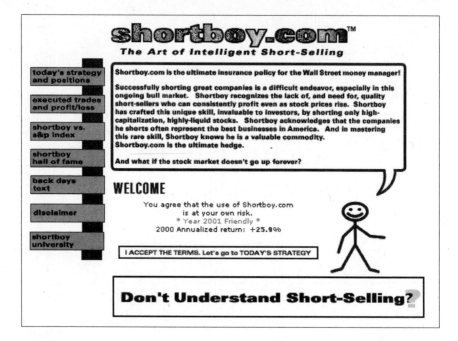

Figure 6.1   www.shortboy.com
Source: Shortboy.com.

difference from the original sale. But if the price has risen, the short seller can be in a heap of trouble. Because securities can theoretically rise infinitely, the short seller may be required to buy back the stock at a much higher price, suffering a significant loss—hence the importance of stop and limit orders, which allow you to specify preset prices for automatically exiting a trade when entering short sales.

"People cannot comprehend how you can sell something you do not own," says Ginsberg. "To me, it's the opposite of going long. There are always two transactions in a stock—there's a buy and a sell. What people don't realize is that you can sell and then buy. You can just do them in reverse. I'm selling first and buying second, rather than buying first and selling second." If anyone should understand the art of short selling, it's Ginsberg. For over six years Ginsberg has donned the persona of Shortboy and kept over 90 percent of his portfolio in short sales.

Even Ginsberg is somewhat surprised by his talent. The first year he started shorting stocks, he racked up a 76 percent gain, even as the S&P 500 index rose 23 percent. He had managed to crush a strongly bullish

---

For May 3rd, 2001

The s&p closed up +1 to 1267.4

The s&p is hovering at the top of the range, and the monthly unemployment report awaits on friday. Which way will it go? Momentum is with the s&p, and the trend is your friend.

Shortboy had a fine posting for wednesday in BJS. The stock was down -5.7 points or -7% on the day. Shortboy posting to sell a measly 500 shares did that? And to the sector as well?

Can the NASDAQ come back to life? You bet. If it seems impossible then it can happen. Did anyone think it would go up +85% in one year? Did anyone think it would then fall all the way back and then some? The NASDAQ always surprises, and that's some of the reason why Shortboy doesn't trade it.

CPN sell 1000 @ 55.90, buy @ 52.10, buy-stop @ 57.10

Figure 6.2   Sample Shortboy commentary
Source: Shortboy.com.

market by betting on the downside. Perhaps it was an anomaly, or perhaps Ginsberg was slowly morphing into Shortboy. Indeed, for the next four years Ginsberg continued to outstrip a rising market by shorting stocks, returning 49 percent, 40 percent, 32 percent, and 25.9 percent in 1997, 1998, 1999, and 2000, respectively.

Along the way, Ginsberg decided to share his pessimistic prowess with the world. He recognized that he had a unique skill and figured that the Internet would provide him with a colorful way to attract some attention. Thus, Shortboy.com was born, complete with the site's signature stick-figure mascot waving happily (see Figure 6.1). Each day, Ginsberg updates his site with bare-bones commentary on the market and an unadorned short-sale pick or two (see Figure 6.2). Some might criticize Ginsberg for providing little or no rationale for his shorts. But it's all part of his bad-guy philosophy. He doesn't want to give a reason. He doesn't want to tout the bad news. Instead, Ginsberg just publishes an innocent little ticker symbol and suggests appropriate sale prices, cover prices, and buy stops.

Shortboy.com is not entirely void of guidance. Shortboy University provides short-sale newbies with some basics on the mechanics of betting on bearishness. In addition, Ginsberg keeps his personal portfolio separate from the calls he makes on Shortboy.com. At least 90 percent of the time, he doesn't personally short a stock that appears on Shortboy.com. If he thinks apparel companies are due for a fall, he'll suggest shorting Kohl's on Shortboy.com, and he'll short Talbots in his own account. If the financials looks shaky, he'll post Merrill Lynch on the site and short Goldman Sachs in his own account.

Surprisingly, Ginsberg only shorts stocks on the New York Stock Exchange (NYSE). Despite the tempting violent downswings in the Nasdaq market, he keeps to the more methodical, predictable companies on the big board. Ginsberg's approach is both admirable and enviable. He maintains a healthy cynicism, attacks the market with discipline, and couldn't care less whether the bulls or bears are dominating Wall Street—his returns are consistently and considerably positive either way.

Ginsberg's mid-2001 decision to cash in on his unique skill by charging for access to the "today's strategy and positions" section of the site was only partially due to pecuniary matters. Tactically, the move helped eliminate some Shortboy front-runners who were hurting the site's performance. Case in point: The Shortboy portfolio is set to sell a $55 stock short if and only if that stock hits $55.9. Knowing that Shortboy followers are going to execute trades at that price, a few start shorting at $55.8 or $55.7. The stock's price gets pushed down before Shortboy adherents can fill their orders at $55.9. Even though the Shortboy online portfolio is only a virtual one, it's performance was being dramatically hurt by the effect, and Ginsberg's reporting scruples wouldn't allow him to recognize any positive performance from these otherwise dead-on calls.

Ginsberg relies primarily on intuition and experience, so he's cautious about articulating any specific trading rules. The following interview provides a few key glimpses into his approach. Log on to Shortboy.com and track Ginsberg day by day to dig deeper into his head. Ginsberg looks at Wall Street upside down. Any investor or trader can benefit from doing the same every once in a while.

Tell us about your first experiences trading your own money.

I had a regular job for about four months right after I graduated from Wesleyan. It was not easy looking for a job right around the time the market crashed, but I found one at a firm that analyzed bankrupt companies. Once I left the bankruptcy firm, I went on to the AMEX [American Stock Exchange]. I was playing with a $50,000 account, which was a lot to me at the time, and I was a little bit reckless. I was out of college, and there I was in a casino. I really didn't know my way around, but I found my way over to the XMI pit, which traded options on the XMI index of stocks. [The XMI is the AMEX Major Market Index, a basket of 20 blue-chip stocks that represent a broad range of industries.] On Saint Patrick's Day 1989, not knowing what I was doing, I sold a bunch of puts on the day before expiration, thinking it was easy money. I'm selling it for $12 today; it'll be worth $0 tomorrow, like it happens 90 percent of the time. But not in this case. Some numbers came out; the market opened much lower; and I was out $40,000, which was almost everything I had. I was shell-shocked, and once I covered my position, I got out of there with just a few thousand dollars left. I cried on the street. It was a traumatic experience, but I've never lost more than 2 percent of my portfolio in a day since then.

You lost all of your money on a single play, but would you really go so far as to call the exchange a casino?

The stock market and the futures exchange are casinos. You're gambling with your money, and as with most casinos, you're going to lose. The bookies in this case are the specialists, and they're the ones that make the money. I learned that in a big way when I got to the AMEX and saw the market makers in the options pits. They were the ones who made the markets; they were the ones who made the money. Even if you were the best trader in the world, you could not make money down there unless you were the specialist. They had it rigged. They made the spreads wide. They knew what they were doing. They were good bookies. I learned a long, long time ago not to trade options unless I'm a market maker on the floor. Everyone lost money down there except the specialists.

So, you go to Columbia Business School and drop out with one semester left. Your friends and family think you're making the wrong decision, but you've had your fill of academia. Where did you head after you left Columbia?

I went back to the AMEX. This time I tried to narrow my focus to individual stocks. It was less risky.

Tell us more about trading on the exchange the second time around.

I would go over to a pit—for each stock, there's a little pit where traders get together and try to make a market in many different options for the stock. When I was down there, the big options were Digital Equipment and Phillip Morris. Wherever I went, they didn't want me. It wasn't personal; it was true for everyone. They want to make their money. I wanted to be one of them; I wanted to be a market maker. What I learned was that you have to go to a stock, stay there, become friendly with the people, kiss a little ass, and you'll be accepted. You can't walk around from stock to stock and expect to walk in and walk out and be bidding on the bids and offering on the offers. I wanted to play their game, but not to follow all of their rules. If I had followed their rules, I would have stuck to one stock. But I didn't want to do that because every day I had different ideas about different stocks. So ultimately, in 1994, I left the exchange because I realized it was fruitless. Either I had to stay in one place, or I had to leave.

Today you almost exclusively short stocks. Where did that fetish for betting on the downside come from? Was anyone in your family involved with Wall Street?

My father was in the box business, and he was always the most negative person on the stock market. After the market crashed in 1987, he thought it was going lower. After I graduated college when the market crashed, he would point out stocks with high PE [price-earnings] ratios and say, "These are the stocks that I think are going down." His negativity about the world and the stock market probably initiated my interest in short selling.

What percentage of investors shorts stocks?

Next to nothing. I'm standing in uncharted water, in a league of my own. I don't want this to sound the wrong way, but I feel like I'm the best. Like Mike Tyson said, he's the baddest man on the planet. I feel that I'm the best short seller on the planet. And, lucky for me, Wall Street's where the money is, and if you're the best at something, you're going to get your reward. You guys aren't my age, but I remember that when the market crashed, a lot of people around the Manhattan area were very unhappy. I don't have to worry about market crashes. I don't have to worry about market corrections. Bear in mind that if I don't beat the S&P this year, everything has to be reevaluated. But I'm only going off of what my track record has been the last five years.

Have you ever been down as much as you are this year?

To me, being down 1 percent is statistically insignificant. At any time, I could break out. All it takes is one day. The reason I have the Shortboy Hall of Fame up [see Figure 6.3] is for people who want to know about risk and reward. I don't lose 2 percent, ever—not since 1989. Now, there have been many days since 1996 when I've made 10 percent in a day, and there have been at least 20 days when I've made 5 percent in a day. I know how to limit my losses. That is what makes me a very good investor. And as you can see, Shortboy has never lost 2 percent, and believe

```
┌─────────────────────────────────────────────────────────┐
│ SHORTBOY HALL OF FAME                                    │
│                                                          │
│ Shortboy's Best Days        S&P 500 Index Worst Days    │
│ Day 1   Jan 24th  (+3.91%)  Day 1   Apr 14th   (-5.78%) │
│ Day 2   Mar 14th  (+2.61%)  Day 2   Jan 4th    (-3.83%) │
│ Day 3                       Day 3   Dec 20th   (-3.13%) │
│ Day 4                       Day 4   Feb 18th   (-3.04%) │
│                                                          │
│ Shortboy's Worst Days       S&P 500 Index Best Days     │
│ Day 1                       Day 1   Mar 16th   (+4.75%) │
│ Day 2                       Day 2   Dec 5th    (+3.89%) │
│ Day 3                       Day 3   Oct 19th   (+3.47%) │
│                                                          │
│        * Minimum 2% change to make Hall of Fame 2000 *  │
└─────────────────────────────────────────────────────────┘
```

Figure 6.3   Days in 2000 when Shortboy and the S&P 500 gained or lost more than 2 percent
Source: Shortboy.com.

me, there have been days the S&P's gone up 5 percent, 4 percent, 3 percent. Those days make the Hall of Fame. [In other words, even though the S&P has registered volatile single-day upswings and downswings of over 5 percent, Ginsberg has never lost more than 2 percent of his position on a single day.]

Consistent gains and seemingly minimal risk—that's impressive. Can you give us an idea of your stock-picking methodology?

I'll try to do my best, but bear in mind, this is me, with intuition, with all my experience, with all my hits and misses over a 35-year period. This is basically what I do each evening: I have about 160 stocks that I follow, 60 of which are on the Nasdaq even though I don't trade them. I just want to make sure that I have a feel for everything that's going on . . .

Why don't you trade Nasdaq stocks? It seems as if they would be a short's dream—especially in 2000 and 2001.

In early 1998 I shorted eBay, and in one day I lost $10,000. I scratched my head because I thought there was nothing to this company; and that's when I realized that there was something bigger that I did not understand about the Internet. From then on, I did not trade another Internet stock, and thank God because the Nasdaq was up 85 percent in 1999. That surely would have put me out of business. I watched the Nasdaq go up 85 percent in 1999, and I watched it go down 40-something percent in 2000. I watched them both; I wasn't there for the wedding or the

Figure 6.4　Kohl's (NYSE: KSS), February 2000–February 2001
Source: Prophet Financial Systems, Inc. (www.ProphetFinance.com).

funeral. Whenever I make a mistake, I make sure I learn something from it. So, even though it took $10,000 from me quicker than anything I could think of in the last five or ten years, eBay saved me a lot of money.

Okay, no Nasdaq. You've got your 160 stocks that you follow . . .

This is where it becomes intuition. I look at a chart, and everyone sees a chart differently. For instance, Shortboy is short Kohl's right now [see Figure 6.4]. I see it being under $50 in November, and it's now over $70; 40 percent in two months is a little much for Kohl's, a department store. It's a big rise, but Kohl's has always been a wise-guy favorite of short sellers because it's trading at 60 or 70 times earnings. That fact alone would keep the price up. Whenever it's a wise-guy short, too many people are short it, and the price stays up. What I'm looking at with Kohl's is a single top on January 31, 2001, when it went over $72 on low volume. Now I see it failing to even get above $70 for two days in a row—I'd be a seller of that. Bear in mind, I'm explaining these things to you, but when I look at a chart, I just see these things. I don't analyze it deeply. It looks like a single top, and that's a red flag for me that there might be selling ahead.

Figure 6.5   Goldman Sachs (NYSE: GS), February 2000–February 2001
Source: Prophet Financial Systems, Inc. (www.ProphetFinance.com).

Are you looking at the same stocks all the time, or is your basket of 160 stocks constantly changing?

It's changing. The stocks I like to trade are high-priced stocks. Every day when I'm at work, I'll look at the biggest dollar winners and losers, and I'll see if there's a good stock in there that I don't have. If there's a stock tomorrow that's up $5, from $95 to $100, on a few hundred thousand shares, that's a candidate for me to follow. It gives me an opportunity to make a few points. I don't want stocks that are in the $20s and are only going to move a point or two. I like high-priced stocks that are going to move five or ten points for the day.

Can you tell us more about your analysis of the charts and the thought process that goes into a decision to short or cover?

It starts out with where I think the market is going. Tonight, with bullishness as high as it is, it's a safe time to be a short seller. I was short Goldman Sachs, so I'll show you what I'm looking at [see Figure 6.5]. But I warn you, everyone sees different things. I look at one-year charts. This is what I've been doing for as far as I can remember, so I'm very used to a one-year chart. What I'm looking at here on Goldman Sachs—two times it tried to go through $120 and failed. That looks like a double top to me. I was a seller around $115 when it failed the second time and went to the bottom of the range.

How long does the typical Shortboy trade last?

No more than three or four days tops, depending on how strongly I feel the market will decline.

Does anything else matter? Do you follow the news of the stocks you are short?

Sure. I don't know how closely you guys are following the site, but you saw me trading stocks recently right before earnings announcements. For instance, Celestica: I had that one dead-picked. As a matter of fact, I wanted to cover it at $65 and change, and the day before the earnings came out, it got down to $66. Then the earnings came out, and they were blockbuster. I knew they were coming out, but I bet wrong and the thing skyrocketed. It got back down to $65 several days later, but I got stopped out in the meantime. So yes, you have to know when earnings are coming out, because that's an X-factor that can send the stock anywhere. And based on my experience, I know how not to get taken to the cleaners with these earnings reports.

You thought Celestica's earnings report was going to be poor?

I thought it was going to be in line with expectations. They blew out expectations.

Do you follow these companies closely enough to make decisions about earnings and other fundamentals?

No. I don't even know what Celestica does. I was just assuming that the analysts' estimates would be right.

And if they were right, you thought it was going to go down?

Yes, exactly—based on the chart. I was looking at a chart with a double top at around $73, and I was sure that I was right until they blew out earnings.

Do you think that if you had followed the company more closely, you could have . . .

No. I'm here to tell you that knowing what the company does will not help you at all in trading stocks, except if you're trading on the long side over a long period of time.

Why don't you take longer-term short positions and shoot for more dramatic moves?

That's just not the way I do it. These are great stocks that I'm shorting. Celestica's come from $45 to $65—that's almost 50 percent in two months. You can get taken to the cleaners if you short these things for more than a few days. Look at my executed-trades web page. All the stocks that I short are the best performing stocks on the New York Stock Exchange. These are absolutely the best companies—I'd be killed. That's the secret to being an intelligent short seller. You get in; you have your cover price; and you get out. If I were to short these things and just let them go, I'd be out of business. If I was short the Nasdaq in 1999, I wouldn't be here today to talk about it. That cleared out every short seller there was. And then, when there were no short sellers left standing, that's when the Internet plunged. We all knew those stocks were worthless, but there were a lot of shorts in them. They all had to be squeezed out. And I'm grateful to eBay for alerting me to that very early.

You just mentioned the short squeeze phenomenon. Is it important to consider the short interest in a stock before you enter into a position? [Short interest is the number of shares of a stock that have been sold short but not yet repurchased.]

I used to look at that. Now I don't, so I have no idea how much short interest there is. But I can assert (like with Kohl's—I'm sure that there's a lot of short interest there) that the greater the short interest relative to the number of shares outstanding, the less chance there is that the stock will drop.

Why is that? Because people are constantly going to be covering?

Exactly. It's just like the more bulls that are out there, the more likely it is for the market to drop. These are great contrary indicators. If a lot of people are short Kohl's, you can bet your bottom dollar it won't drop, because these guys have to buy the stock back. Like eBay, I couldn't understand it. Forty million shares outstanding in the beginning, but only a three-million float. [Shares outstanding represents the total number of shares of a company's stock that exist, whereas the float represents the total number of shares freely trading on public markets.] It was criminal to me. Of the three million that were floating, there were two million shorts. There was one day where the stock went from $200 to $300 in a day. That's the power of there being over 50 percent of the float short. They floated a very small number of shares, so there was nothing to do but buy. That's what fueled the Internet run up to begin with—the shorts getting squeezed. You can thank the short sellers and all the money they lost for the tremendous run up of the Internet. Now it's all been leveled out. But the Internet will survive.

These squeezes must scare a lot of people away from short selling.

I'm probably the only short seller who stays away from the Nasdaq. People look at the Nasdaq and say, "That's really overpriced." And they're right. But then again, knowing that the Nasdaq is overpriced and being able to sell short on it are two different things, as a lot of people learned in 1999. I was lucky; I learned my lesson from eBay. But there were dozens of companies that went up like a rocket, based on nothing. So, knowing that these stocks are overvalued and being able to short them don't go together. These things can have a mind of their own. That's what got me off of the Nasdaq—the fact that when there were short squeezes, you couldn't buy back at any price. You could put your price two dollars above the offer, and you wouldn't get it. The market makers wouldn't answer their phones. They would change their markets. It was corrupt. I know you don't get that on the New York Stock Exchange.

Why do you say that if everyone is bullish on Wall Street, the stock market is going to go down?

The majority is never correct. It's been proven over time that whenever there's a consensus—a majority of bullish people—the market will either go slightly down or sideways or down. The last specific incident I can recall was in 1998, right before the S&P went down about 20 percent. Bullishness shot up to 55 percent, and bearishness was in the low 20s. That was a pretty clear signal that bullishness was too high; then, when bullishness and bearishness equaled each other, the market bottomed. It's been a very beautiful indicator over time. [Ginsberg measures bullishness and bearishness by consulting a survey conducted by Investor's Intelligence. The poll measures the percentage of investment advisers who are bullish and bearish.]

You favor short-term trades on the NYSE. But if you've mastered your own version of technical analysis, why not apply your techniques to the long side? What's the difference between going short a double top and going long a double bottom?

Half of my talent is in sidestepping rallies, so I do identify double bottoms. Anyone can buy a stock and go long. I'm working to craft my short-selling skill, since I'm standing here alone. Look at Celestica—there was a nice double bottom at $46 right before 2001 [see Figure 6.6].

Figure 6.6 Celestica (NYSE: CLS), February 2000–February 2001
Source: Prophet Financial Systems, Inc. (www.ProphetFinance.com).

It went down to $46, went up a bit, then came back down to $46, and then shot up. That looks like a double bottom to me. If I saw that on the S&P chart, I would say it's not a day for shorting. And that is half the reason why I'm able to produce such high returns. The days that the market has risen are the days when I do not lose money. That goes back to the Shortboy Hall of Fame. Every year there are days when the S&P goes up 2, 3, 4, or 5 percent—it went up 5 percent on January 3, 2001, that crazy day when the Fed stepped in and lowered rates. But I didn't get taken to the cleaners. You have to be able to sidestep the rallies. You're asking why I don't go long some stocks? To me, it's just as good that I don't lose money on those days, seeing as I'm looking at the entire world in reverse.

On your web site you recommend that people go long the S&P 500 index with half of their account?

My advice to most people is, don't invest. And if you must invest, know what you're doing. Of course, I don't recommend that anyone be 100 percent short or 90 percent short like me. I don't have half of my money in the S&P; I don't have any money in the S&P. But I'm trying to keep people safe. The biggest worry about the stock market is, "Will it drop?

What's going to happen to my retirement account?" People have to understand that what I do is a safeguard against a plunging market. If you do what I do, you don't have to worry about a collapse in the stock market. And believe me, you never know.

Do you trade before or after hours? [Standard market hours are 9:30 A.M. to 4:00 P.M. Various alternative electronic exchanges have made it possible to trade before and after these hours.]

No, never.

Are the after-hours markets more difficult for short sellers?

No, it's based on principal. Believe me, 9:30 A.M. to 4:00 P.M. is more than enough time looking at a computer screen, pressing the submit button, and gambling on stocks all day.

Do you still feel that it's gambling even though you have been able to pull off 20 percent to 40 percent returns every year?

I don't want to say it's a sure thing.

You painted a picture of the type of company you like to short. Are there any specific sectors that you tend to follow?

Anything that moves that's high priced with high liquidity. That basically limits me to the best companies—the ones that trade a few hundred thousand shares a day minimum, and that are $50 or above. It's not the stocks or the sectors; it's the charts and the prices. If I can make five points on a chart, that's a stock I'm interested in.

What has been your biggest personal one-day gain?

In 1997, the day they closed the market at 3:30 P.M., I had two of my best days. I made 10 percent on Wednesday and then 9 percent the following day. That was extraordinary. I haven't been able to replicate that since. [On May 7, 1997, the Dow Jones Industrial Average fell 554 points, triggering the NYSE's newly implemented circuit-breaker rules for the first time and halting all trading on the big board.]

What was unique about those two days?

I fed off of the fact that there was a fear factor in the markets closing early. I saw it coming. As the thing was dropping, they started posting that if it got to a certain number, they would close the market. It was a self-fulfilling prophecy. Once they started announcing the number, things started accelerating toward it. And they actually did close the market, which means that then on the news, they were going to start talking about how they closed the market early and instilling fear all around the country. I made a hundred grand, and the next day I did very well too, and that changed the whole landscape for me. I didn't realize that I could make that type of money in a day or two.

Do you plow back the money you've made all these years into your trading account, or do you play with a set dollar amount?

I like to trade with a bit more than a million dollars—that's the best way my system works.

Why not use more money? Why not short thousands of shares of stock every time you trade?

That's a great question. There's something in everyone's stomach that tells them what their limits are and how much pain they can endure. There were some days when I was short 4,000 or 5,000 shares. I remember the day when the market closed down in 1997; I might have been short 20,000 or 30,000 shares—4,000 or 5,000 shares in five or six different stocks. But my normal amount is 1,000 shares. If I'm short 2,000, my stomach gets queasy, because I don't like to lose. That's why I don't lose the 2 percent: I don't like to lose. My stomach always tells me when I'm shorting too much. When you get that bad feeling in your stomach that says, "Uh-oh, it ticked up a half point; I can't take it; I've got to cover," you know you're short too much.

Are there high transaction costs associated with shorting stocks?

No. If you have $100,000 in your account and you are long $100,000 worth of stock, you don't collect any interest at the end of the month because it's all tied up in stocks. If you have $100,000 in your account, and for the entire month you have $100,000 worth of shorts, then you're going to collect interest on the $100,000 that's in your account and the $100,000 that you have in shorts. If you just short stocks and don't go long stocks, you're going to collect interest on the entire amount of money you have in your account, plus you'll be collecting interest on any stock that you shorted that you held overnight. And interest is interest. So that definitely plays a role. Every month I'm collecting interest. It's not the biggest thing, but it's just a little added enticement.

If you have done so well as an investor, why go through the trouble of maintaining an Internet site and sharing your tips, tricks, and picks with the general population?

I have a skill that no one else has. And one day, I'm sure I'll be recognized in some form or capacity on Wall Street. Who knows where this run might take me? There are trillions of dollars invested on the long side of the market. The goal of every money manager is to outperform the S&P. I'm killing the S&P from the short side. I have a unique skill. That's why you don't see any Shortboy copycat sites. No one else can do this. I can beat the S&P from the short side, and what that means is that I never have to worry that the market's going down. You might think that I would do better in declining markets. Unfortunately, that wasn't proven true last year. The market went down 10 percent, and I only did as well as I did the year before when the S&P was up 20 percent. My feeling is, I'd rather the market rise slowly because when the market rises, stocks go up, and it gives me an opportunity to short them. When stocks are all going down, and they're all depressed, and they're all at the bottom of their range, I can't short them. I can short a stock that's launched itself up and is ready to go back down.

Do you handle all of this trading by yourself?

I work on my own. I'd rather not disclose the name of my brokerage house. I'm a short seller, and no matter what, short sellers are bad guys. That's why I never give a reason on the site for the stock I'm shorting. I don't say it's a bad company. I'm in it for the short-term. I only short the highest capitalization stocks. I don't want to be known as someone trying to push down prices. I've just crafted a skill that enables me to profit off of some good companies. I hope that in five or ten years, Wall Street is around, and the stock market is higher than where it is today. Then we'll see what my performance is. I've become well-off. I live in Manhattan; I'm living well. I'm certainly not anti-American or anti–stock market. I want the stock market to go up. I don't think it will affect the way I trade, and I guess the proof is last year. I didn't do any better than I had been doing the previous four years, and it was the first year the market didn't go up 20 percent. Actually, it went down 10 percent. If you had told me at the beginning of 2000 that the market was going down 10 percent that year, I would've said, "Wow, I'll probably make 60, 70, 80 percent." But that wasn't the case at all.

Why wasn't that the case?

Maybe I'm losing my touch; I'm not quite sure. But is 33 percent something to sneeze at? No. You have to look at it in perspective. I made 33 percent. That's a great return. That was probably one of the top returns on Wall Street.

Chapter 7

CONFESSIONS OF A
CONSUMMATE CONTRARIAN

Aaron Brown

Internet Alias		Investment Style	
Aaron Brown		Long-term	
Year of Birth		**Location**	
1956		New York, NY	
Education			
BS, mathematics, Harvard University; MBA, University of Chicago			
Web Site (Free)			
eRaider: www.eraider.com			

In the world of finance academia, professors battle their points—usually about market risk premiums, multifactor index models, and similar fascinating topics—in a war of published papers. By showing a passion for truly understanding market dynamics, many of those professors at Wharton drove us to pursue careers in finance and investing. Nonetheless, it's rare that their works and ideas ever strike a nerve among actual market participants and jump from the page of the prestigious *Journal of Finance* to the mass-market *Wall Street Journal*. But Aaron Brown and Martin Stoller, professors at Yeshiva University and the Kellogg School of Management, respectively, did more than publish a paper. They set out to fix the whole system of for-profit corporations in the United States. And you probably didn't even think it was broken.

We'll start with Aaron Brown, cofounder of eRaider (see Figure 7.1), who has an impressive finance bio. Aside from the professor gig, Brown

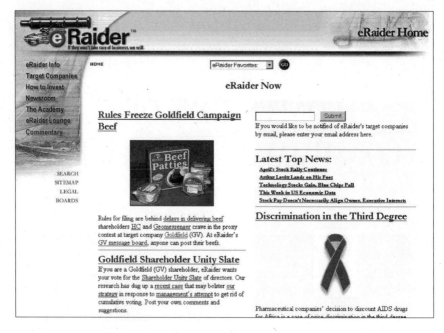

Figure 7.1 www.eraider.com

Source: eRaider. Copyright © 1999–2001 eRaider.com Inc. used by permission. Website Designer Nicholas Hofmeister, Art Director Francis Klaess, Editor Eliot Cohen.

has been a systems analyst for American Management Systems; portfolio manager for Prudential Insurance; head of mortgage securities for LePercq, de Neuflize; and consultant to J. P. Morgan, Citigroup, and Rabobank. At eRaider, he does the "investing"—although that's probably too passive a term.

ERaider is all about making deficient managers actually do their jobs, which—as many executives have forgotten—is to make decisions that maximize shareholder value. The value lost when manager interests and owner (i.e., you, us, and every other stockholder out there) interests come in conflict is typically referred to as an agency cost. This issue is often discussed in business schools among academics, and the presence of such costs is used as one justification for corporate acquisitions and takeovers. When one executive team isn't managing to maximize value, another team can purchase stock, oust the old management, and fix the problem. ERaider wouldn't consider an outright takeover; according to Brown and Stoller, the Internet and online message boards make that desperate and costly action unnecessary. ERaider hopes that more often than not, showing managers an angry mob ready to strike—causing the voices of irate shareholders to ring in their ears— will scare them into submission. If that fails, eRaider hopes that it will get enough shareholder backing on its message boards to wage a legitimate legal battle to fix corporate snafus.

And managers aren't the only problem. Hearing Brown talk about Wall Street is like listening to Al Pacino in *And Justice for All*. This whole system is out of order. Thankfully, Brown eloquently sums up just a few of his grievances against the modern corporation on the eRaider web site. The following is just part of Brown's "Brief History of Getting Things Done":

> It took an elaborate system of auditing and bank oversight, backed by tough legislation, for the business corporation to be successful. The culmination of this process was the Securities and Exchange Acts of 1933 and 1934 and the Investment Company Act of 1940. The first transparent, efficient, and honest stock market dates to the 1950s.
>
> It did not last long. By the early 1980s the legal protections were being repealed. Investment banks were chasing deals and profits rather than watching investors' money. Some investment banks went bankrupt; most of the rest switched from partnerships to subsidiaries of "financial services" corporations (companies that try to extract fees from investors). Accounting standards slipped every year to the point that companies could legally report almost any numbers they wanted, and increasing numbers of companies skipped even the "legally." Corporate boards abandoned any pretense of oversight and devoted themselves to golden parachutes, greenmail, and dead-hand poison pills. Instead of companies raising capital and investing in profitable projects, it seems that the cycle has become hot-IPO, frantic trading, money frittered away on deals and fees, and class-action lawsuit.
>
> Fortunately, technology may bail us out. The Internet has evolved a new way for people to make group decisions: the public message board. These boards are treated with fear or contempt by people who get on once and write an article. They see misinformation, rudeness, and anonymity. If they stuck around a while, they'd realize that message boards like that die out. No one comes back day after day to post venom or nonsense. The boards that survive develop a community. Newcomers often vent anger, but if they stay, they calm down, learn, and teach. Anonymity disappears. You may not know the real names of the other posters, but you know their ideas.

Like most hopeless battles, this one got started over some lost (or perhaps stolen) money. For that story, we turn to Martin Stoller, leading national expert in crisis management and full-time professor of communications. His bold spirit, his initial call to arms against corporate injustice, and his cash (he raked in $51 million from the sale of Plextel Communications in 1997, a company that he both founded and managed) made eRaider possible. Here's a short excerpt from Stoller's manifesto:

> In late 1998 I bought several thousand shares in a New York Stock Exchange–listed firm called United Companies Financial (UC). Having taught crisis management at Northwestern and consulted in the field for years, I had learned that the stock market has a pronounced tendency to overreact—to bad news *and* good. So I had developed the practice of taking stakes in troubled companies, when research satisfied me that whatever had suppressed their share price was temporary, exaggerated, or likely to be fixed. In the case of UC, I based my investment decision in no small part on the stated book value of the firm, expressed in an audited bill of financial health issued by one of the Big Five accounting firms, Deloitte & Touche.
>
> Within months, over 90 percent of the value of my investment had disappeared. Forget the market cap (the stock had traded as high as $35 within the year; I bought my initial shares at $1; two months later, the stock was trading for 10 *cents*). What was truly amazing was that the company's *book value* had declined from half a billion dollars to less than zero—$17 per share to bankruptcy, a breathtaking collapse. But most stunning of all, *no one would tell me where the money had gone.* A public company of the United States refused to answer calls from a shareholder. I couldn't open them up with a crowbar.

Thus, eRaider was born. Well, not quite. There were many more intricate twists and turns in the tale, but we'll let you discover them yourself. The two professors are embarking on a noble quest, and they desperately want some devoted passengers on board. Read the interview, visit the web site, and join the team. For now, we'll leave you with Aaron Brown and the eRaider dream:

> Each successful takeover will persuade a dozen other companies to go along with the message boards voluntarily. As these companies' stock prices go up, even more companies will fall into line. ERaider will develop credibility among investors, and they will begin to vote for eRaider [board] candidates as automatically as they now vote for management candidates. In a few years it will be considered normal for shareholders to spend a few hours examining the companies they own and sharing their work with other shareholders. Management will consult the message board on major issues of strategy and report to the message board on the day-to-day activities. After more than 800 years, the for-profit business corporation will become a viable form of organization.

Start at the beginning. How did you get interested in investing?

I've always been interested in numbers. As a kid I would go through the investing columns, try to beat the market, and try to figure out some of the nuances. I convinced myself very early on that there is no quantitative financial analytic way to beat the market. It didn't matter how much research you did on stocks, how many numbers you looked at; there was just no way to do it. What struck me as comparatively easy was improving company performance. Showing up at shareholder meetings, engaging directors and management in intelligent conversation about the company, and showing them somebody was watching seemed to make an enormous difference.

Where did that revelation come from? Most people can't even conceive of having enough power to affect the policies of a large company.

It seemed like common sense at the start. People talk about shareholder meetings as being a waste of time, but that's because they are judging it by the effect on the investor. It always seemed to me that the reason you go to a shareholder meeting is for the effect on management and directors. If somebody works for you and you don't show up to watch him, don't expect good performance. If you go to a company and see people joking, laughing, wasting time, not taking money very seriously, and then suddenly you see them shape up and start producing better work, you can tell in five minutes that you are having an effect. It takes a bit longer to persuade yourself that that actually translates into a better stock price. A real problem for most investment managers is that they get no reliable feedback, which is why they start getting superstitious and believing in technical analysis and things like that. They can pick stocks wisely and lose a lot of money, and they can make random picks and make a lot of money; but when you do what I do, you see the results right away. People either react the way you want them to react, or they don't. In any case, it's much more rewarding than being a hostage to the ticker tape.

In your opinion, the stock market in general is perfectly competitive, making it impossible to produce substantial excess returns. How competitive is your niche, the market for corporate control?

Not at all. The simplest actions—writing letters, showing up, being intelligent—bear enormous consequences, but you have to have some feeling for business, for people. It's not something to be done en masse. The Internet is like a small town where employees, investors, and management can come by and chat. Everybody knows everything in a small town. You make that into a big city if you try to do the same thing with General Electric, and it's not at all the same atmosphere. There are plenty of secrets in a big city. The market for corporate control for companies under a billion dollars in market cap is completely noncompetitive. Larger companies—I don't understand them. I don't understand what they do; I don't understand how they make money; I don't understand why they survive—so I leave that analysis to others.

We want to hear stories about companies you have taken on, but let's first talk about why a service like eRaider needs to exist, why companies aren't open and honest. Start with accounting numbers; in general, how useful are they?

The issue that concerns me is quality. Can you go through the notes, dig into the numbers, and figure out what is going on in a company? For small companies, there is enough steel in auditing rules that a knowledgeable investor who reads the notes and has some experience with manipulation can figure out what's going on—absent fraud, of course, which is distressingly common. On the other hand, stated accounting numbers, reported earnings per share, reported cash flows, and reported return on equities have become close to worthless. The more people focus on a number, the more it gets manipulated. Accounting statements were never meant for amateurs.

How do you feel about Regulation Fair Disclosure (FD)? How does that look to impact companies' clarity and transparency in reporting the numbers?

Regulation FD was the first piece of securities legislation that was called for by shareholders. It was a groundswell, on nobody's radar screen, and it was enormously popular with individual investors. That's why it got done. We got into this silly game where analysts would guess the quarterly numbers, the numbers would come out a penny up or down, and the stock would move a lot. Quarterly earnings of a couple of cents mean almost nothing. The long-term effect of Regulation FD is going to be to reduce quarterly volatility and destroy the earnings game where investors watch and interpret every move. Investors will start to realize that what really matters is a long-term value of business, not what happened last quarter, and not analyst upgrades or downgrades.

How about the traders who play the earnings game? Is that a valid approach to the market?

Day trading is reckless—it's silly; it's gambling. It does provide a certain amount of liquidity for the market, but liquidity from people who can't afford to provide it. My real objection: They create rules to protect themselves. Five years ago a shareholder lawsuit had a class made up of people who bought the stock over an 18-month or two-year period. Today, shareholder lawsuits are brought by people who bought on Tuesday between 12:00 and 12:21—all because some trader bid the stock price way up, then bid it right back down, and one bunch of day traders made a lot of money from another bunch. Suddenly the company has got to pay off the losers. That means the long-term shareholders are paying off the day-trading losers. There is absolutely no excuse for that. If they want to gamble, that's fine, but they've got to accept their losses. They can't come to the company, and they can't get the SEC to pass regulations that are hypersensitive to tiny amounts of information that might get in the way of serious investors communicating with their companies.

Can you give a specific example?

The great Emulex hoax: Mark Jakob submits a false press release saying that Emulex is under investigation by the SEC and that the CEO has resigned. In an hour and a half of trading the stock price goes from $110 to $40, and then back up to $100 when the rumor is denied. And we get a lawsuit about it—not against Mark Jakob, but against the company. Why should the company have to make up the losses of the people who overreacted to a false press release?

Was the company held responsible?

It's in litigation, but they'll settle for $10 million or some amount. Very rarely does one of these suits go away completely. Even when the suit is dismissed entirely, the company usually pays to avoid having it refiled.

Your eRaider manifesto, which appears on the site, discusses boards of directors, whose job it is to protect shareholder interests. Are they succeeding?

Corporations were invented in the twelfth century, and up until the 1930s for-profit businesses were never successful as widely held public corporations; insiders always stole the money. It was only with the adoption of accounting standards—the Securities and Exchange Acts of 1933, 1934, and 1940—that we got the existing system of corporate governance. It worked for about 20 years, from 1945 to 1965, after which management quickly learned how to co-opt the boards. CEOs are very, very good at taking independent board members and making them dependent—finding directors that won't rock the boat. Corporate boards in most companies have become rubber stamps. There are exceptions. People like Warren Buffett and Henry Kravis watch over their companies carefully, but the biggest problem for corporate boards is that there is virtually no support for them. If they do decide to question the CEO, they have no backup, no information flow from the company, and in many cases no independent legal advice. They feel isolated and powerless. ERaider shows them that there are people out there who want them to do their job right, who will support them if they take aggressive action. The Internet basically functions as a shadow board, something that board members can use as a resource to find out how shareholders feel.

I have been in board meetings where a single shareholder letter was what allowed a director to stand up. The CEO didn't want to hear it, and none of the directors were brave enough to bring it up until one got a letter. Two hours later, the board voted for the shareholder's proposal. The Internet multiplies that enormously. A director can go find well-argued positions and questions to ask the CEO. For all of our companies, the directors read every post and take them very seriously. The old golf-buddy, back-scratching board members are going to quit because no one wants to be embarrassed. You are already seeing a new breed of directors who are brought up to take the responsibility seriously and will stand up to CEOs.

Executive compensation is an issue that follows that question nicely. First of all, have multimillion-dollar executive salaries gotten out of hand?

Executive compensation is clearly too high. We got a rash of option compensation in the 1990s that was rigged so that CEOs and top executives couldn't lose. Shareholder activists wanted indexed options, wanted managers to have to hold the stock for a long period of time after exercising. They wanted out of the money options and options deep down in the organizational chart. The real point of options is to focus the attention of mid-level and lower-level employees on the good of the company.

What's the best way to align the interests of top management and shareholders?

Top managers who are relatively wealthy should own a lot of stock. I don't believe in big base salaries. Look on Wall Street, and you'll see that very few people make more than about $125,000 a year in salary. Everything is tied to bonuses and options. I think the CEO of General Electric ought to make a comparable salary—enough to pay his bills at a fairly high lifestyle—and take the rest of his salary in stock. And he ought to hold his stock as long as he is employed with the company and for two years afterward.

How does eRaider change the current picture? Where do you derive your power?

Our biggest single effect is through the employees. The employees read the message boards. They hear people making sense. One of the ways management stays powerful is by keeping all interest groups apart, telling each that it can't do something because of another. Employees can't have raises because shareholders wouldn't stand for it. They tell shareholders that we can't get the product out on time because the employees aren't good enough. Customers, suppliers, everybody gets a story that some other group is causing the problem. On the message boards we cut through all that. We hear from the customers: "Here is why I bought, but now here is why I am not happy." And this kind of information is incredibly valuable to everyone, including the CEO. It's very hard to run a company badly if everything is out in the open.

It took a year to convince the SEC that eRaider was legal, but they have been enormously supportive of us—individual SEC members, not necessarily the Commission as a whole. But from the SEC commissioners all the way down to the staff people, we have gotten an enormous amount of free legal advice because people understand that what we are doing is right.

Aside from the legalities of starting eRaider, have you faced any legal threats from any companies that you've mentioned on your boards?

That's a routine tactic, a disgusting tactic that ought to be illegal. Most small shareholder activists will go away when they get a letter from a law firm because they know that a suit could cost them thousands of dollars. ERaider has a real law firm; companies get a letter back from a real law firm, and in most cases they go away. What we are doing is honest, and there is really nothing for them to put their hooks on. California passed the slap law that says if a lawsuit is filed to silence someone against public policy, there is a way to collect damages. That's only in California, but I think that the basic idea has spread and that people are more careful about bringing completely baseless lawsuits than they used to be.

What's your motivation for "raiding" companies? Especially now that your fund is closed to the public, how does eRaider make money? [At one point, eRaider offered a publicly available shareholder activist mutual fund.]

We never made money from find fees—never intended to. We actually lost quite a bit of money. The only way that we make money is by appreciation of our target company stocks. There is so much distrust on the Internet that we wanted to be absolutely clear that if those stocks go up, we make money because of our investment. Anybody can invest on the same terms we do. If the stocks go down, we lose money. All of the costs of the site plus all of the costs of any proxy solicitation we do—any costs of organization—that's all born out of our profits.

How does the traditional mutual fund industry measure up to the standard that you've put in place?

The basic problem is very simple: Active management doesn't pay. Whether you believe in efficient markets doesn't matter; it's very clear that after expenses and taxes, the entire actively managed mutual fund industry is selling a loser's product. They are charging people $125 billion a year in fees and another $125 billion in hidden fees you don't actually see, such as brokerage commissions, many of which get kicked back to the fund company. And they are delivering less than nothing for it. There are exceptions. I think Vanguard Group is a very good company—low-cost index funds that make sense for almost every investor.

How many target companies has eRaider identified?

We've announced five publicly. I think I've learned quite a bit about what kind of companies to focus on. And one of these days, within the next six months, we are going to go after a large company—something in the $1 billion market cap range.

What size have the others been?

Under $100 million. The idea was to target companies of approximately $200 million in market cap, but because we wanted to get a 5 percent stake and wanted to conserve our investment resources early on, we started with smaller ones.

Have you gone through a whole cycle of buying and selling with any of them?

We had one go bankrupt, and we did sell out after the stock had become worthless. That was our first company—very close to being our greatest

Figure 7.2 Employee Solutions (OTC: ESOL), May 1998–May 2001
Source: Prophet Financial Systems, Inc. (www.ProphetFinance.com).

success, and instead a complete failure. We did what we set out to do, but it didn't save the company. With this sort of investing, out of ten companies, two or three go bankrupt, four or five yield good returns, and two really take off—go up five or ten times.

What was the company you are referring to that went bankrupt?

Employee Solutions [see Figure 7.2].

What happened?

It was a private company that found an inactive company and merged into it just to get the public listing. So it never went through all the paperwork and due diligence of a public company. It was wildly hyped by analysts on Wall Street, and the stock went up to $30 per share. After a big shareholder lawsuit, the whole thing collapsed . . .

The following passage, which tells the story of professional employer organization (PEO) Employee Solutions, was written by Aaron Brown and is taken directly from the eRaider web site.

> Employee Solutions went public in 1993 and enjoyed three years of great stock market success. Business success was mixed. They built the

best-quality PEO in the country and expanded rapidly. 1995 to 1997 saw a tangled series of transactions and allegations of financial fraud. To quote from the analysis we posted when we first announced eRaider's interest (April 2000), "The kindest description of these transactions are complex deals with insiders, involving large contingent payments that spawned expensive litigation and chewed up shareholder value. They saddled the company with $85 million of unnecessary debt, diluted the stock by 40 percent, and brought the stock from a high of $41.50 to a low of $0.21. But a new management team started cleaning things up a year ago. They have brought costs under control, improved service and profitability, and focused the business precisely where the long-term value is. We love the way they run the company, and we love that the new CEO bought 100,000 shares of stock with his own money."

It's important to remember that none of the $85 million of debt ever went to the company; it just cleaned up some old mistakes. $6 million went to settle the HDVT lawsuit, $4 million to settle the shareholder class action, and $23 million to take care of workers compensation liabilities (the shareholder lawsuit alleged that these losses had been hidden). $3 million was paid in investment banking fees for arranging the loan, and $50 million was used to pay off existing loans also undertaken to clean up problems. That adds up to $86 million. The interest from this debt plus the amortization from wildly overpriced acquisitions caused large losses.

Employee Solutions could not prosper while it owed $85 million. The interest payments on the $85 million of debt ate up all the cash flow, so there was nothing left for growth. Moreover, the high debt load created an impression of financial distress, which scared away customers. Had the $85 million been used to acquire worthwhile assets, the cash flow from those assets would have helped the debt service.

At this point, we introduce Quentin Smith. Smith was an Arthur Andersen consultant who joined the Employee Solutions board in January 1998, assumed the chairmanship in August 1998, and became CEO in February 1999. He eased out the old directors and management and installed allies in all the positions of power. He was the architect of the plan to save Employee Solutions.

I think there were three main choices at this point: sell the company, grow the company and the stock price so you can raise new equity capital, or slash costs and increase profitability enough to make the company attractive to lenders. This is where I enter the story. I started investigating the company, looking at its history and business. I already liked the PEO business. Our research told us that Employee Solutions had the best product not only among PEOs, but among all types of employee servicing companies.

And now back to the interview . . .

The reason we got involved is that it looked as if Quentin Smith was going to cut a restructuring deal that had more benefit for insiders and employees than for shareholders. One of the things you can do in a situation like this is to find somebody to buy the company and pay off the debt, and shareholders get cash. And we found some people who wanted to buy it. We were confident that we had a situation where we could do something—either get restructuring negotiations done to our satisfaction or find a buyer. We sparred for a while and eventually got a place at the negotiating table for the restructuring; unfortunately, we targeted the company in March 2000 at the high of the Nasdaq. At the beginning of March, the company was worth $350 million as a going concern, and the $85 million debt was pretty easy to restructure. By the end, in December, the company's value had gone down to about $125 million just by action of the stock market. So we won in the sense that we got a place at the table, we got our equity investors listening, and we negotiated a much better deal for shareholders than I think they would have gotten without us. But it all went for nothing because by the time the deal actually got done, the market had moved enough that there wasn't anything left, and the company ended up liquidating.

Employee Solutions was a distressed company, but almost every other company we go after is sitting on too much cash. Management won't do anything with the money. They won't take any risks. They are not getting a good return on equity.

Can you discuss more generally how a shareholder's rights are impacted during bankruptcy?

Nobody is really representing shareholders. In principle, the board of directors and management represent shareholders, and in some companies that's true; the management and directors might own a lot of shares and act in shareholders' best interests. But increasingly we are seeing companies that file for bankruptcy not because there is no value left, but because management sees it to their advantage for one reason or another. The minute they file for bankruptcy, managers get appointed debtor in possession, and I think the courts are much too quick to appoint existing management as debtor in possession. You've got to think long and hard before putting the guy who got you into bankruptcy back in charge. They gain a fiduciary duty not just to shareholders now, but to all stakeholders—employees, creditors, everybody.

Usually it's tough to get an equity committee appointed to represent shareholders independently because the idea is that management and the board represent shareholders. Management is often looking out for their own interests, for their own jobs, for their own ideas. The creditors typically just want to get paid quickly. You have to go through this process to understand how little promises mean to them; they will take a penny today over an almost certain promise of 100 tomorrow. Employees get a lot of respect in bankruptcy court if they organize, but shareholders really don't. I see company after company that goes bankrupt, the creditors get paid off, management gets a lot of money, and employees keep their jobs. A company will come out of bankruptcy and make a fortune for the new investors, including stock options for managers. Often bankruptcy is a threat. We get that a lot: "If you organize, we will go bankrupt, and all of your SEC rules go out the window." Another problem is that the SEC has been very deferential to bankruptcy courts. For example, when companies go bankrupt, they routinely say they can't file financial statements—the effort would be too much. It's never true, but the SEC doesn't want to be accused of adding to the problems of a distressed company or sending the company into liquidation. I think the SEC has to go in and say, "As long as you've got public shareholders, as long as your stock is trading, you've got to give them full information."

The whole process is set up as if public shareholders have already been written out. Part of that is historical: It used to be that companies didn't go bankrupt until there was no hope for public shareholders. And part of that is that public shareholders are dispersed and relatively powerless; creditors are relatively homogenous and can put together good legal representation very quickly, and management planned the whole thing. It was their law firm, their strategy.

How do the Internet, message boards, and the eRaider site help to accomplish your goals? Why couldn't you just continue your investment strategy without this entire communications platform?

We get 15 percent to 40 percent of the target company shareholders on our message boards. We post information about our opinion; other people come with different opinions. We usually go out and meet with the CEO and the board; we slowly achieve some sort of consensus, and at some point we take some kind of action—a shareholder proposal, a proxy fight, a letter writing campaign—to get something done. We don't go in with something specific we are planning to do; we wait and see what consensus develops.

Who does most of the traveling, meeting the boards, and leading the fights?

It's been all me, and that's the problem. This was never meant to be all me. We have got to get more people involved; people are just very shy about doing it. With five companies it's a lot of work, and I'd like to get up to 40, so we need more people.

How long do you expect a single raid to take?

I tell people three years. It takes a couple of months to get the message board together, another couple of months to establish some sort of relationship, and then a proxy season or two to prove we've got organization. A lot what we do results in turnover of ownership. We may go in feeling that we've got only 20 percent or 30 percent support, but we feel that every year that goes by we get another 10 percent. People who don't care sell, and people who do care buy.

What has been your biggest success to date?

Our most spectacular success was an odd situation—a company called Transmedia Asia Pacific, not a target company for the fund. A large investor came to us and asked us to advise him, and we discovered that the company had just issued toxic preferred stock, a security that can convert to an unlimited amount of common stock and that is almost always disastrous for shareholder value. Even if we took over the entire company, the problem was a contract with outsiders. So the investor said to us, "Be that as it may, I will give you 100,000 stock options on the company to analyze the situation." It was a long and hard-fought campaign. We went to the FASB [Financial Accounting Standards Board], the NASD [National Association of Securities Dealers], and the SEC, and I think we put a substantial dent in the amount of this kind of security that is going to get issued. I think we had a big part in changing the accounting rules with the FASB and the SEC.

Twelve days before the stock was going to explode and destroy the company, we forced an agreement with the holders of the toxic preferred stock; they would exchange it for 15 percent of the equity in the company. And what was amazing about it is that at the time of the agreement they could have turned in their stock that day for a little over 50 percent of the equity. They looked to get 99.99 percent of the equity if they just held on for another 12 days, but we convinced them that 15 percent of a liquid surviving company was worth more than 99.99 percent of a worthless one. That's never been done before. Nobody has ever beaten a toxic preferred.

Were you able to make any money from the 100,000 options given to you?

Not yet, but we've got them, and we'll see what happens. By the way, the options were donated to the fund, so the public mutual fund holders got the benefit. But they didn't pay anything for it.

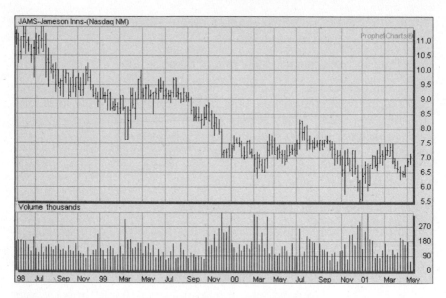

Figure 7.3   Jameson Inns (Nasdaq: JAMS), May 1998–May 2001
Source: Prophet Financial Systems, Inc. (www.ProphetFinance.com).

Jameson Inns was our third company [see Figure 7.3]. They have been entirely impervious to us, and this proxy season we are going to go after them with a shareholder resolution. I think we are going to get the company sold.

What is the problem there?

Jameson is a real estate investment trust, and like a lot of REITs, it contracts all of its management service; it has no employees. But the management company used by Jameson is 100 percent owned by the Jameson CEO and chairman. They have a conflict of interest on every contract they sign, every construction project they undertake. The management company makes money by constructing more and more inns, but the REIT only makes money by returning more than its cost of capital. Recently, Jameson has been acquiring and building inns beyond the interests of the REIT. The new Remodernization Act allows the REIT to bring the management company in-house as a taxable subsidiary, and that would be one solution. Another solution would be to take the owner of the management company off the board and fire him as CEO of Jameson.

The lesson we learned with that one: REIT shareholders don't care about the share price; they just care about the distribution. [REITs are required to pay at least 95 percent of taxable net income to investors in the form of dividends, also called cash distributions, that typically range from 7 percent to 10 percent.] You can explain to them over and over that distribution won't continue unless the company improves its financial performance, but until they actually cut the cash distribution, the REIT shareholders won't support any action.

What would be ideal for eRaider? It seems as if none of your actions work exactly the way you envision.

The ideal is that we create the message boards, all kinds of intelligent people visit, we achieve a consensus, management reads and agrees, we make the changes, and the stock goes up. We never expect anything that easy, but I don't think it's as crazy as it sounds. Each company is teaching us one thing that can go wrong, so one at a time we are learning what to avoid. We designed the site to be as confrontational as it was because we were afraid of being ignored. Now the problem is scaring them too much. When I was doing this privately, my problem was getting patronized and ignored, but that's not at all the issue once you do it in public. I had not appreciated the difference between calling somebody up and saying "I'm a concerned shareholder" and setting up a message board on eRaider.com.

What does the market in general think of eRaider's actions? Have you noticed any stock market reaction to an announcement that something is a target company on your site?

We have watched that very carefully. There is certainly an increase in volatility, a short-term price increase, but it's very transitory. At the time we launched, people were very concerned about manipulation and pump-and-dump schemes. And even though eRaider doesn't dump, they still don't like us pumping. A lot of people see the stock on eRaider and decide they are going to get into it slowly, because when a company is small, there is such little information. It's comforting for investors to know there is somebody that has really looked at it, that has talked to the managers, that has been to visit.

Has it been more difficult to find target companies in this bearish market?

No. This is our natural market, and when we get going full steam we will pick up a lot of new companies in downturns, and we will hold them for the upturns. We will be contrarian investors because we look at fundamental value.

Are there any other issues that you consider before targeting a company? Even if a company has a problem that looks fixable, what might keep you away?

Family ownership is the worst. If you find something that's family controlled, you can just walk away; not only do insiders control it, but typically they don't care about the share price. In fact, often they want the share price low for estate planning reasons. You can't fight a family; a lot of activists get themselves trapped because some of the worst-governed companies in the country are family controlled and publicly owned. Somebody braver than me will have to take them on.

We also look at trading volume. We try to see what kinds of investors are in the stock. A lot of clearing for Spear, Leeds, & Kellogg might indicate less serious investors than if you see trading through some of the other market makers. We look at the time of day people trade, as well; a lot of serious investors tend to trade near the opening or the close. A lot of trading around 11:00 A.M. to 2:00 P.M. is not necessarily good—it shows a lot of weaker hands. In addition, we look at Internet message boards and see who is posting about the company. We like to see a stock that seems to be mostly owned by serious, long-term, buy-and-hold investors. We also need to be able to sell the story. There are a lot of companies out there with problems we could fix, but we couldn't explain them well on a message board. There has got to be a clear path for what we need to do.

Recently, your web site had an article about Staples, Inc. Why is a big-cap company like Staples on your radar screen?

We cover corporate governance in general, and that's one of the issues that gets us a lot of traffic; people come to our site to get the truth about some of the issues that don't always get covered in a neutral manner. Staples spun off Staples.com in November 1999, which was close to the peak for that kind of company [see Figure 7.4]. They sold shares to insiders and favored venture capitalists at $3.25. They canceled an IPO in early April 2001 and said that they would buy back the stock for $7 per share. Every other Internet company in the world has lost 90 percent of its value, but Staples.com more than doubled for some reason. It's a web site—in taking orders it loses money. Nobody would take it for nothing, because nobody would finance the operating losses to have it.

What happened was that Staples had arranged for a bank loan to get the actual capital and then guaranteed the bank loan. The people who were "sold" stock never put up any money, never took any risk; it was just supposed to be an insider deal. What I find particularly unpleasant

Figure 7.4 Staples (Nasdaq: SPLS), May 1999–May 2001
Source: Prophet Financial Systems, Inc. (www.ProphetFinance.com).

is that I have no doubt that they were planning to flip this thing in an IPO for $20 to $40 per share, so the original deal was supposed to be an easy-money giveaway. And then when it didn't work out, they still decided that these people were entitled to some easy money. We have gotten a lot of Staples shareholders coming to the site and asking what they can do about it; they can vote against it, but it will probably get approved regardless. It's a problem of getting organized too late. If they thought that somebody was going to do this a year ago and had gotten organized then, they could have blocked it.

You mentioned that you want people to get more involved with eRaider. What is the best way for an interested individual investor to get involved?

Post for a year, meet some people on the board, and participate vicariously in a few raids. The first time you call a CEO, the first time you submit a proxy, it's intimidating; but after a while it's easy. Nobody really believes the stuff that goes on until it's happened to them. A lot of people come to eRaider, and it's the first time they have heard intelligent people validating that corporate managers do cheat. There are a lot of crooks out there.

Chapter 8

CLEARING THE AIR
Kris Skrinak

Internet Alias		Investment Style	
kris		Medium-term	
Year of Birth		**Location**	
1959		Mill Valley, CA	
Education			
BS, economics, King's College; studied computer science at New York University			
Web Site (Free)			
ClearStation: www.clearstation.com			

Recently, we received a copy of *E*TRADE Magazine* in the mail (not e-mail, but real mail, delivered by the U.S. Postal Service; remember them?)—a quarterly publication sent to holders of accounts with the on-line broker. The magazine is more or less a 50-page advertisement for E*TRADE's suite of services, and we normally don't even bother with it. But we flipped through it this time, and somewhere in the middle an interesting picture caught our attention. It was an advertisement for ClearStation, the education- and community-based web site that E*TRADE acquired in 1999 (see Figure 8.1). We were stunned to see a full-page picture of "Kensey," also known as ClearStation cofounder Doug Fairclough. The photo might not have even been Fairclough—the man's face was purposefully obstructed, perhaps a keen metaphor for the anonymity of ClearStation's online environment. It was the first time we had seen a major player in the online investment space advertise the value of insight from one amateur guru communicating in a large-scale investor-to-investor community; there was also a quote from Kensey—

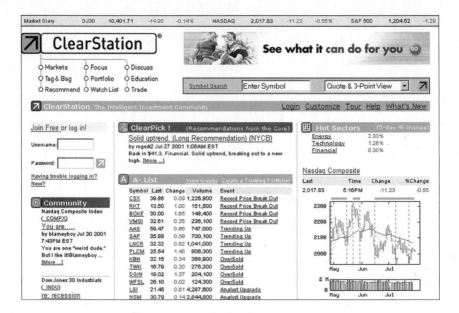

Figure 8.1   www.clearstation.com

Source: ClearStation, Inc. © 2001. All rights reserved. ClearStation is a wholly-owned subsidiary of E*TRADE Group, Inc.

who is no longer even employed by ClearStation or E*TRADE—giving his thoughts on the current state of the market. E*TRADE's marketing campaign is a step in the right direction of solidifying the value of virtual neighborhoods of online investors. During the Nasdaq boom, it seemed as if everyone thought he or she could get rich buying four-letter symbols posted to message boards or chat rooms; after the crash, the pendulum swung the other direction, and investor-to-investor communication got bashed and blamed. But E*TRADE finally got it right with the ClearStation advertisement emphasizing Kensey's analysis. You might be sick of hearing this from us, but the true value of online investment communities—the real money to be made—comes from the few smart guys. Finding them is the hard part.

Access to Kensey's stock picks and analysis is one of the key reasons to log on to ClearStation, a free site built on a three-point investing foundation that combines technical, fundamental, and community analysis. But Kris Skrinak, headliner of this chapter and the other half of the ClearStation founding duo, is no slouch. He has worked with some of the top individuals in finance at Goldman Sachs and other big-name

Wall Street firms. He knows how to invest in all types of markets, across all sectors, and on all levels of the market-cap food chain. And he loves to educate; nearly every investment Skrinak makes is communicated to more than 400,000 ClearStation members, and he welcomes feedback: "I don't speak in public because I am right every time. I speak in public because I'm not right every time. I get the majority of my sanity checking and ego checking from the people that I meet and the people that choose to write back to me on ClearStation."

Skrinak might be a little too modest. There's no doubt he can be wrong, but with yearly investment gains that range between 75 percent and 300 percent regardless of market conditions, there should be nothing stopping you from heading to ClearStation, navigating to his recommendations (under the alias "kris"), and subscribing to receive e-mail updates every time he adds or deletes a stock from his watch list. In fact, everyone in the "ClearStation Core," which is immediately identifiable after clicking "Recommend" at the top of the site's home page, is worth monitoring.

During our interview, Skrinak was constantly concerned about getting off track, about confusing his strategies and straightforward advice. He didn't want a muddled and roundabout conversation to confuse a topic that he has spent the past five years trying to demystify. His core message is this: "Keep things really simple. If you want to have a single barometer of how a stock is going to perform, ask what are the expectations for the profitability of the stock. Unfortunately, that particular question is not answered by a single school—not by fundamental analysis, not by technical analysis, and certainly not by the news media. The only way to answer that question is to choose tools from each school and apply them with discipline."

Our Skrinak interview appears toward the beginning of this book because of its simplicity and clarity. His strategies touch on all investing disciplines, and his comments are logical and insightful, especially within the confusing realm of technical analysis. This interview is a perfect introduction to some of the more complex strategies you'll read about later. Technical analysis is often looked at as stock market voodoo, but Skrinak yanks it back from the netherworld: "There's really nothing technical about technical analysis. Technical analysis is the language of group psychology in the stock market. If you look at technical indicators not as having some inherent, quantitative meaning, but as having a group psychology meaning, all of a sudden, these indicators come to life. Suddenly they become things that you can use. They become advisors."

Take us through your Wall Street tour of duty. To say the least, you've worked with some impressive folks. How did those experiences help you form your current investment philosophy?

My first job out of college was cold-calling at Lehman Brothers. I was cold-calling doctors in the Midwest. God, that was a terrible job; it was degrading, to say the least. Then, as a programmer with Lehman Brothers, I worked in fixed-income instruments—definitely very hot in the eighties, but now a little bit passé. That's where I started reading research reports and looking at competitive investment philosophies. I had the typical investment instruction in college as an economics student, which was none, really. I didn't have any philosophy at all until I started working at Goldman Sachs. There I was fortunate enough to work in Quantitative Strategies—part of Fischer Black's group—and that was the first time I found some useful tools that seemed to work in the market. What Fischer Black was doing was index arbitrage, and you could actually do that back then, because a couple seconds of difference between Chicago and New York yielded some actual opportunities. The good thing about that particular position was that I had the full range of Goldman Sachs products, including Fischer Black, to experiment with. Working on the trading floor—the 27th floor of 15 Broad Street—was awesome; that's when I started meeting top traders, because Goldman had quite a few of them. That's where my investment philosophies were formed. For the first time in my life I was able to do what you're doing right now—talk to traders who did well, to find out what they were thinking, what they were doing. Most of the knowledge that I gained was not on the trading floor itself, but at Delmonico's, the steak house around the corner. You would go there to drink beer and finally get a chance to ask a guy a question you'd been dying to ask him for three weeks.

Were the Goldman traders open to sharing strategies? Was it easy to mold their advice into your own trading philosophy?

It took a couple of years to begin to decipher their code, but one obvious thing was that this was not an environment for contemplation and intellectual research. It was a tactile environment, with more of a Vegas feel than anything. Some of these guys would be trading all day, hundreds of millions of dollars, and the first thing they did when they walked out of the building was buy a lotto ticket.

You can study folks a lot, and you can study techniques a lot, but you don't learn how to invest until you put your own money on the line. I was at Goldman for about five years investing other people's money, and I didn't learn a thing about investing my money until I moved out of New York City to California. I finally had to fend for myself.

What did you learn? What is the basis of your investment philosophy?

Nothing influences the future of a stock price more than the expectation of future profits, as we saw more than a year ago in the tech sector. Every stock has support at zero, and that's basically where the whole tech sector went. A number of smarter investors started investing in oil and utilities, which at that time were showing greater expectations. Part of that was due to the energy crisis, which was forming in San Diego at the time, and another part was the expectation that George Bush might become president. It was obvious that Noble Drilling and Precision Drilling were companies to invest in a year ago. And it was a very good idea to sell companies like Sycamore Networks, which had a PE [price-earnings] ratio of 400 or 500 and a single customer. These are fundamental indicators that I'm mentioning right now, but when you go to ClearStation and look at any tech stock, especially well after April, when the march was really on the downside, every single one had a fat red bar over it. There was just no reason to hold on to those stocks.

What are those red bars?

The initial purpose of ClearStation was the demystification of technical analysis. Technical analysis is a relatively simple field—primarily an academic field. A market technician tends to want as many tools in his back pocket as possible, but one of the things that I learned very early was that you really don't need many. In applied technical analysis, support lines, resistance lines, a trending indicator like MACD [moving average convergence/divergence], and a timing indicator like stochastics are all that you need. [Skrinak explains the use of the indicators later in the interview.] To give people an intuitive sense of how to use these tools, Doug Fairclough, the cofounder of ClearStation, came up with the idea of putting red and green bars over the graphs [see Figure 8.2]. When MACD is bearish, you get a red line. When it's bullish, green. Most people can intuitively understand what those red and green bars mean.

We always ask this question, but we rarely get a satisfactory answer. Why does technical analysis work? How can these indicators possibly show where a stock is headed?

Technical analysis is a way to read group psychology. That's the way I use technicals, almost exclusively. The reason a support line exists is not

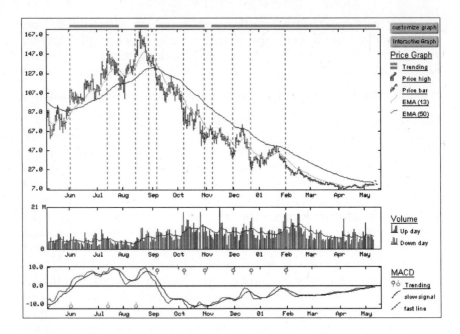

Figure 8.2   ClearStation chart for Sycamore Networks

Note: Bars at the top represent bullish and bearish conditions as indicated by MACD.

Source: ClearStation, Inc. © 2001. All rights reserved. ClearStation is a wholly-owned subsidiary of E*TRADE Group, Inc.

because of any technical phenomenon or quantitatively based phenomenon. It's purely group psychology.

There's a company, Barrett Resources, that tested $44 four times and bounced back every single time [see Figure 8.3]. There's nothing magic about that number. It just so happens that investors remember numbers. They remember the number 44. When Barrett hit $44, they were ready either to buy more or to refuse to sell. It's no more complicated than that. Now, the reason 44 was an important number for investors is because it used to be resistance. If you went back to late September 2000, Barrett was coming up through the $30s, and it hit $44. Forty-four was the number at which this group of investors refused to pay more. That's where people began to sell. Forty-four was a number that became ingrained in the minds of the tens of thousands of people who invest in Barrett and the millions who invest in oil and gas operations. If you were to read any more into it than that—that it had something to do with a particular number on their balance sheet—you would probably be giving too much credit to the people who are buying and selling the stock.

Figure 8.3   Barrett Resources (NYSE: BRR), September 2000–April 2001
Source: Prophet Financial Systems, Inc. (www.ProphetFinance.com).

The same stock, Barrett Resources, gapped up in March from about $45 to $60; it's at $64 right now. There was an incident, perhaps the discovery of a new oil field, which caused that gap to happen. What's significant was not that the gap up was predictable, but that the gap up occurred to a previous resistance level. Back in early January 2001, the stock had gone to a high of $60 and retraced down to $44, and the March news caused the stock to gap back to $60 immediately. I don't think there's a more basic technical indicator than support and resistance.

Why shouldn't those resistance and support points change over time as expectations change?

That's a good question, and it folds seamlessly into the next issue, which is trending. Trending is the single most important issue in the market. Spotting a long-term price trend in the market is the key to the kingdom. When you find support and resistance lines changing over time consistently in any one direction—successively higher highs and higher lows or successively lower highs and lower lows—then a trend is in effect. That is the reason that Doug and I decided to focus primarily on MACD as our main trending indicator. What MACD measures is the acceleration of price action over time, and a well-tuned MACD, like the

Figure 8.4   Adobe Systems (Nasdaq: ADBE), October 2000–March 2001

Source: Prophet Financial Systems, Inc. (www.ProphetFinance.com).

one we have at ClearStation, is going to give you opportunities that exist in the week to month timeframe. That's where the largest profits are in stock investing.

In early 2001, Adobe Systems, like the rest of the tech sector, was on a downtrend [see Figure 8.4]. It was trading in the 70s at the beginning of the year and then down to 30 in the middle of March. If you look at the chart, you see two steps backward, one step forward, throughout that entire downtrend. The number-one implication is that this is not a stock that you want to continue to hold. It was very obvious by Christmas that this stock was in a downtrend. It had every single characteristic of a downtrend, including fundamental factors such as downward earnings revisions. All of these signposts are pointing to reduced investor expectations. When a company is consciously reducing investor expectations by revising earnings downward, you have to get out. There is no reason to be in a stock where the company itself is trying to get investors out.

Adobe was genuinely an excellent company with an excellent product that was well positioned in the software market, and it continues to be; but on a technical basis and on a fundamental basis, all the signposts were weak. All the stars crossed on Adobe Systems around Thanksgiving 2000. The stock went MACD red and took a pretty significant dip, going from $85 to $65 in a two-week period. But then, as every stock does, it bounced back up from that particular trend. The right time to get into a trend is not in the two steps forward; it's on the one step back. When Adobe started this one-step-back motion in its downtrend, that was the time to get out. Everything at that moment said that this is the time to short. This is the time to buy puts or sell calls.

Are most investors aware of these simple technical indicators? It seems that if something so simple were so powerful, everyone would use it. You'd get a game of everyone trying to beat everyone else to the trigger.

Yes and no. The number of participants in the financial markets is so large that I think it precludes the possibility of ever having that kind of zero-sum game. That's been proposed often, especially to people who are trying to sell systems: "If your system is so good and everyone buys it, it wouldn't work anymore." If there were ever a black box invented that really did work, just based on a mumbo jumbo of technical indicators, I believe it could continue to work. Over 50 percent of American households have money in the market, most of which is passively invested through pensions. On any given day there may be 10 million market participants in the United States alone. If it's possible to make that black box, you should still make it, because the invisible hand is going to continue to work. Of course, there is no system out there that works every single day. If it did, I'd be using it.

We've got the basics of technical analysis down, but a lot of the talk surrounding ClearStation has to do with a three-point approach to investing—the synthesis of technical, fundamental, and community analysis. We will talk more about the ClearStation community later, but can you give us an example where fundamental analysis enters the equation?

Consider Scios: If you take a look at the prospects for this company—who their customers are, who their vendors are, what their revenue growth rate is—things just start looking up. Scios is a local stock out here in Sunnyvale, California. [Scios is a biopharmaceutical company engaged in the discovery, development, and commercialization of novel human therapeutics.] I found out about them in the local newspaper, saw the chart, waited for a breakout, and bought, and this is a stock that's now turned into a long-term position. A long-term position doesn't exist for me unless I've held stock for an entire year, and the only thing that's going to cause me to hold stock for more than a year is that it never suffers more than a 10 percent to 15 percent weekly price decline. That's my sell rule.

All the pharmaceutical and biotech stocks right now look extremely strong for a number of reasons. Ninety percent of the drugs that don't make it to the market fail in the last phase of clinical trials, and they fail because there was some group out there, less than 5 percent of people, who had an adverse reaction to the drug. Drug companies have tens of thousands of these patents in their stable, and they can attempt to rerelease them with the help of biotechnology. These are the kinds of things that investors really respond to. This is the kind of thing that can get people excited. Pfizer has a market cap right now of $272 billion. I think we're going to see these stocks replacing the Ciscos and Intels as the market cap leaders.

There is another company called SFBC International that takes drugs to clinical trial. You have thousands of biotech companies, and with all their innovation, they need to have their drugs tested. SFBC is growing at a 100 percent to 200 percent top line rate because of all these customers out there, and that trend is going to continue. That's the kind of thing that's getting me excited right now.

What moves biotechs, oddly enough, is press releases. It's kind of a crazy business. Human Genome Sciences has designed its fiscal year to have regular and steady press releases on its products. They've timed acquisitions in such a way that they can keep the market relatively well fed with press releases, and that's the reason I've got a position in that stock. Because it works. It absolutely works.

Let's start with the sell rule you mentioned. Could you explain that a bit further? Do you use automatic stops?

I have a 10 percent sell rule, and I refresh it once a week. I don't do stop orders because volatility has been so high and because I check my portfolio at least once a week, a Friday ritual. One of the beauties of living in California is that by the time I get out of bed, the market has already been open for a half hour, so I'm not bothered by all the premarket analysis. I wake up and see the results of actual trading concerns, not speculation on what's going to happen based on futures. Once a week, every Friday, I take a snapshot of my portfolio, and that's the gauge that I use in the coming week for my sell rule.

If there is one single piece of advice that I could give to every investor in the world—if they only got one message from me—it's to have a sell rule. People ask Warren Buffett, "When do you sell stock?" And he says, "Never." You know what that is? That is the arrogance of the rich. The arrogance of the rich is this notion that you can tell somebody who's finally saved up $5,000—and they don't want to get 4 percent on a money market—to buy and hold. That is just as extreme as any day-

Tag & Bag

All Sectors   All Industries   Help on Sectors   Technical View   Fundamental View

Sector: All (Technical View)

Name	1-day % Change(1)	5-day % Change(1)	13-wk % Change(1)	13-wk % vs S&P(1)	RS Rank(2)	Vol % Change(1)	% >50-day EMA(3)	New Highs(3)	New Lows(3)
Capital Goods	1.42%	3.61%	10.43%	17.10%	1	12.30%	63.93%	8	3
Energy	-0.81%	3.31%	4.42%	10.85%	3	-0.45%	67.37%	9	0
Basic Materials	1.19%	2.99%	8.32%	14.99%	2	15.55%	68.05%	2	3
Conglomerates	0.97%	2.55%	2.56%	8.88%	4	-29.16%	81.82%	1	0
Transportation	1.19%	2.10%	0.14%	6.31%	6	5.41%	60.87%	1	0
Consumer/Non-Cyclical	0.52%	1.43%	-5.05%	0.79%	11	-10.30%	61.98%	5	1
Healthcare	-1.04%	1.16%	-4.66%	1.21%	10	-10.53%	65.98%	10	3
Utilities	-0.14%	0.62%	2.43%	8.74%	5	-10.33%	66.67%	3	0
Services	1.06%	0.12%	-0.84%	5.26%	8	9.26%	58.90%	34	6
Consumer Cyclical	0.51%	-0.01%	0.02%	6.19%	7	25.53%	62.43%	6	2
Financial	0.15%	-0.09%	-2.49%	3.52%	9	-2.83%	70.75%	35	1
Technology	-1.18%	-0.56%	-10.27%	-4.74%	12	-4.08%	49.94%	5	8

Figure 8.5   Sample of the "Sectors" view in the Tag & Bag section of ClearStation
Source: ClearStation, Inc. © 2001. All rights reserved. ClearStation is a wholly-owned subsidiary of E*TRADE Group, Inc.

trading philosophy. I happen to know a lot about TheStreet.com and CBS MarketWatch because they were potential suitors for ClearStation; if you were buying and holding them, you're deep under water right now.

People used to call my radio show in San Diego and ask about Webvan. Webvan has never shown any positive characteristics. It's never shown a positive technical or fundamental characteristic, ever. But people—they like the trucks. I don't know what it is. What can you do to avoid all of that? What can you do to avoid the misleading but entertaining expressions that you hear in the media? What gets you out of this mess? Having a sell rule. Refusing to own a stock after you lose 10 percent is the most powerful portfolio management tool you can possibly have. It gets you out of that mistake every time. And once you get out of a stock, it's not like you're back to zero. You have cash. You don't have to sell the farm. Instead, a lot of these people are buying these battered tech stocks, holding them and hoping for them to recover. If you go to the market with hope every day, you should seek an investment advisor.

You said that you found out about Scios in a local newspaper. Is there any systematic way that you keep yourself educated and informed of potential investment opportunities?

Tag & Bag at ClearStation was designed to screen stocks primarily for Doug and me [see Figure 8.5]. The industry screens and sector screens in Tag & Bag are some of the most valuable places to look right now. For example, if you regularly go to Tag & Bag and search sectors, you see that energy has consistently been the top sector. Health care is up there today, but energy is number three. Energy has been competing for the first spot for so long now, that if you do not own energy stocks, you just haven't been watching, you haven't been paying attention.

In the top analysis, Tag & Bag lists the 15 basic sectors from health care to capital goods, and then you can continue to drill down on either a technical or a fundamental basis. I tend to continue to drill down on technicals. If you click on Healthcare—still in the technical view—Biotechnology & Drugs is the top subsector. Maybe this is the first time you've ever looked at this list and you want to get a fundamental view, so you go ahead and click on Fundamental View, and then you surf the entire biotech industry by market cap. Then you can dig down into some of these top companies, and if you understand a little bit about their business, you can go ahead and pick individual stocks. That is what I tend to do. My routine—and I probably spend only half an hour per day with this routine—is that I'll take a look at the major indexes first, including the Dow and the Nasdaq, to understand what they're doing on a macro trending basis. Then I go to Tag & Bag and do what I just described—drill down on the leading sectors. I look at maybe 200 or 300 stocks per day.

The fact that you have the confidence to play in many different sectors is rare. A lot of people have been obsessed with tech lately—blind to any other investment alternatives. What stocks in other sectors have you bought, and what are some stocks and sectors that you might avoid?

The basic answer to that is I trade with the trend. I look at that sector analysis page at ClearStation, which is a very simple analysis showing the percentage changes of each sector over the past day, week, and quarter. There was only one reason I was in chemicals and bought International Paper back at Christmas: That sector was rising to the top of the heap in the ClearStation sector analysis.

I do think there are some special exceptions. There are some innovations right now, such as those I mentioned in biotech, that merit special attention. I think the energy crisis merits special attention. Whenever you hear the word crisis, there is some opportunity. In general, though, I'll do my top-down analysis on ClearStation. I'll look at the major averages. I'll look at what sectors are moving. I'll dig into the relative strengths of the sectors. But I'm not excited about the return of Cisco. I'm not excited about the return of Microsoft or Intel. Frankly, I could care less. There's very little upside on stocks with that kind of market cap.

After you browse the sectors in Tag & Bag, how do you zero in on a few individual securities?

The nomenclature Tag & Bag means you go in, you tag a couple stocks by putting them on your watch list, and you eventually bag them by throwing them in your portfolio. When a stock makes it to my watch list, that's when I'll go to the fundamentals. There's a web site, Market-Guide, that has a page called "Description," that will tell you the vendors, competitors, and strategy of any company. ClearStation doesn't carry that content. The last stock I put on my watch list is Amdocs, because it has a very nice looking uptrend.

But it's just as likely that when I put Amdocs on my watch list, doing a bit more careful analysis will take me to a stock like Activision, which is at a new high. The Activision chart looks a thousand times better. This is the kind of stock that's going to catch my interest and turn into a core position in my portfolio. If one stock in a particular sector catches your interest and then, all of a sudden, you find this small family of stocks that is doing better than the stock that got you there in the first place, you just dump the original security like a blind date and move on to the more interesting stocks.

How many stocks will you own at a given point in time?

I'm rarely going to have more than 16 positions. I don't understand why anyone would; it's too much work and not enough upside. I understand you are supposed to be diversified, but that's one of those bullshit things that they tell you in school. Diversification is just a hedge against stupidity and not doing all of your homework in the first place. Give a stock a two- to three-week analysis from when you discover it, keeping it on your watch list, until you actually take a position. That's just good due diligence. The only question after that is, when do you accumulate?

I tend to buy stocks that have a relationship with their moving average. If the stock has a relationship with the moving average, that makes it very easy to accumulate. Your first position may be just 1,000 shares. The stock will take a small run up, and then it will come down to the 13-day exponential moving average. [A moving average is simply a curve that represents the average price of a security over time, in this case the previous 13 days. It is used to smooth large fluctuations in prices to help to spot a trend. An *exponential* moving average (EMA) simply places more weight on recent prices.] If it bounces at that point, then you know you can continue to accumulate on that 13-day EMA bounce. That makes it easy to take very large positions in some of these stocks. This is just basic technical trading. Like I said, I stick to the basics.

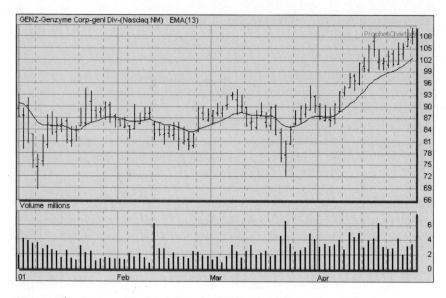

Figure 8.6   Genzyme (Nasdaq: GENZ), April 2000–April 2001, with a 13-day EMA
Source: Prophet Financial Systems, Inc. (www.ProphetFinance.com).

Elaborate on that accumulation strategy. Do you have an example?

If you take a look at Genzyme [see Figure 8.6], it has a relationship with the 13-day EMA: Every time Genzyme touches its 13-day EMA, especially in the recent trend [starting at the end of March], it bounces up. It seems to refuse to do anything but get stuck on one side of that EMA. Now, it looks like it's about 8 percent above the 13-day EMA, so you wouldn't buy at this level. You'd wait five days or seven days, whatever it takes to retrace, and then buy it again on that 13-day EMA.

You've mentioned to us in the past that your yearly returns might range from 75 percent to 300 percent annually. Would an investor following your advice on ClearStation be able to duplicate those numbers?

Look at Amazon's chart [see Figure 8.7]. I look at that chart, and it looks as if it's bottoming out. It also looks like it's got a relationship with the 13-day EMA. When it was trading negatively, it looked like icicles hanging off of the 13-day EMA—all the way until April, when something happened: The trend reversed. When that trend reversed, Amazon went MACD green. Now, all of a sudden, it looks like mountain peaks on top of that 13-day EMA. Today, as we speak, it's right at the 13-day EMA, and it might be a good day to buy Amazon. But if I recommend Amazon to-

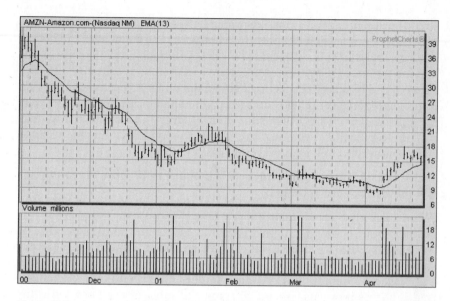

Figure 8.7 Amazon.com (Nasdaq: AMZN), November 2000–April 2001, with a 13-day EMA
Source: Prophet Financial Systems, Inc. (www.ProphetFinance.com).

day and give that recommendation to 10 people, then depending on what they do with the information and on how they accumulate their stock, they would get 10 completely different results. If I recommend Amazon today, I wouldn't suggest that anyone buy it for at least another two weeks. I'm putting a stock on your radar. I would hope that you would do the same due diligence that I do, and then wait for the next retracement.

How do the specific picks and investment advice that you give on ClearStation compare to your own personal investments?

I have a philosophical commitment to make everything that I'm doing personally a subset of what I'm doing publicly. So, every position that I have privately is in the public record at ClearStation, with the exception of some options plays. I've been selling a lot of covered calls lately, just because the premiums have been so good. [Skrinak means that he has been selling call options while maintaining a position in the security underlying those options—also known as a covered call. Selling the calls results in recognizing an immediate profit, but the strategy limits Skrinak's upside potential in the underlying stock; if the stock rises above the strike price on the options he sold, he still must deliver stock to the option holder at the strike price.] I just sold 2,000 Qs yesterday because there was a 9 percent premium between now and less than 12 trading days to expiration. [Qs, traded on the American Stock Exchange under the symbol QQQ, represent shares in a trust meant to track the value of the Nasdaq 100. Skrinak sold calls on QQQ because the strike price was 9 percent higher than the current share price. He believes that the calls will expire worthless for their holders.] There was just no reason not to take that. I'm not going to post that on ClearStation, because there's no way to talk about covered calls.

We've talked about your returns. What about risk? How do you quantify the risk of your approach?

When I say that diversification is a hedge against stupidity, what I'm talking about is having 30 positions and $1,000 in the market. One of the easiest ways to diversify is to buy an index. Beginning investors should probably own the Qs, Diamonds, or SPY. [Much like QQQ with the Nasdaq, Diamonds (DIA) and Spiders (SPY) represent exchange-traded shares in a trust meant to track the value of the Dow Jones Industrial Average and the S&P 500, respectively.] Then, when you start beating that index with some of your individual picks, you can move on to other positions.

I have 10 percent risk at any given moment. That's the way I view my positions. I will mitigate that once in a while with some call options or some naked puts. I might let naked puts get me into a position rather than just outright buying the stock. Selling options is a nice way to balance out the risk, especially when you're managing 10 digits. You've got to do something to take the sting out of the day-to-day movements of the market. [A naked put, also called an uncovered put, exists when an investor has sold a put option and retained no accompanying short position in the underlying security. In a follow-up to our interview, we asked Skrinak to explain more about selling puts to get him into a long stock position: "Selling a put obligates you to buy the underlying security if its price is below the exercise price on the expiration date. That is, the contract has value and the buyer will seek to redeem that value. I would never sell a naked put on a security that I wouldn't buy outright at the time of the transaction. There are two notions I'm promoting here: First is that of selling options, rather than buying; the second is that this approach to buying actually gives you more flexibility. Too many traders make the mistake of only thinking of buying when it comes to options. There is plenty of profit to be made in selling. Also, you can always buy back your puts if you change your mind on the trade. You'll pay a small penalty in that the option will have gone up in price, but that penalty is usually a fraction of that if you had made an outright purchase of the security."]

Selling covered calls, you're pretty much guaranteed 8 percent to 12 percent per month because of the volatility. That's a pretty good return in and of itself—over 100 percent. The market for options on the Qs is unbelievable. The options market is much more vibrant today than it's ever been, and it's incredibly underserved. There are very few resources for the options investor.

Besides the sell rule you mentioned earlier, are there other key messages that you'd like to get across to investors?

When you succeed in the market, it should be a natural result of your investing discipline. But every so often, you will do something like short Nortel the day before it loses 30 percent or buy Amazon the day before it goes up 30 percent. You can't help on those days but think that you're some kind of brilliant guy, an amazing investor. "Man, I saw that coming. I can do this every day." If anything, the most dangerous trap is admiring your handiwork. When you admire your handiwork, you lose track of the market—you lose track of your discipline and your instincts. I try as often as possible never to admire my handiwork, and one of the easiest ways to do that is to post on ClearStation because people reply from all different angles, angles that I never considered. Some are fairly predictable. Some people are just hecklers, and when you make a mistake, they really get under your skin. But the one thing that I don't do every day is walk out the door and think, "God, I'm just the best investor in the world!" Interacting with the 400,000 people at ClearStation is one of the best ways for me to keep from buying my own hide.

It's interesting to hear that ClearStation, a site built very much around technical analysis, has so many members. Traders—and technical analysts, more specifically—tend to be treated very negatively in the press and among the general investing public. Do you agree?

Have you heard of Peter Lynch? He's a technical investor. He came up with the 100-day EMA as a means of managing his funds. That's technical investing. Technical investing is maligned primarily because nobody has demystified it. The technicians themselves are responsible for a lot of this bad press because they tend to want to relay that's there's a deep science here. The reason ClearStation is called ClearStation is because this stuff is not complicated. It's not hard. It's clear. Just understand the basics. What is a trend? What are the characteristics of a trend? You can throw 99 percent of the technical garbage that other people bring up— mostly because they want to sound important—right out the window.

One of the beauties of the Internet is that you can claim the truth. There is a platform, and there is a voice. The old hype was that you have to value invest and trust experts with your money—disempowering messages that are primarily marketing collateral. Now that the market has taken a downturn, all of the people that spread that propaganda are back out there again, only doubly strong now.

The Internet is its own form of free speech, but that free speech needs to be financially supported. In the absence of the ad revenue that was supporting the early phases of the Internet, there's not going to be a channel for empowering voices for a very long time. If you look at the landscape of the financial web today, you can see that the technical sites are back to spewing their old lines about technical trading—like it's this miraculous black box that, for $200 a month, is going to make you 200 percent per year—which is a line of bull. All the old line brokerages are back to selling their loss-leader research, and one of the worst places you can go to for financial analysis is the leading brokerage firms. They were the ones who still had buy and strong buy on stocks that lost 80 percent to 90 percent of their value. I think Kensey at ClearStation [cofounder Doug Fairclough] was one of the most important people in finance in the last 10 years. He was usually right and spent almost all of his time educating the people who chose to receive his e-mails. When people disagreed, there was no product that he had to lose. ClearStation has always been free. We've always made our money with ad revenue. There was a period when there were quite a few web sites like that, but that period is long gone now. It's sad that the era is over. It was an exciting era, and I'm proud to have played a part.

Chapter 9

ALL YOU CAN EAT BUFFETT
Bob Bose

Internet Alias	Investment Style
Bob Bose	Long-term
Year of Birth	**Location**
1945	Swanton, VT
Education	
BA, economics and government, Trinity College; MBA, finance and marketing, Columbia	
Web Site (Free)	
Green Mountain Asset Management: www.stockresearch.com	

The Nasdaq crash of 2000 and the steady decline of all major indexes in 2001 may have seemed like the end of a long, wonderful dance to most investors, but Bob Bose knows that we still have it pretty good. Bose, a self-proclaimed old-timer, revels in being one of few in the business who was around for the last real bear market of the 1970s and early 1980s. During that time, Bose figured out that the whims and whirlwinds of technology companies and technology stocks make investing in the sector nearly impossible, especially when times are rough: "You try selling new technology in a bear market, and it doesn't work too well—like a lot of the dot-coms today. Investors' portfolios are underwater. Who the hell is going to take a chance?"

If the markets remain rocky this time around, Bose isn't likely to disappear—he's been at the stock market game for more than four decades, earning his junior investor stripes at age 12 with paper route money. With an MBA from Columbia Business School, Bose got in-volved in investment banking and rose to the ranks of vice president of

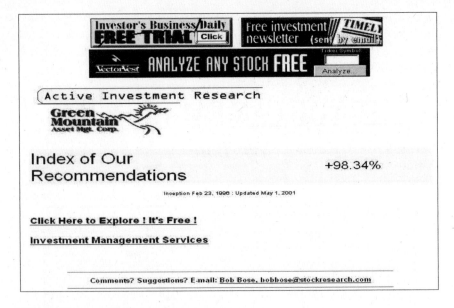

Figure 9.1   www.stockresearch.com
Source: Green Mountain Asset Management.

economics at Hornblower & Weeks, Hemphill Noyes. He left New York
with his wife in 1974 to escape the crime, crowds, and chaos of the Big
Apple. These days, Bose heads Green Mountain Asset Management (see
Figure 9.1), a small money-management firm far from the Street—in
Vermont. In addition, he operates StockResearch.com, where he keeps
the world in tune with his most recent stock picks and economic commentary. He lives and breathes the stock market. Our interview with
Bose was interrupted by a credit card sales pitch from MBNA. He dis-
patched the telemarketer with the quip, "I seriously don't need another
credit card... but I love your stock. Thank you very much."

Bose, a long-term investor who rarely sells a position, is a Warren
Buffett devotee—a designation that fits perfectly with his tech-stock
aversion. "We are growth-stock investors, but we try to be very cog-
nizant of the price we pay. We believe that Wall Street never, ever, runs
out of inventory, and our job is simply to find the right merchandise, at
the right price, in the right quantity, and at the right time." That translates into two or three mid-cap or large-cap stock picks per year. Sounds
like an easy life, but Bose finds ways to keep busy, thanks in part to his
web endeavors. StockResearch.com offers a weekly economic update as

well as quarterly postearnings announcement reports on each company that the site profiles.

Bose is a finance guru—a whiz with an annual report. He relies on extremely traditional numbers-based analysis to value stocks; he uses discounted cash flow models—the bane of any finance student's existence—which involve projecting the net amount of cash that a firm will take in each year and discounting to the present value by using an interest rate that reflects the risk of the investment. When Bose is wrong, it's not the numbers that get him; it's the fundamentals—qualitative assumptions about a company's competitive positioning and products. His biggest burns recently have been in Worldcom and Campbell Soup. "I knew going in to Worldcom that the voice business was brutally price-competitive. I don't want to be in a commodity business—it's just too damn difficult to make money. I thought that their data products were more or less immune because they were such a dominant player. Well, I was wrong."

Thankfully, Bose is right far more often than wrong. The recommendations on StockResearch.com have easily outperformed the S&P over the past five years while maintaining Bose's extremely low-risk requirements. And, as he loves to remind us, there aren't too many professionals who can make that claim.

It seems strange that someone who manages money for a living would give away all his thoughts and picks online. Isn't StockResearch.com competition for your asset management business?

Not at all. The people who want me to manage money want it hands-on. They want me to pull the trigger. In Fall of 1998, when Long Term Capital Management was imploding, Fannie Mae went from $58 to under $50 and closed at $57 all in the same day [see Figure 9.2]. You had about a two-hour window to buy the stock under $50. And we did. On the web site, we just can't do that—there's no way. Some visitors to the site are going to have discipline—take my research and go do their own thing. Other people want to be led around by the nose and told exactly what to do.

One of the stocks that we like is Cintas. Not too long ago, the stock went from $46 to $36 on nothing that I would consider to be a significant change in fundamentals. The last five points in that downdraft were company guidance, changing the [quarterly earnings forecast] range from $1.32–$1.35 to $1.30–$1.33. Now, you've got be kidding me that people react to that nonsense, but they do. I've gotten old enough

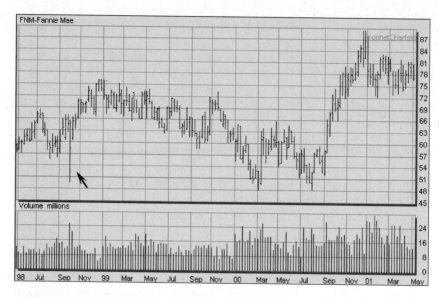

Figure 9.2　Fannie Mae (NYSE: FNM), May 1998–May 2001
Source: Prophet Financial Systems, Inc. (www.ProphetFinance.com).

and wise enough to just ignore that garbage. I would suspect that a lot of newer investors would react to that—overreact. It's shaken a lot of people out of good long-term positions for the wrong reasons. Another one of our stocks is State Street—volatile as all hell. That stock is all over the place, and people probably think they're smart enough to try to trade it. Well, maybe they are, but there aren't many good traders. If I've got a company like State Street that's been able to compound money at 17 percent to 18 percent per year and that, in my opinion, still has a reasonably attractive outlook, I don't want to be shaken out. It's difficult to find companies that can compound at that kind of growth rate where I think I understand the business.

What do you look for in a potential new position?

We look for consistency in earnings. We don't care about market cap. Normally, the way we do things, the market cap is going to tend to be large, certainly medium-sized. We are going to want consistency—no mistakes—but there are always exceptions. We want up earnings for at least five years. We want good returns on equity, relatively low levels of debt, and we'll see what shakes out.

Is identifying attractive investment candidates as easy as using a simple stock screen? Where else do you look?

We're not proud; we'll take them from anywhere we can. We subscribe to ValueLine. But I'm not Fidelity. Realistically, how many good ideas do I need? If I have two in a year, that's fine, because the chances are excellent that the other companies I've got are still working for me. I've owned Automatic Data Processing since 1988. Still love it. In my own account, it's the biggest position I've got. It's the biggest position for clients. We've held it when it has floundered around for a year and a half and done nothing, except the earnings were going up, and ultimately that's what I care about. Sooner or later the price is going to go up. I looked at Automatic Data for a client one time, and I bought it for him in 1990—300 shares at $46. The stock is now $59 and change, but the 300 shares went to 600; the 600 went to 1,200; and the 1,200 went to 2,400; so now he's got 2,400 shares at $59. And he hasn't paid any taxes yet. We like that. That keeps me going while I'm looking for the new ones.

Looking at your web site, it appears as if you haven't bought any stocks recently. When was your last purchase?

Johnson & Johnson probably would have been the most recent one.

That was over a year ago?

Probably not quite a year, but it was a while ago.

Has there been a drought in terms of the way you invest, in the sense that there are fewer investment opportunities these days?

We were up 18 percent last year. I'm not going to kill myself looking for new things when our existing picks are all working. I might look at Schwab, but there's no push in terms of a Schwab because I've already got a chunk of financial stocks. I've got State Street. I've got AIG [American International Group]. I've got Fannie Mae. Those are three big liquid financial stocks, and I own them. I've got Automatic Data Processing [ADP]—they process trades. You want online? ADP processes trades for six of the top ten Internet brokers. It's a backdoor play. They've had 160 quarters of double-digit earnings growth.

I'm willing to buy growth rates rather than sectors, so once State Street began to look like it was going to get out of the banking business, I was interested [see Figure 9.3]. They were still carrying a finance stock multiple. I don't own a bank stock—never owned a bank. But State

Figure 9.3   State Street (NYSE: STT), May 1997–May 2001
Source: Prophet Financial Systems, Inc. (www.ProphetFinance.com).

Street is really not a bank. They're an investment manager like me; that's a business I think I understand a little, and I like that business. They also keep the books for a whole bunch of other folks. That's a good business. And the cost of the stuff they need, except for the bodies, keeps going down. They need faster and faster computers—well, the cost of that technology keeps getting cheaper. When you've got a State Street with a far superior record to the overall S&P 500 but you can buy it at a market multiple or less, do I worry that it sells at a premium to the finance sector? Not at all.

How do you determine a fair price for a stock?

Usually we use a free cash flow model, discounting free cash flow. We'll make some estimate of the growth rate of free cash flow for the first five-year period, then for the second five-year period, and then in perpetuity. We try to be reasonably conservative about those estimates. Cintas refers to itself as being in the corporate identity business [see Figure 9.4]. They're a laundry; they rent uniforms. Delta Airlines is one of their customers; they go in and put together a uniform package for the company—logos, pants, shirts. That's a business I think I can understand. I can't spell biotech, and I can get my socks blown off in biotech. I fol-

Figure 9.4 Cintas (Nasdaq: CTAS), May 1997–May 2001
Source: Prophet Financial Systems, Inc. (www.ProphetFinance.com).

lowed Cintas for a long time but never wanted to pay what it was being guided at even though I loved the company. It had up earnings every year for 31 years. That's my kind of company. Then they made an acquisition of Unitog. When they made the acquisition, they flat out said that it was going to take them two years to get things up to their standards—to get rid of some of the sales force that wasn't ever going to be brought around to Cintas standards. All of a sudden, the growth rate in that year went from what historically had been 18 percent down to around 12 percent. That's enough for Wall Street to cream a stock. And the negative reaction was justified if there was a long-term change in the growth rate. But my view was that it wasn't, so we bought a ton of the stuff. And it's done very well—in a business that I think I can understand.

Talk a little about understanding a company's business. How far does that need to go?

I ask, "Am I going to be at an informational loss? Am I starting off with a couple of strikes against me?" There's always somebody that's selling me that stock; they could have good reasons for selling me the stock— maybe they know more than I do. After you've been in the business as long as I have, you build up a whole bunch of prejudices that help you filter out a lot of information so you can focus on what's important. For instance, cyclical stocks—we just don't own them. [A cyclical stock is sensitive to the natural business cycle and overall macroeconomic conditions and variables, such as interest rates.] You have got to make too many decisions and be correct too many times to make any money. We don't own papers; we don't own oil stocks; we don't own chemicals; we don't own airlines—they're all off the radar screen. Now, when it comes to biotech, I'm at a clear disadvantage. But let's go back to something like an Automatic Data: Am I at a disadvantage there? They do payrolls for people. Why should you give them your payroll business as opposed to doing it yourself? If you're a Fortune 500 company, chances are pretty good that you operate in more than one state, for starters, so Automatic Data can minimize the cost of redoing those tax tables. Every time they change the damn form in state XYZ, Automatic Data can redo the software once, and all of their clients share that benefit. So, is somebody likely to outperform me in understanding that business? Probably not. Payroll processing is about 50 percent to 60 percent of their business, which means that a lot of revenue is recurring, which we like. Automatic Data also gets about a third of their earnings from float, which is what an Exxon or somebody has to give them before Automatic Data has to turn it around and give it to the Feds for tax filing. They make money from [the interest on] that float. That gives you a stable base of earnings. If interest rates are going down, they might lose a little on the float. But if interest rates are going down, chances are that the stock market is going to do better, so you're going to have an offset with their trade processing business. That's a nice company. I don't think anybody is going to really outfox me on Automatic Data. Think Warren Buffett: This isn't baseball. You don't have to swing at every pitch. You can play it more like cricket. You can deflect the ball without actually swinging at it.

How many hours a day do you work?

A lot. But I like what I'm doing, so for me it's not really working that hard.

Does most of your work consist of following existing positions or looking for new ones?

I'm not sure I would separate the two. I completely ignore most Wall Street research. Some of it is interesting reading for background information, but Wall Street is a much different business. Wall Street is a marketing-driven business. Mine isn't. I'm not into relative performance. If the S&P is down 20 percent and I'm down 15 percent, I don't consider that a good year. That's a bad year. But if I'm a manager in Fidelity's group, then I had a good year, and money will come pouring into my fund. 2000 was absolutely fantastic—a down year for the S&P, and I'm up. I like that. I think we benefited at the end of the year from a flight to quality that pushed our stocks up short-term more than they should have been. I think they're good companies, but just because they're 10 percent overvalued, I'm not going to blow them out.

The other thing I do that's significantly different from traditional mutual funds is that I'll concentrate positions, à la Buffett. If you're trying to beat the S&P 500, all you've got to do is own the best of the S&P 500. It's really that simple. So, don't own any utility stocks. Why? Because they're not growth businesses. They can't possibly grow much faster than GDP. In some cases, you run into big problems because it's a regulated industry. So don't own them. Get rid of the airlines; they're a cyclical business. Unless you're trading those stocks based on the price of oil and you get lucky, it's a tough way to make a buck. A while back, everybody was touting Boeing: "What a great investment!" No. It's a terrible business. They make huge airplanes that are highly cyclical. Why not focus on some of the good goods? Good businesses are not difficult to identify. We have 90 percent of our customer assets in 20 names. That's a pretty high concentration for an asset management firm.

Do you quantify risk in any way for your customers?

In a word: no.

Why not?

First of all, nobody asks. Secondly, how are you going to quantify it? I can absolutely guarantee you that I don't have a single client that would object to the volatility of our returns last year, because they were volatile to the upside. Nobody would object to that. They'll object to volatility to the downside. And they should. Everybody would love to have a 20 percent CD return that never varies—ain't gonna happen. But Automatic Data has 160 quarters of consecutive double-digit earnings growth—think about that for a bit. Cintas: 31 years. State Street: I think they're at 20. We have a sizable position in Colgate and AIG, companies with long-established track records.

Wall Street has a very short-term focus. When we first bought our Pfizer position three or four years ago, it was off a second-quarter earnings announcement [see Figure 9.5]. Pfizer made the numbers and then went on to say, "We want to guide you—meaning the Street—down for the second half." Why? "Because we're hiring more salespeople. That's marketing expense, and it's going to shrink our expected growth rate."

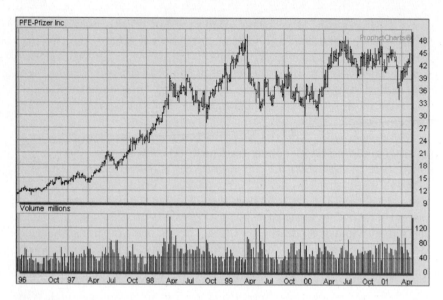

Figure 9.5 Pfizer (NYSE: PFE), May 1996–May 2001
Source: Prophet Financial Systems, Inc. (www.ProphetFinance.com).

Wall Street hated it. They trashed the stock. Well, let me see if I can figure this out. Why are they hiring more salespeople? Because they have more products to sell. You don't have to be too bright to figure this out. They had three new products coming to market at approximately the same time. Oh! We need more people to push the stuff out the door. What would Wall Street like—that they spend $2 billion on R&D and have nothing to sell so they don't need to have a sales force? They trashed the stock—hit it hard for a month—then finally figured out that one of those drugs was Viagra. Then the stock took off.

A lot of your analysis relies on understanding the numbers. Take us through an annual report—what do you look for?

First would probably be an impression. I've literally thrown out annual reports when I didn't like the first two pages. Never got to the balance sheet. There was one where the chairman and president both had full-page pictures of themselves. The executive VPs—there were about four of them—had half-page pictures of themselves. The senior VPs were down to quarter-pages. They're spending the stockholders' money doing this nonsense? Kaboom! It hit the circular file. Why bother?

I've gotten some annual reports that basically put one or two or three pages around a 10-K. That's okay. I can live with that. There are an unlimited number of opportunities out there. If you're willing to do the work, you just keep turning over rocks—that's what we do for a living. We keep turning over rocks until we find something we like. After the first impression, you get back to the financials. The really good guys will normally show you 10 years of data. What does that tell you? It tells you they're bragging.

We like to see decent returns on equity—20 percent is nice—and not a lot of debt to do that. Obviously, if you combine financing flexibility by not having a lot of debt with a decent amount of free cash flow, your company has a lot of flexibility. Buy a business that's easy to manage—something you don't have to walk on water to manage—because as Buffett says, sooner or later, somebody's going to come along that doesn't walk on water, and then you've got a problem. A good example of that would be IBM and Xerox; when those folks had everything under lease, they were part of the Nifty Fifty. But when you sell new products every year, every single year you start off at zero. That's a different business, and they didn't make the adjustment very smoothly. Xerox never made it at all.

The annual report always includes a Management Discussion and Analysis; you'd like to see management deal with any problems and explain them to you. You want them to deal honestly with you. There are some companies that will say, "My god, we really screwed up this year. Here's why." We held Colgate through the Mexican crisis in 1994 [see Figure 9.6]. Why not? Here's a company that if the only place they were doing business in were North America, the growth rate would be zip. So, they have to operate in Latin America, South America, and other parts of the world.

In terms of the balance sheet, I mentioned the debt ratio, and there are other standard things depending on the particular company. You obviously don't want to see inventories growing like a bat out of hell and sales doing nothing—a sure sign that you've got a problem. Are the margins going up, down, or sideways? Is the tax rate reasonable? Or did they, for some reason or another, manage to finesse the tax rate so that all the earnings came from the assumption of a nice, low tax rate?

Have you found over the years that the value of accounting numbers has deteriorated?

I would say the quality has deteriorated in part because you've got a much higher use of options as a form of compensation. And yet, companies like to pretend that isn't true—that options don't cost them anything. It gets buried in the footnotes. I'm somewhat surprised that the

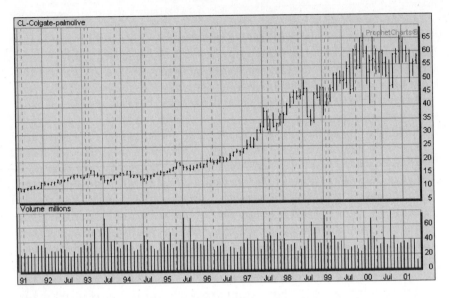

Figure 9.6   Colgate-Palmolive (NYSE: CL), May 1991–May 2001
Source: Prophet Financial Systems, Inc. (www.ProphetFinance.com).

analysts on Wall Street don't pay a little more attention to that, but they need to keep their lines open to corporate management, so they don't want to beat on that issue. The truly outrageous practice is resetting options. You're the corporate CEO, and you get issued some options at $40; the stock goes to $30, and they reset them at $30. The stock goes to $20, and they reset them at $20. Then they pretend that it's not costing them anything. It's nonsense. For some of these companies, you can take a pretty good haircut to their reported earnings based on options— 10 percent to 15 percent would not be outrageous.

What's the best way to gauge the effect of options?

The only way really is the annual report. Usually it's a footnote.

When do you sell? When is it time to take some profits?

I never sell just to take profits. That's the dumbest thing you can do. If you've got profits, things are working. If I'm taking profits, I'm selling my good guys. The retail broker will call you up and say, "We've got a profit in XYZ, and I'm sorry we've got this little loss in ABC here. Why don't we sell XYZ to offset the loss in ABC?" Well, let's see: I've got two commissions there. Now I've got the money from those two sales, so

I've got to reinvest it. There's at least one more, maybe two more commissions. Numerous times in the past decade-plus, I could have sold Automatic Data and taken my profits, but then I've got to go find another company that can grow at 15 percent per year. Not only that, but what I have left to reinvest in an economic sense is the net after-tax proceeds. So if I buy Automatic Data at $50 and sell it at $100, I now have 50 points worth of capital gains. Even at today's somewhat lower rates of 20 percent, I now have only 90 cents on the dollar to reinvest. That 90 cents on the dollar must outperform the buck. Now, honestly, that's a damn difficult decision to justify—that is, as long as you're not getting paid on a commission basis. In that case, you don't explain it that way.

There are some people out there, like William O'Neil from *Investor's Business Daily*, who say, "Hey, put in a stop 8 percent below the price that you paid for. It'll take you out automatically." They're right, it will. But you miss an awful lot of good guys that way, because to assume that you're so smart that you're going to be able to get in and not have 8 percent variation in the price of the stock, why do you think you're quite that bright? History would prove otherwise on average.

Overall, have you been happy with your returns?

Definitely on a risk-adjusted basis. Even on our web site, with one company that went bankrupt on us, we've outperformed the S&P. There are not many managers who have done that over five years.

Where can an investor go wrong following your methods? Can anyone do what you're doing?

I started my career getting beaten up. That does taint you. There are people out there managing incredible amounts of money that have never seen anything close to a bad market. Think about that. When was the last time we had a bad market? 1987 wasn't a bad market! The S&P was up 5 percent! That's half the average rate of return on common stocks. If you bought stocks on August 25, yes, you had a problem. That was the high, and then we had that little crash. But everybody forgets that it was a big up year until then. If you bought stocks December 31, 1986, and held through the end, you made money. That's not bad.

So, when was the last bad market?

Back in the early 1980s when you had the price of gold and inflation taking off. Then the market took off in August 1982, and it really hasn't looked back. Other than some old-timers like me, you've had nobody that has held their feet to the fire. Hoping for 15 percent in 1987 and making 5 percent, is not exactly challenging your beliefs. We're getting a few people out there who have been focused solely on the tech area who are getting a little challenged now. To the extent that they have a good, sound fundamental set of beliefs to go by, they'll probably be better off.

Why are you so negative on high-tech stocks? Most investors would say that those emerging companies offer the greatest opportunity for above-average returns.

Hornblower was the underwriter for a company called Cartridge Television in the early 1970s. I was a young guy just out of school, and thought I could figure all this stuff out. Cartridge Television—hey, this is kind of a cool idea. What do they do? They put stuff on cartridges. And where do those cartridges go? They go in your TV set. Oh jeez, isn't that neat? Now, what do we call that today?

A VCR.

Right. Have you heard of Cartridge Television? I think not. I have some stock certificates in my office that have Cartridge Television written all over them. Now, Hornblower didn't have an unfavorable research report; let's put it that way. Cartridge Television was the first on the block to do it—the first company with the technology. And they got killed; they went out of business. Unfortunately, I lost some bucks, but it did teach me a lesson about technology, about Wall Street in general, and about how to watch out for the competition. Cartridge could never get to critical mass. Whenever you introduce a very high-end consumer electronics product—like digital cameras today—you always have some rich folks that will adopt early. They'll try it early, and that drives manufacturing costs down. Then you get a few more people to buy it, and eventually you end up with a mass-market product like VCRs. Well, Cartridge Television was never able to get to that critical mass. See you later, Cartridge Television! That taught me a lot early on. Here I thought I was quite smart. It seemed like a great thing to me; it seemed like the next Xerox. I thought it was going to be great. And I was right, except I lost everything on that investment.

You claim to follow the strategies of Warren Buffett, but isn't it fairly simple to hire the real thing—give your money to Buffett—by purchasing Berkshire Hathaway stock? What do you make of Berkshire Hathaway as an investment?

I probably would not buy it for the same reason that Buffett would not buy it. It's too big. He tells you he's not going to get the same returns going forward. I think I can sit here and do better than Buffett going forward. Not because I'm brighter. I'm not even close. But I have less money to play with—a lot less. The sizes of his investments have to be huge to have an impact on what he does. That's not true for me. I can find a Cintas with $2 billion in revenues. That's not a big company—not these days. Can they double and double again? Sure they can. Can they export this concept to Europe? Sure they can. But for Buffett to buy that, it's chump change. Why bother? He needs big stuff to keep generating those kinds of returns. I don't. I have an advantage. I have an advantage over Fidelity. I'm not running $100 billion. When I go in and buy things for people, I don't disturb the market. Every now and then you see some truly idiotic things. You see pressure on a stock for one reason or another that makes no sense. Chances are very good that it is some big mutual fund taking a position or exiting a position. They get started and they keep going. The last 500,000 shares of what could have been a multimillion-share position get tossed into a market where there could be very few buyers. You see a big swing in the price at the tail end of the transaction. I can move quickly, not have an impact, and buy it. But can the guy at Putnam do the same thing? No, because he needs more than 500,000 shares of Fannie Mae. He needs 5,000,000 shares of Fannie Mae. Back to Peter Lynch: He'll tell you the little guy can do better. That depends on how hard they want to work, how smart they are, and whether they stick with a philosophy.

I do well when it's beginning to look like the economy will slow. That was true in 2000 because there was a flight to quality. If the economy is slowing or there's a serious risk of recession, what do you want to own? Automatic Data looks like a good bet. How about Colgate? That's a good bet. How about Pfizer? They sell drugs on patent. Their earnings will hold up. So, people buy those stocks. If you're sitting there with no philosophy, there's a tendency to get impacted by a magazine article about the 10 best picks for 2001. You read it and say, "These guys publish a financial magazine, so they must be good." Then they quote some mutual fund fellow who was up 20 percent last year, but they forget that the market's going to change in 2001. Those are the pressures on people. They're real; they're there. How people deal with them is going to determine their performance.

Chapter 10

THE WALL STREET RENEGADE
Brandon Goyette

Internet Alias	Investment Style
WallStArb	Short-term, medium-term

Year of Birth	Location
1970	Nashua, NH; New York, NY

Education	
BS, computer science and finance, Rensselaer Polytechnic Institute	

Web Site (Free)	
FinancialChat: www.financialchat.com	

"I am a contrarian, I like to look where others are not," explains Brandon Goyette, hedge fund manager, Internet chat room moderator, and hybrid trader-investor extraordinaire. In Financial Chat's ActiveTrader chat room, thousands of traders and longer-term players gather each weekday to tackle the markets in a free, open, and often chaotic forum (see Figure 10.1). Goyette makes use of the thousands of pairs of eyes in the chat room to help him find the next big thing. And Goyette has found a number of big things, racking up triple-digit gains in many of the past years, all the while sharing the majority of his diamond-in-the-rough stock picks with the general investing public in ActiveTrader.

Like many of the investors in this book, Goyette caught the stock market bug early in life. In college he watched CNBC rather than MTV and managed to lose half of his $20,000 portfolio by investing in the market. "It was money better spent then the $100,000 I spent on college," notes Goyette about lessons he learned from his substantial early failure. After college Goyette joined Goldman Sachs as a junior analyst, jumping ship after three years to join a hedge fund. He started out at the

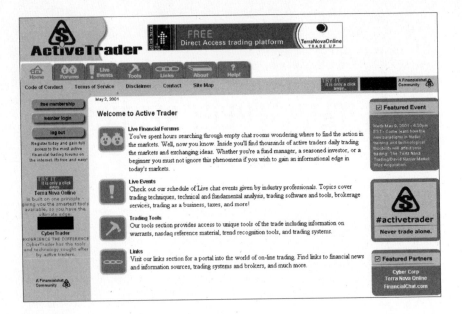

Figure 10.1   www.financialchat.com
Source: FinancialChat.

fund by trading fixed-income arbitrage but quickly discovered that his best gains came from playing individual stocks.

Goyette has come a long way from his Goldman days. He no longer has any respect for the word of the Street. Like others within these pages, he believes that analysts at major firms are merely pawns for investment banking endeavors, rather than investor advocates. In his opinion, the prominent analysts aren't paid to find the next big thing; they are paid to study the fortunes of big capitalization companies that are their employer's banking customers.

In order to tap alternative sources of information, Goyette founded ActiveTrader in 1996, and the chat room grew to become one of the largest free trading forums on the Internet (See Figure 10.2 for information on accessing ActiveTrader). ActiveTrader is a true virtual version of the traditional trading floor. There are friendships, fights, folklore, and fortunes. Participants in the chat room are known only by their nicknames, which range from "theMaxx" to "buyinlow" to "Presto" to "DaddysMoney." It's an underground world with a vibrant history and culture. On July 29, 2000, a day trader in Atlanta shot and killed nine people in two brokerage offices. That same evening, we logged on the ActiveTrader chat channel to listen to the reactions of the other traders around the country. Not long after we logged on the channel, a gentleman with the nickname "Wareal" joined the chat room and told everyone that he was a trader in the office where the shootings had occurred. Wareal had logged on the chat channel to seek comfort from fellow traders and share the horrific story of the massacre. He was also providing the chat participants with the very first eyewitness account of the shooting—a poignant display of the Internet's ability to transcend other information sources. The conversations that took place that evening on the virtual chat channel were a powerful example of the Internet's impact on society and culture.

Sociological discussions aside, ActiveTrader is a hotbed of insight and information. The participants in the channel were investing in Internet stocks long before anyone on Wall Street had even caught a whiff of the dot-com revolution. They were also well ahead of the curve when it came to optical networking, fuel cells, biotechnology, and other investing fads. Investment philosophies and approaches in the channel vary dramatically. While Internet Relay Chat (IRC) and ActiveTrader in particular seem best suited to the hyperactive trader, the ideas generated through real-time chat and constant interaction can be useful to longer-term investors as well. Ironically, Goyette himself preaches analysis, research, and patience—unusual tenets for the man who oversees Active-Trader's active traders. "I find that the traders in ActiveTrader are too myopic," explains Goyette. "They can see five minutes into the future, whereas I am trying to look weeks, months, or years out. I'll use my background in technology and my ability to read a balance sheet and analyze cash flows combined with the story to come up with something that I think will get others excited when they finally figure it out."

Goyette looks for a risk-reward ratio of one to five—he wants to make $5 for every $1 of downside risk. He buys in before anyone else is paying attention and sells out once the rest of the world starts bidding up the prices of his companies. Goyette almost never sells at the top, but he's content with a double or triple even if he misses out occasionally on the tail end of a rocketing stock homerun. He follows industries closely by reading trade magazines and web sites, keeping ahead of the mainstream financial media. When the big guns in a sector start to run, Goyette has the ticker symbols of all the smaller players in the back of his head. He knows that investors who miss the initial run-ups will eventually stumble upon his small-cap jewels, and he'll be ready and waiting with thousands of shares in hand when the time comes.

The mIRC program with the #activetrader channel open.

In 1988, a year before Tim Berners-Lee invented the World Wide Web, Finnish programmer Jarkko Oikarinen designed what remains even today one of the most interactive and unique applications available on the Internet—IRC, the Internet Relay Chat network. Relatively unknown for several years, IRC came into its own in 1991, enabling users around the globe to exchange information during the Persian Gulf War. IRC again proved its worth during the coup against Boris Yeltsin in 1993, allowing Moscow natives to broadcast live reports to the international community. Over the past five years, IRC has emerged as a battleground for the day-trading revolution. The ability to communicate with thousands instantaneously and exchange information and insight is particularly attractive to day traders, who make a living off speed and speculation. Unlike popular web-based message boards at Yahoo! and Silicon Investor, IRC offers real-time, back-and-forth chatter with no rules and few limitations. Day traders in particular relish the anonymity IRC allows; the thousands who gather daily to share tips and trades know each other only by odd nicknames and peculiar reputations.

    In order to access IRC servers, you need to download an IRC client (or program). The most popular IRC client is mIRC, which is available for

Figure 10.2   A Brief Introduction to Internet Relay Chat

Figure 10.2 *(Continued)*

> download at www.mirc.com. MIRC is a shareware program, which means that you can try it out for free temporarily but are bound by an honor code to pay the developer a fee if you use the program regularly. The web site provides help and information on downloading the program for a number of different Windows platforms. Mac users should browse to www.ircle.com and download the Ircle IRC client for the Macintosh.
>
> In order to access the ActiveTrader chat room, you need to configure your IRC client to connect to the FinancialChat IRC server at irc.financialchat.com. Once connected, join the ActiveTrader chat room by issuing the command "/join #activetrader." If you log on during the trading day, you should see hundreds if not thousands of other traders chatting away. If you have trouble connecting to the chat room using IRC, you can also make use of a web-based chat program at www.financialchat.com. Web chat isn't quite as fast or seamless as IRC, but connecting is usually easier for beginners.

Always willing to offer his opinion on a company, Goyette (or WallStArb, as he's known on ActiveTrader) will gladly converse with anyone who sends a message his way. His presence on ActiveTrader provides investors with a unique opportunity to chat with a professional hedge fund manager. The following interview provides a glimpse of Goyette's investing style. If you like his approach, log on to ActiveTrader and introduce yourself. The unusual virtual world known as IRC is waiting for you.

You got your start at Goldman Sachs and then left to work at a hedge fund. What was your position there?

I started out as an assistant portfolio manager, trading fixed-income arbitrage. Hence my nickname: WallStArb. I took on that persona even before getting into any online stock channels or financial forums.

How was your performance at the hedge fund?

I used to trade billions of dollars in short-term U.S. treasuries—buying short-term U.S. treasuries and shorting Fed funds futures or Euro dollar futures. We were taking a duration-neutral trade and essentially isolating the credit risk out of it. We were buying something backed by the U.S. government and selling something backed by a European bank. We essentially lent money to the U.S. government and borrowed money from European banks. When you get any kind of flight to quality, the stock market crashes, and all of a sudden people buy the better credit risk and sell the lesser credit risk, and those spreads widen out. We were essentially long the interest-free differential between those. We used to have a lot of sophisticated computer models, some of the best on the Street. I eventually became the senior portfolio manager there before I left. We were one of the bigger players in the U.S. treasury market and used to chew up a lot of the competition. The treasury market is much, much different than the equity market, so there is no real comparison there. We weren't taking speculative positions.

Why did you decide to leave?

To start my own equities-based hedge fund. The Fed didn't move for quite a while, and fixed-income arbitrage returns started to dry up. It was hard to make money, so I started going back to my equities roots. And I did very, very well—not doing much day trading but taking large positions in smaller, unfollowed, and unloved stocks. I was looking for the next sector that was going to be interesting or hot, trying to get ahead of the curve. My firm offered to spin me off and create my own hedge fund. I've been doing that for almost a year and a half now.

Let's dig in a little bit and discuss how you find these investing opportunities. You said you like to find unloved, small companies. Where do you look?

I do a lot of reading of nonfinance-related news sources—especially trade magazines. As a computer person with a background in technology, I understand and even fool around with and implement a lot of the new technologies. I'm always playing around with the latest web servers and latest software from dozens of different companies—just keeping up on technology because that makes me a better investor. Here's one instance: Recently, we have been beta testing Interwoven's new product, and to be honest, it's a piece of garbage [see Figure 10.3].

What does it do?

It's an add-on for one of Microsoft's new e-commerce servers. Essentially, it does content management. If you had a bunch of people contributing news to a web site, it gives them separate logins and manages the content, putting it dynamically to the web site from a database. It would be fantastic for something like TheStreet.com, and a lot of big

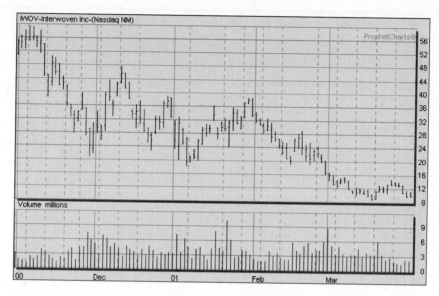

Figure 10.3 Interwoven (Nasdaq: IWOV), November 2000–March 2001
Source: Prophet Financial Systems, Inc. (www.ProphetFinance.com).

corporations use it, but Interwoven has a new product coming out that's a slimmed-down version, and it's horrible.

Is that a good reason to stay away from the stock?

We were actually shorting Interwoven starting in late January 2001 in the mid to high $30s, but I am not a person who shorts a lot.

There are times when I will be reading an article and find something interesting that will get my wheels turning. A sector is expected to be hot by these non–stock market people for the year 2001; they might list half a dozen names, and I will look for something that's got a decent balance sheet that seems to be totally under everyone else's radar, and I'll start looking into it. That's the type of research that I find valuable.

How do you know that a particular company is not on people's radar?

You can tell by price action or just by reading the balance sheet—look at its earnings compared to the rest. Look at its price-to-sales ratio, or a general stock chart. If you've got a stock that's gone from $2 to $200, you can tell that people have probably figured it out. But if you have something in the same sector that's been languishing or having short-term problems . . . A year ago, a perfect instance was Linux. A couple of hot Linux IPOs came out, and we knew that Linux would be hot. I didn't

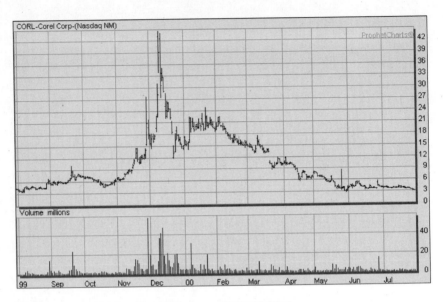

Figure 10.4   Corel (Nasdaq: CORL), August 1999–July 2000
Source: Prophet Financial Systems, Inc. (www.ProphetFinance.com).

have access to the IPOs, so we were buying Corel at two or three bucks, knowing that they had a product that was competitive to Red Hat. Corel was unloved—everyone hated it—but they had this Linux angle, and eventually everyone picked up on it [see Figure 10.4]. It far surpassed our estimates. I think we probably sold the last of our position for $10. It continued to run to $40.

Why would that happen? Why weren't more people on the Street paying attention to Corel?

Because they are not paid to. Most big brokers and analysts are paid through investment banking fees. The high-powered analysts at Merrill Lynch and Goldman Sachs who are making the big money are not being paid by getting retail clients to buy Cisco at $50. It's a loss leader, this research. They are recommending companies that they can make money on from the investment banking back-end.

You sold Corel at $10, and it went to $40. Why $10? What had changed that made you want to sell?

At that price I wasn't a buyer. It started to get a little bit ridiculous. But Corel had a fantastic short squeeze. I ask myself, "Would I be a buyer

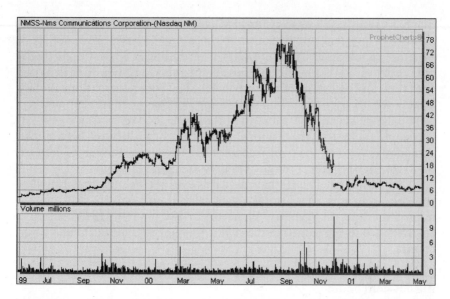

NMSS-Nms Communications Corporation-(Nasdaq NM)

Figure 10.5 NMS Communications (Nasdaq: NMSS), May 1999–May 2001, adjusted for a two-for-one stock split

Source: Prophet Financial Systems, Inc. (www.ProphetFinance.com).

here?" And if the answer is no, then I've got to ask myself if other people are going to be buyers. You can't fight the tape when you are trading a large position; you've got to start to sell as they are buying. You've got to feed the ducks while they are quacking. I am seldom ever going to pick a top on a stock. A lot of people like to get the middle part of a run; a lot of people like to get the end part of a run. I like to be first. Nobody ever went broke taking a profit, and when you have a large position, you are almost trading like a quasi market maker. You are selling into rallies, buying on the dips—working in or out of a position to get the best average price. One of my biggest misses of 1999 was a company in the telecom sector called Natural Microsystems [see Figure 10.5]. We bought several hundred thousand shares in April 1999 after they warned one quarter. The stock was $3, and within a year it went to over $150 a share. It had about $3.50 in cash when we were buying in. And the multiples got ridiculous on the run. There is no way you can even believe the stock is worth $150 when it was trading at $3. Natural Microsystems would not stop running, and we were selling all the way up. I don't think we sold one share above $20.

But that's generally what we are looking for—something unloved that has value. In this case, Natural Microsystems was a highflier, missed a couple of quarters, and was down to three bucks a share. You could pick a hundred companies that were $200, now trading at $3. But there might not be any value there. A lot of those companies are laden with debt and don't have any real value. They were just bid up with a lot of funny money. That is what I try to do—find something that has good fundamentals, a good balance sheet, and, more importantly, a good story that's going to get people excited. If you're wrong, your down side is limited because the company isn't going to go into Chapter 11. They have enough cash to get them through whatever rough spot they are going through.

Very infrequently will these laggards ever become leaders. But what you are hoping is that people eventually figure out that, "Damn, I missed the boat on Vignette. Vignette's at $30, but this little Allaire is $5. They are in the same business, but this one is trading at such a discount."

Do those $3 to $150 jumps happen anymore? Was that just a product of the dot-com boom?

I think it was exaggerated, but it happens all the time. Dell at one point was a $2 or $3 stock. There was a point when 3Com—when I bought it in the early 1990s—was nine bucks. Everything is undiscovered at one point. JDS Uniphase—you can't have a stock going up 10,000 percent like JDSU did without it being cheap and underfollowed at one point. It's just a matter of looking for the next one. For instance, Puma Technology [now known as Pumatech] was a major position of ours [see Figure 10.6]. We were long Puma because of this vaporous thing called Bluetooth, which seemed interesting back in 1998. [Bluetooth is a wireless technology that allows portable computing devices to network with each other.]

When did you buy Puma?

It was around $2 a share in mid 1999. It was the only small player in this Bluetooth consortium, which included Motorola, Intel—all the heavyweights. Puma used to do infrared ports for laptop computers so that they could talk to your printer. But they were transferring over into synchronization software for Palm Pilots. Bluetooth was going to be the de facto standard for communications protocols. Puma was a little tiny company where you could isolate this one particular event and make a bet. In 1999 Puma Technology happened to be the number one stock of the entire year, even better than JDS Uniphase. A little stupid stock went from $2 to a little over $100 by the end of the year. It was absolutely amazing.

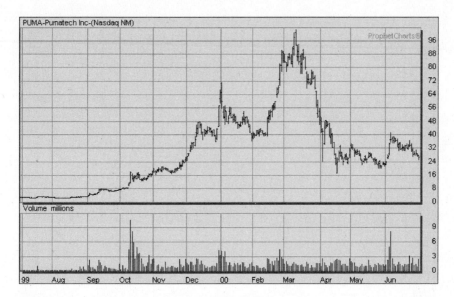

Figure 10.6 Pumatech (Nasdaq: PUMA), July 1999–June 2000
Source: Prophet Financial Systems, Inc. (www.ProphetFinance.com).

Did you really think it was a good company, or did you just want to play a speculative craze?

They owned a bunch of shares in Amazon.com. They had about three of four bucks in cash when it was trading at $2. So, it wasn't a bad risk. Did I think it was going to go to $100? Hell, no. Did I think it was going to go to $10 or $15? Absolutely. One of my mottos when I am doing a trade, especially a large trade or a position trade, is that I am willing to risk $1 to make $5. I am looking for a company with an interesting story, an interesting technology, no debt, and a balance sheet or cash position to back it up. I've been wrong before, and I got trapped in one dot-com last year, which was probably my biggest mistake of the year.

What stock was that?

Musicmaker.com [see Figure 10.7].

You say you got trapped. What does that mean?

Well, I lost.

Were you hanging on to the stock, hoping it would turn around?

They had cash, and I had a decent sized position . . . I got caught. I didn't

Figure 10.7   Musicmaker.com (Nasdaq: HITS), November 1999–October 2000

Source: Prophet Financial Systems, Inc. (www.ProphetFinance.com).

buy it at its high, but we were buying the stock at $3 a share, and I think we ended up getting out for a buck or a buck and a half. It was a position we were carrying around forever—150,000 shares. That was a decent loss.

What made you decide to sell at $1.50?

It just wasn't turning around.

That's a lot to lose on a single trade. What about diversification? How many positions are you typically holding at one time?

Anywhere between 20 and 50. It really depends on the market climate. If I think a sector is going to be interesting—for instance, proteomics is going to be a hot sector like genomics was. There are a lot of small companies out there trading near cash, and I probably have a dozen different proteomics companies in our portfolio right now.

What is proteomics?

Proteomics is essentially the sequencing of the proteins instead of the genes. Once people start saying "proteomics, proteomics, proteomics," and once CNBC starts talking about it, people go out and start looking for these companies. It may take six weeks, six days, six months, but we are going to be positioned in them at a reasonable level so that there is not much downside for us.

How can you be the first? Why aren't more people on Wall Street paying attention before CNBC starts talking?

I think you have a lot of laziness on Wall Street. Analysts are paid to push whatever they are pushing for a reason. They overlook a lot of stocks and focus too heavily on the same few stocks. How many analyst opinions do you really need on Cisco? Do you need 80 different opinions on Cisco? Obviously, Wall Street thinks you do. Personally, I don't think you do. If their real job were to advise investors on what is going to make them money, instead of putting a different spin on the same information, they would actually try to go dig up information. That's the big problem I see with the major Wall Street institutions. They are all concentrating on looking at the same 50 or 100 stocks out of a universe of 10,000. It leaves a lot of potential opportunities out there for either the informed investor or small hedge fund manager like myself.

Is there a valid economic reason why these depressed companies rebound or are discovered and appreciate in price?

Yes, if the business sector is hot, if the business sector is sound, and if the company is having a short-term problem. You get these companies, especially in technology, that screw up a product cycle by a quarter, maybe two quarters, and their stocks will get absolutely decimated. The sector is still a decent sector; other companies in the sector are being valued highly, but this particular one isn't. That's a good buy, and that's what we are looking for.

What do you make of traders who spend all their time focused on technical analysis? Is that a mistake?

If they make money, it's fantastic. Do whatever makes you money. For me, I'm willing to risk $1 to make $5. You're not going to find that opportunity by reading a chart. You are going to do that by having more and better information than the next guy.

Do you use technical analysis at all?

Support and resistance lines. When I am selling, I'm selling to other people. So I want to know when they are going to start buying. If I'm sitting on a couple hundred thousand shares of XYZ Corp. and XYZ Corp. is bumping up against a resistance area where the momentum guys are going to start to leave it or shorters are going to start working it, then I'll start selling there.

Do you follow any strict trading or investing guidelines?

I won't touch companies with any significant amount of debt. If a company ever goes to be sold, the debt holder is the first to be paid. The equity holder is always the last guy in line. I hate to be the last guy in line. You look at a company like Lucent—their debt structure is so disadvantageous for the equity holders. If they screw up a quarter, that's fine. If they screw up a quarter too many times and have debt, that starts eating into cash reserves and becomes a major problem. And it doesn't really become a problem until it's a problem. Northpoint went out of business because of their debt. I never got caught in Covad or Rhythms or any of those other DSL or CLEC stocks because one thing I always knew was that these companies are losing money and that they have a ton of debt. [DSL stands for digital subscriber line and is a means to connect homes and businesses (covering the last mile) to the Internet. A CLEC is a competitive local exchange carrier, a telephone company that competes with the present local exchange carrier.] As the stock falls, it puts more pressure on; the whole downward spiral feeds on itself, and it's accelerated by debt. A lot of times, debt holders essentially do the trades I used to do in treasuries; they have a better credit quality instrument, and they are shorting an equity that is a lesser credit quality instrument. If they can force the company into bankruptcy, they may get back 20 cents on the dollar, but their short is going to go to zero. I used to do junk bond arbitrage at a hedge fund I worked for. I no longer do it, but that was the name of the game.

Do you do any intraday trading? Is it possible to catch the wave into some of these stocks on the day that investors start pouring in?

Absolutely. I'll trade on news; I'll trade on momentum—on a number of different things.

What's your game plan when you are trading?

I focus a lot on news and knowing what sectors are moving and what companies are in that sector. If there is something coming out that's going to make these genomics companies move, you can position ahead of that news. You get the uninformed traders or uninformed analysts buying, and you are doing the selling into it.

I've been doing this for so long and know the technology sector so well that, for instance, if Plug Power has great news about some fuel cell, in the back of my head I can probably name off a dozen other fuel cell or alternative power companies. If Plug moves enough, people will start saying to themselves, "I missed Plug, but maybe I should be getting into some of these other ones because they are going to move." You get this whole herd mentality. The sectors move in sympathy with something that acts as the catalyst.

If the hot sectors can change daily, how does a trader know what the sector of the day is before the moves have already happened?

If you are looking at CNBC or the *Wall Street Journal* for your news and information, you are not going to get it. You can get a lot of great information—like what sectors are moving—live in the financial forums. With ActiveTrader, you get a lot of that information because you have thousands of pairs of eyes. You will see people talking about a particular sector; you'll see some news and more people talking. You can see the interest in a particular sector building.

Talk a little bit about why and how you started ActiveTrader.

Like a lot of things in this world, I just kind of stumbled into it. I was a fixed-income arbitrage trader, and we wanted to create an online forum for talking about stocks. So, I set up a whole network for financial related forums: FinancialChat. ActiveTrader just happens to be the largest forum on that network. My goal was to create a place where people who are interested in equities and are professional about it can share ideas and share information. A lot of times someone will mention something that I have never heard of. I may not buy it, but I'll start watching. For example, I wouldn't have known about proteomics; some of my friends whom I chat with got me turned on to that sector.

Is there a lot of hype in the chat room? Can thousands of people possibly interact intelligently?

Let me put it this way: During the day I warn a lot of people. A lot of people love to mention the stocks they are following. They'll just mention a symbol with no information. And we are constantly warning people. They'll type in "Cisco." What the hell does "Cisco" mean? That's not information. That's not helping me at all. If Cisco has news, post the news. If there is some kind of information or rumor going around, post that. But just posting a symbol or writing that it moved up 1/8—that's not information. And we are constantly warning and essentially making sure that people know that hype, whether positive or negative, isn't tolerated. The big problem the market is having right now, especially for the day trader, is that there is no discernable pattern. You get two up days and three down days. You get three up days and two down days. This market is schizophrenic. It's sector rotation upon sector rotation; they love this name one day, and they hate it the next. People hate alternative fuel cell companies; they are all going to zero. Then, literally, the next day they are all up 100 percent. The optical companies are like that. They're all going to zero, and then next month or next week, they're all up 150 percent. You get a lot of frustration from the traders.

Is it the day traders who are blowing these moves out of proportion? How much impact do individual investors have on the market?

I think dumb money was moving the markets a lot more in the past than it is now.

Why not now?

Dumb money is dumb money for a reason . . . and now it's no money. It's been a capital preservation market. The smart traders are the guys who know how to cut their losses, know how to do risk management. I think a lot of the dumb money that was really moving the markets up was trading on the bigger fool theory: If I buy something that's overpriced, and can sell it more overpriced, that's fantastic. That's not the way I trade. It might have worked for them, but a lot of them are out of the market, and a lot of those stocks are now trading at a buck.

You've got two types of money: hot money that's looking to go somewhere and money that's not—capital preservation money. And the hot money just keeps chasing different sectors. The e-commerce thing lasted a year. The Linux thing lasted three months. Now, three or four days is a sustained rally in one of these sectors. It's hot money looking for a place to go, and in a bear market you get huge time compressions in these rallies. Nobody wants to hold a hot potato—but everyone is looking for it. Linux plays were hot for three days last week. [Linux is a computer operating system that competes with Microsoft's Windows. By "Linux plays," Goyette is referring to companies that make software or provide service for the operating system.] Two weeks ago, VA Linux was trading at $7, had a three-day rally, and went to $12. Plug Power, for instance, was $15 on January 10. In five days it was $32. And now it has lost almost all of those gains.

Why the time compression of these rallies? Is it because people are scared of getting stuck?

To be honest, I've been making a lot of money recently—taking large positions at the beginning of these rallies, selling into the ends of them. I can only speak from personal experience, but I'm not holding for that last penny. Making a profit in this type of stock environment isn't an easy thing, and like I said before, you've got to feed the ducks when they're quacking.

You have some interesting information on your web site concerning block trades—large buy or sell orders. It's something that a lot of people talk about but no one explains particularly well. Do you pay attention to block trades? [A block is a sizeable trade, typically at least 10,000 shares of stock.]

I focus on block trades only when the price declines on no news. Say you have a $10 stock. All of a sudden, it drops down over two days to $6 for apparently no reason—no news. It has a quick dip down and prints a lot of big blocks a couple of different times. That is generally indicative of a very, very solid bottom. What happens is that you've got somebody who is a desperate seller. The stock is not very liquid; it trades 200,000 shares a day. For whatever reason, the seller wants to get out of a big block. He will negotiate a price, and the market maker may know about the order a day or two in advance. The market maker will work in a short in that position. He will start shorting the stock, shorting it from $10 down to $9, $9 down to $8. The stock will get close to the negotiated price where this million shares is going to come out, and the market maker will essentially cover his short with these big block trades and get long a certain amount. This situation is generally good for a decent bounce in the stock. The price is being pushed artificially by one big seller.

Say somebody owned a $200 stock that is now trading at $10. In the big picture for him, the difference between $8 and $7 in the price is not that big a deal. The market makers know this and take advantage of that situation. They are willing to take these big, big blocks of shares off his hands at a discount—buying these shares wholesale. So a weak hand is out of the stock. The market maker is in with a lot of shares at a very attractive price. He is going to try to push the stock back up relatively quickly to sell out of those shares for a decent profit. So you have that working in your favor when you find these types of situations. I find it's generally really meaningful only when it happens in a very quick V-bottom type of a price action on a particular stock.

How often do you see these block patterns?

You see them a lot—a quick drop on huge volume in heavy blocks and then a quick bounce back, generally to the level before that sell-off happened. Pull up a chart on Puma Technology right at the end of December. A lot of big funds had to get out by the end of the year because they bought it at $30 or $40 or $50 or $100, and they've got it in their portfolio. It ain't going up. So in the last couple days of the year, these portfolio managers say, "Enough is enough. I've got a million shares to sell.

Figure 10.8   Vyyo (Nasdaq: VYYO), November 2000–January 2001
Source: Prophet Financial Systems, Inc. (www.ProphetFinance.com).

Where are you going to buy them?" Puma was at eight bucks a share on
December 13. Four trading days later, it was trading in the $3s. It had a
big, big volume spike in those days in the $3s—1.5 million shares ver-
sus 300,000 per day the week before. The January effect was just the opposite. There is no longer this huge selling pressure, and any amount of
buying pressure takes the stocks back up.

Here is another one: Vyyo [see Figure 10.8]. The stock was $30 in
November and traded down to $5 on some monster volume in the last
couple days of December. The stock then popped back up to $15 within
two weeks. It traded almost a million and a half shares four or five days
in a row, and once that selling pressure was alleviated, the stock rallied
back by January 15. That is when these blocks are good indications. It
doesn't happen all the time, but when it does happen, it makes for an incredible risk-reward ratio. I'm looking for the capitulation. I want to be
a buyer of last resort.

**Can all types of traders and investors benefit from ActiveTrader and
from following day traders and the short-term movements of stocks?**

Absolutely—I don't consider myself a day trader. I am more of a position
trader or a swing trader. I am not necessarily an investor. Because tech-

nology changes so much, I think it's almost impossible to say what technology is going to do 10 years from now. I'm not bright enough to know what technology is going to do *two years* from now. Anybody who thinks they can tell you where technology is going to be in five or 10 years is either oblivious to the pace of change of technology, has got his head up his ass, or is lying. These companies and these analysts that come out with five-year revenue projections for companies that just started last week—it's asinine. Think about the companies that were around five years ago. What were the leading companies five years ago in technology? You can't really think of them. Microsoft was there. Cisco—well, maybe. But the landscape has totally changed. Informix is pretty much dead. Novell is pretty much gone. You had a couple of other networking companies back then—Banyon, 3Com, and Cabletron. You had all these ATM companies, which have either gone under or been acquired—ATM being the network technology. Look at e-commerce companies. Most of them came public in 1999. They are gone. Most of them are Chapter 11.

I think investors can get really good information from ActiveTrader and financial forums in general. It's a way to get a lot of information in a finite space where you don't have to look around a lot.

Chapter 11

EXPLOITING FEAR AND GREED
Oliver Velez

Internet Alias		Investment Style	
Oliver Velez		Short-term/medium-term	
Year of Birth		**Location**	
1967		Westchester County, NY	
Education			
Studied accounting and English at Hunter College in New York; dropped out after three years			
Web Site (Free/Pay)			
Pristine.com: www.pristine.com			

In the beginning of his investment career, Oliver Velez could only muster up $4,000 of his own money to devote to his brokerage account. Luckily, Velez was able to convince each of two outside investors to lend him $20,000, increasing his pool of cash to $44,000. The brokerage firm in New York City with which Velez signed up offered him a 10 to 1 margin, suddenly upping his buying power to nearly half a million dollars. With enough capital to make a killing in the market, the world was Velez's oyster.

But there were rules. The brokerage firm took the original $44,000 and stashed the money in an escrow account. Any losses that Velez incurred would be culled from the $44,000 of hard cash; any gains would be split 50/50 with the firm. The brokerage firm slapped an exorbitant interest rate on all of Velez's trades, and if he lost half of his initial $44,000, the firm had the right to kick him out.

The pressure from the rules of the game impaired Velez's trading savvy initially, and he lost well more than $22,000 within a few days.

Velez exuded natural talent, however, and the firm let him stay on. Good move—within three months, Velez turned the initial $44,000 into $250,000. Eight months later, he checked out of the brokerage firm with $1.4 million, cashed out of his agreement with his partners, and has been on his own ever since.

Raking in a million bucks, however, wasn't the best thing to happen to Velez at the brokerage firm. As Velez handily beat the market day in and day out, other traders began to take notice and ask for his advice. Velez remembers one gentleman's inquiries quite vividly. "Oliver, I never see you upset or perturbed or anything like that," remarked John, a trader in the firm. "You always seem calm, just reading the paper. What is your secret?" Velez pondered the question for a moment and then responded, "John, it's really quite simple. You see all the other traders here? You see them staring at their monitors, their hands reaching for the phone to call the order desk? You see these people reaching for the phone, putting the phone back, bobbing and weaving and not sure what to do? These guys are letting the market play them; they're not playing the market."

Velez continued his response to John, explaining his more contemplative approach: "What I do is, I go home and come up with four or five stocks that meet my personal criteria. I set the rules. If on the following day the stock crosses a certain price, then I buy. If it does not, I sit and read the paper. Now the market is playing my game. If it refuses to play by the rules that I've set up in the quietude of my home the prior night, then I don't do anything. If it does decide to play by the rules that I've outlined for the market, then I instantly leap into action. I know precisely what to do because I set the rules."

John was stunned at the profundity of this tactical market approach and asked if he could take a look at the stocks and parameters Velez had picked out the night before. Velez didn't have a problem with sharing, and he kindly explained his daily game plan to John. Word spread around the office that Velez was tackling the market without biting his fingernails, and soon the entire office of 200 traders was receiving a daily advisory from Velez. Shortly thereafter, Velez was faxing his four stocks of the day and his trading rationale to hundreds of strangers. If not for his wife, Velez may have continued to hand out his valuable advice free of charge to the world at large. But Velez's wife began to wonder why her husband wasn't charging for his highly demanded insight. Velez was making so much money trading at the time that he had never given any thought to charging for his daily comments. But he decided to improve the format of his newsletter and to tack on a reasonable fee, and before long *The Pristine Day Trader* advisory was born.

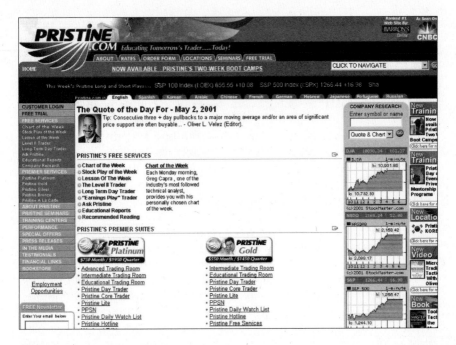

Figure 11.1   www.pristine.com
Source: Pristine.com.

Today, *The Pristine Day Trader* bulletin continues to be Pristine's flagship service. The philosophy of the newsletter remains the same: provide investors with four daily stock picks along with detailed buy and sell instructions for each trade. Pristine doesn't want its subscribers to swallow the stock picks like automatons and jump into a play without thinking. Instead, the newsletter is intended to teach investors the rationale behind each stock pick so that they can hone their skills and identify other opportunities. Even today, Pristine.com remains a beacon of light in a sea of competitive newsletters loaded with hype (see Figure 11.1). Back in 1994, when Velez initially launched *The Pristine Day Trader*, it was truly a unique offering in the investment field. While other newsletters touted "proprietary" and "secret" methods of beating the market, Velez blew the door wide open by publishing his complete rationale for identifying specific opportunities and giving investors the tools to beat the market on their own.

Pristine.com has come a long way since Velez helped trader John revise his market philosophy. With more than 85,000 subscribers in 62 countries, Pristine is one of the largest daily advisory services in the world. The firm now offers multiple advisory services, various chat rooms, and a formal seminar program for offline training. They even host a "grueling six- to nine-month boot camp . . . designed to be the Harvard University of trading training, with course materials, tests, and evaluations." Pristine is a big business, and the company charges for its services; at the time of writing, subscriptions to the site's services sold for $75 to $750 per month. The top-of-the-line Platinum service provides traders with multiple daily and weekly newsletters, access to several advanced real-time trading chat rooms, and various other perks. Thankfully, Pristine offers a noteworthy slate of free content as well, including regularly updated columns and stock picks, and provides a free trial for its for-fee content.

Pristine has an impressive track record to back up its pricey fees—all the firm's advisory services have racked up triple-digit gains in past years. Velez admits that it is nearly impossible for people to replicate Pristine's picks precisely because countless variables can affect a transaction. But even shaving off one third of the company's stated performance record, as Velez recommends as a prudent practice, still puts Pristine's stock picks up in triple digit territory. The firm's stock-pick track record, however, is not Velez's crown achievement. He is considerably more satisfied when Pristine helps individuals develop their own skill sets and become independent investors.

In 1998 a middle-aged Asian woman attended a Pristine seminar in San Francisco. With a fairly sizable $300,000 to invest, she wanted to hone her trading skills and increase her nest egg. After spending some time in Pristine's real-time trading rooms and learning the firm's strategies, the woman ballooned her $300,000 into $8 million within seven months. It's an astounding success story, until you learn that the woman swiftly turned the $8 million into $6 million, $4 million, $2 million, and, finally, $1 million. Frustrated, but content to earn her winnings back, the woman enlisted Pristine's traders to help her identify her weakness. Pristine discovered that she had the buy side of the equation down pat, but was severely lacking when it came to pulling the sell trigger. She spent more time perfecting her trading technique and improving her sell tactics. With her confidence restored and her trading tool kit fully stocked, the woman proceeded to turn her $1 million into $22 million.

This is not an isolated success story; Pristine has churned out many millionaires. Velez claims that numerous Pristine traders have made more than half a million dollars in a single day. A larger number of folks have scored $20,000, $30,000, and $40,000 days.

With so much success to his name, you might expect Velez to be on the arrogant side. But he's very much the opposite and prefers to play the role of market philosopher, doling out his commentary in a soft, hypnotic tone. In the following interview Velez expounds his practical market approach in considerable detail, discussing strategies that range from minute-to-minute "micro" trading to many-months-long "core" trading. Don't get hung up on the details of his technical examples; Velez has numerous fundamental principles that are invaluable to any type of investor.

You worked as an accountant for a law firm on Wall Street in your early years and became captivated with the markets. What about the stock market intrigued you?

Number one, most individuals could not do it well, and that presented a very nice challenge for me. If you could manage to attain some type of proficiency, you were regarded as being smart. So, in a very real sense, it was a great deal of ego that pushed me into the arena. Once I began to dabble in the market, I recognized early on that I was basically born for it. The markets were something that I would never master, and therefore would always retain my interest. As a child, I always had a problem with attention span. I would become very fascinated with one specific thing, but it would fail to grasp my attention for a long period of time. The market is the first thing in my life that can captivate me indefinitely.

Did you begin your investing career with a technical short-term focus or a more traditional fundamentals-based long-term approach?

As an accountant, I recognized that a great deal of creativity goes into producing numbers for annual reports and earnings. With some legal fancy footwork on the number side, you can push various expenses from one corner to the other. You can delay income or speed income up by electing one rule versus another rule. Numbers, in and of themselves, are not the true picture of current reality. Even when the numbers are somewhat accurate, fundamental pictures give you only a snapshot of what the company did sometime in the past. And what *was* in many cases is not consistent with what *is*. A fundamental picture is a snapshot of what *was*. I became frustrated with this gap between what *should be* and what *is*, what *was* and what *is*, what the numbers suggested that the company *should do* and what the stock *was doing*. It became evident to me that the most important thing was not what the numbers said about the company in the past. The most important thing was not what the numbers suggested the company's stock *should* be doing now. The most important thing was what *is* the company's stock doing at this moment.

As I moved to a more technical approach to the market, this realization began to grow: Astute technical traders are not concerned with what was or what should be. They are concerned with what *is* at the current time. I developed this very strong belief that successful market play is all about playing people; it is not about playing stocks. It takes people and their emotional reactions to events, numbers, and news to move stocks. Numbers do not move stocks. News items do not move stocks. Analysts do not move stocks. They can be the catalysts, but in and of themselves, these items do not move stocks. It is the human reaction to these items that moves stocks.

By studying price alone, we are studying the patterns of two dominant emotions: fear and greed. An opportunity in the market is found when you can spot the transition from one emotional state to the other. In my philosophy, technical trading is nothing more than developing the skill to spot the transition from fear to greed and then from greed back to fear. Those are the two forces that move prices. Fundamental analysis is the study of those things that ignite fear and greed, like news and earnings. Those things can ignite emotional states in people, but technical analysis goes right for the jugular. It goes right to the core of the matter and studies the actions that result from these two emotional states.

Where did you learn how to play that psychological game?

When I was starting out, there were not a great many books on the market that dealt with the how-to of technical analysis, especially related to stocks. There were a number of futures technical analysis books, and you had your classics like Edwards and McGee. But there was not a great deal of information. There were certainly no seminars and no gurus at the time that focused on the how and why of investing. Most individuals who were supposedly leading experts did not want the public to know their methods or approaches. So, it was quite honestly a great deal of trial and error, looking at literally thousands upon thousands of charts every week. Once a week, I would get a package mailed to me with three thousand different weekly charts—there were so many on one page that you literally had to use a magnifying glass to see the charts of each individual stock. It was through this process of getting this package every week and going through every single one of the charts, that over a relatively long period of time—four and a half to five years—I began to recognize certain events or patterns that were recur-

ring quite frequently, pictures that happened over and over again in almost the same way every single time. I began to take extensive notes
on this phenomenon and even took it to the point of looking at intraday time frames to see if the same patterns or events would happen in
multiple time frames. To my amazement and my excitement at the
time, many of them did, and I began to collect notes on these specific
patterns.

When I made the connection between these patterns and the emotional states of people, it was a phenomenal breakthrough for me. There
are a variety of pictures and patterns that I discovered—I certainly didn't
invent them—that are the pictures of two points of opportunity. For instance, fear is currently dominating the landscape, so there is more selling than buying. There's fear, there's fear, there's fear. At a moment, at
an instant, there's a change where fear loses its grip and greed shows itself or becomes dominant for the first time. That transition, that point,
that change—if you were to take a snapshot of that picture, it would be
the same every single time.

The other point is when you've had runaway greed for a period and
there is more buying than selling. Many people are willing to buy at a
higher price than the last group of buyers. But there is going to be a moment when greed will lose its grip and give way to fear. Fear will overcome or become the dominant force for the first time. If you were to take
a snapshot of that moment in time, the picture would look the same
every single time. It was through a long process of looking at hundreds
and hundreds of charts that the similarities of the pictures became very
clear to me. Then I began to develop specific trading strategies to exploit
these transitional pictures or chart patterns.

**If technical analysis and trading are rooted in sound financial and psy-
chological principles, why does the mainstream media treat day traders
so negatively? We've heard statistics saying that 95 percent of day
traders lose all their money? Do you find that to be true?**

I have heard statistics from 75 percent, 85 percent, 95 percent; I have
even heard that 100 percent of day traders lose all their money, and I
think to a certain extent that the negative view is warranted. The self-
directed trader community has been one of the fastest growing subsets
of the financial markets, and whenever you have a very rapidly growing segment or industry, it will attract scrupulous and unscrupulous
firms and individuals who want to capitalize on the trend. What the
day-trading industry began to get was a lot of businessmen who stepped
into the arena and tried to capitalize on this rapidly growing segment;
they did not do the industry a great justice. A lot of firms were very

irresponsible and sent people to financial ruin by causing them to step into a professional arena. They considered short-term trading a hobby or something you could do with only a minimal amount of education.

As a result, the industry did get a bad name. Day trading is a very challenging endeavor; it is not a pastime, and it is not a hobby. It is a profession. Anyone who feels as though he or she is going to step into this world that we call active self-directed day trading—a world that is primarily dominated by market makers and traders like me—and compete by virtue of opening an online account is at the height of naïveté. The number one message that people forgot or missed a few years ago is the fact that this is a very professional game, and it is no place for the faint-hearted. It is certainly no place for the ill-informed or the novice.

It's also a very complex game with several distinct approaches. What are the different styles of trading?

We teach a four-pronged approach with four styles: core trading, swing trading, guerilla trading, and micro trading. Micro is the style of day trading that has gained the greatest degree of popularity among the media and the public at large. It is what is commonly referred to as day trading. I call it micro trading, and from my perspective it is only one of the many styles of short-term-oriented play.

Core trading and swing trading fall under the wealth-building styles of trading. The core trader focuses on capitalizing off of moves that can last anywhere from weeks to months. That is certainly not investing; it is a form of trading. Swing trading tries to capitalize on stock movements during two to five trading days. That has become a very popular style of trading, and it is the style that some of the country's top traders practice. The other two styles—guerilla trading and micro trading—fall under a category that I call income-producing styles. Guerilla trading covers holding periods anywhere from one to two days max. Micro trading is your typical intraday trading that everyone is somewhat familiar with—you buy a stock today and you sell it today before the close and virtually never hold a stock overnight.

We at Pristine feel that a true professional market player applies all four of these approaches to the market. The age-old question, "Should I hold a stock overnight, or not?" is a futile one. We teach traders that they should not be one-dimensional market players; there are times when the market is very conducive to micro trading, and there are times when it is not. There are times when it is very intelligent to core trade a stock for several weeks. And there are times when the core trading style will annihilate you and when shortening your time frame is the correct mode of operation.

How do you go about turning amateurs into successful traders? What is lesson number one that you teach in Pristine's educational seminars?

The first thing we try to do is change the way that people think about the market; we try to teach them that they trade people. Each time you buy a stock, someone is on the other side of the trade selling it to you. Each time you sell a stock, someone is on the other side stepping up to the plate to buy it from you. The $64,000 question is, who is smarter at this moment in time? Is it you or is it the person or entity on the other side? If we can get people to think in terms of other people, then we've taken the first big step toward moving them into the realm of professional market play.

When an order comes across the screen of a Nasdaq market maker or in the pit of a New York Stock Exchange specialist, that professional is not thinking, "What's management up to? What are the products? What were last quarter's earnings?" No. When a 5,000-share buy order comes across the screen of a Nasdaq market maker, his first question is, "Who is this order from? Is this order from someone who knows what they're doing? Or is it from an idiot?" The answer to that question will determine how he treats the order.

The first thing that we try to get people to do is to ask the same question. Who's in control of the stock now? Is it the buyers or the sellers? Have they been in control for a while? Are they showing signs that they're losing control? We get them to stop thinking about earnings, to stop thinking about the fundamentals, and to start looking at the price action as a gauge for determining who is in control. Once we get them to think that way, we start showing them specific patterns that happen over and over again in all time frames. What is very unique and convenient about the style of trading that we teach and practice is that these patterns can be applied in all four time frames. For instance, if I teach one trading pattern that happens over and over again, it can be used in the core trading style, the swing style, the guerilla style, and the micro style.

Let me give you an example. One pattern is the Pristine Key Buy. It is a three to five consecutive bar pull back after the stock has made a new 20 bar high. Let's say that the stock has made a new 20 bar high—it's registered the highest high in the last 20 bars. If we are talking about a daily chart, then the stock has made a new 20-day high. Then the stock experiences a three to five consecutive day pull back. Basically, fear can only last on average three to five consecutive days before another wave of greed hits. So, we have three to five consecutive down bars followed by an up bar that takes out the high of a prior bar for the first time. That represents a shift back to greed and indicates an appropriate entry price for a short-term swing trader. This single pattern, if applied to weekly charts—a 20 week high and then a three to five consecutive week pull back to the downside, followed by another week that for the first time takes out the high of the prior week—would represent an entry in a core trade. On the daily chart, that same pattern would represent an entry in a swing trade. On a 5- or 15-minute chart, that same pattern would represent an entry in a micro trade. The patterns are the same. These pictures, the transition between fear and greed, happen in every time frame consistently. We teach a collection of these patterns and then show people how frequently they occur in all of the primary time frames: weekly, daily, and intraday.

Can you give us an example of a pattern you identified in a recent trade?

Absolutely. This is a little bit different, but the same patterns appear in reverse as well. Our traders have done phenomenally well during the end of 2000 and the beginning of 2001. Most skillful traders will do a lot better in a down market than they will in an up market, simply because stocks fall faster and harder than they rise. But the patterns are the same on the reverse to the downside as they were when we were experiencing the bull run.

Let's look at the weekly chart of the Qs [QQQ; see Figure 11.2]. If you look at the beginning of this year, January 2001, I want you to note that there was a three-week rally during the first week, second week, and third week. One, two, three, and then what happens? We resume the downtrend. If we were to flip this chart upside down, you would see three bars down and then a rally to new highs. Well, it's just upside down now—a three bar rally and then we move to new lows. This was a multiweek trade where we shorted the Qs once it broke for the first time below a prior week's low after three or more consecutive up weeks. So, the fourth week was our entry week. That was the first week that QQQ broke below a prior week's low after a rally. We rode QQQ all the way down for seven consecutive weeks. Now, if you note the beginning of April, this is what we call a Climactic Pristine Buy setup. It is after the stock has moved significantly to a new low, and for the first time the stock trades above a prior week's high. On the week of April 8, we have a multidollar move in the Qs back up. Now we've had two consecutive weeks to the upside, and, of course, if we have another week to the upside, we've then had three in a row, and we're looking for the resumption of the move to the downside.

This is a very simple approach where we're counting bars. The QQQ weekly chart shows very clearly that for the past five, six, or seven

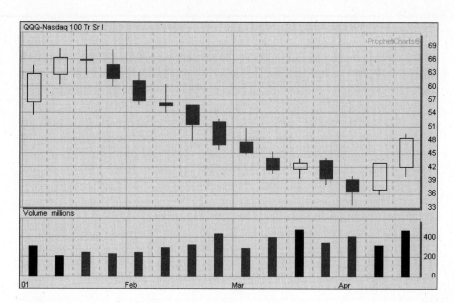

Figure 11.2 Nasdaq 100 Trust (AMEX: QQQ), January 2001–April 2001
Source: Prophet Financial Systems, Inc. (www.ProphetFinance.com).

months, the sellers have been in complete control of the market, and that three- to five-week rallies are nothing more than phenomenal shorting opportunities. The bears allow the bulls to have a brief, temporary, three-week rest, and now they're coming back to the party.

I could show example after example in all time frames. The micro trader uses the same pattern. Take a look at Sanmina; in the middle of the day today, around 12:00 EST, there is a multibar pull back—one, two, three, four, five [see Figure 11.3]. If each bar represents 15 minutes, you will see five 15-minute bars that drop to the downside. After five, there's an explosion from $25.75 to $28, and that's nothing more than the same pattern. After a rally to a new 20-bar high, you have three to five consecutive down bars on the 15-minute chart. Now we're looking for the instant the stock trades above a prior 15-minute high for the first time, and that's our entry price. That is going to represent the moment when greed resumes control.

You referenced a prior 15-minute high. On this SANM chart [Figure 11.3], what price are you talking about, exactly?

The prior 15-minute high is $25.92, so we entered around $26.

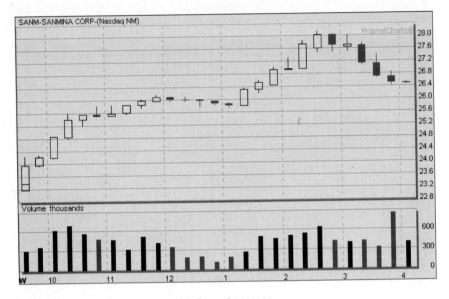

Figure 11.3   Sanmina (Nasdaq: SANM), April 25, 2001
Source: Prophet Financial Systems, Inc. (www.ProphetFinance.com).

How do you determine when to sell?

There are a variety of different sell signals. We use a trailing stop method. If we're in the current 15-minute bar, the stop is below the last 15-minute bar's low. Then, as we go into the next 15-minute period, we move the stop to the low of the previous 15-minute bar. We continue that process until we get stopped out.

In the case of SANM, it would be seven bars later?

That's right.

Does volume play an important role in your analysis?

I would like to see the stock pull back on light volume, which tells me that we are getting more selling than buying, but it's still light compared to the volume that accompanied the rise. If you look at Sanmina, the volume is very small during the midday dip, and then there is an explosion in the volume on a move up. Of course, we don't see the explosion in the volume until after the fact, because we are already in the stock.

What happens when things go wrong? These technical studies can't possibly be correct 100 percent of the time.

There are two types of losses: a loss from a mistake and a loss from mathematics. In a loss from mathematics, you've done nothing wrong. This is a numbers game. I explain it to my traders this way: If I were to give you a coin that was guaranteed to flip heads 7 or 8 times out of every 10, what would your bet be? Your bet would be heads every time you flipped it. If we can find something that happens 7 or 8 times out of every 10, we can make a fortune in the markets. It is not going to happen *every* time, but you don't need it to happen every time.

We've identified patterns or events that happen 6, 7, sometimes 8 times out of 10, and we exploit them every single time we spot them— it becomes a numbers game. So, some of your losses can simply be, "Hey, this is the 1 or 2 or 3 times out of 10 that it's just not going to work." Nothing is going to be 100 percent. We tell our traders that every single time you experience a loss, it is imperative that you separate the loss into one of two categories. You can put a loss into a category called normal, numerical losses—"I've done nothing wrong." Then, there's another column that says, "I'm stupid. I made a mistake." As you collect five, six, seven of these items in the "I'm stupid" category, you must look at them and find the common denominator in all of the losses, because it will be there. You have either entered too late, anticipated or entered too soon, failed to use proper money management techniques, picked the wrong stock, traded too big of a size, picked the wrong time of day—it could be a variety of different and wrong reasons. Once you find the common denominator in all of your losses, your sole mission in life is to kill it and make sure it never happens again.

Regardless of the reason behind the loss, what should a trader do when a stock begins to tank?

Before an astute trader gets into a trade, the price that he or she is going to quit should already be known. When you enter a stock, if you do not know where you will call it quits, you are gambling. It is only when you know this point that you are not gambling; you are moving in with a well-defined plan. With our method, if your stock drops to your "uncle" point, you sell it. Period.

What about an overnight gap? What if a stock gaps way below your selling point?

That is a disastrous situation, and there are specific techniques that we use either to come out of that disaster or to help mitigate some of the pain. I wrote an article in *Active Trader* magazine on how to handle disaster. A recent statistic indicated that 1 in every 20 overnight trades results in an unexpected disaster. If it happens that frequently, one must have a disaster plan. In the event the stock gaps viciously to the downside, the first thing we tell our traders is to do nothing for the first five minutes. You're already crushed; five minutes is not going to be the end of the world. You let the stock trade for a full five minutes. This will give you five minutes to get over the shock, as much as you possibly can in five minutes. It will also help you gain at least part of your composure. It will give the stock the ability to get rid of the bulk of the overnight or premarket selling—a lot of it happens in the first five minutes. Oftentimes, that five-minute period establishes an intraday low. In some cases, it establishes the low for the entire day. Because of the high probability that this will occur, we tell traders not to panic in the first five minutes. After the first five-minute period is over, mark off mentally the low of the day. What is the lowest price the stock trades at in that five-minute period? Mark that off.

If the stock breaks to a new daily low after the first five minutes, sell 50 percent of your position. Then, wait for a full 30 minutes, including the first five minutes, from 9:30 to 10:00. After 10:00, you are going to mark off the absolute low of the day once again. Giving the stock 30 minutes after a dramatic drop to the downside gets almost all of the panic selling out of the way. Then bargain hunters start to come in, and oftentimes stocks are dramatically off of their lows after 15 or 20 minutes of trading. After 30 minutes, mark off the low of the day, and that is going to be your absolute "uncle" point. If at any point later in the day, after 10:00 EST, the stock moves to a new daily low, then the selling is not over, and you should dump the whole thing. Those are the steps.

Now, oftentimes the stock will have a strong intraday rebound, and the most challenging part of that scenario is figuring out when to sell. Odds are that the entire loss is not going to be made up; a portion of it can be made up. Some of the loss can be narrowed, but this is damage control. It's not profitable trading when a stock dramatically gaps to the downside.

Let's talk about your security selection process. Do you tend to follow whatever is moving on a specific day, or do you prefer to stick with certain stocks?

I focus on what is moving and ask, "Does this stock give me one of the pictures that I know and that I play all the time?" I'm not one to pick something that's moving, anything that's moving, and jump on board.

That is gambling. But if something is moving and I know the pattern, I don't have to think about it; I don't have to guess; I don't have to shoot from the hip—I know the strategy. That's appropriate, intelligent, successful market play. With a detailed plan, you know precisely what you're looking for. You're playing the stock; the stock's not playing you. That was the problem a lot of people got into in 1998 and 1999, when the game was to find out what was moving, make sure it had four letters in its symbol, and then buy it. It worked for a while. But there is a right way to make money and a wrong way to make money. When you make money the wrong way, it's not really a profit—it's a loan. Ultimately, the market is going to ask for it back, plus interest.

You mentioned earlier that when you were learning the trading game, everyone kept their techniques to themselves. There must be a reason for that secrecy. If a successful trader let his or her strategies out in the open, every market participant would eventually capitalize on the approach, and the anomalies that the system was originally intended to exploit would disappear. Why doesn't this "no money machines in the market" theory affect Pristine's trading strategies?

I have never bought into that concept. I think people—especially the so-called gurus of the past—have used that excuse to keep people dependent. Fear and greed have been around for a long, long time. Oliver Velez and his trading tactics are certainly not going to change that. People always react the same way. Individually, we're intelligent; collectively, we're a mob that acts the same way every single time, over and over again. We're Pavlovian models who salivate at the tinkering of the bell. I can take you back to charts in the 1980s, in the 1950s, in the 1920s, and you will see the same exact patterns. You see these same patterns in everything that people are involved with: the bell-shaped curve that we see in stocks is the bell-shaped curve in relationships, the bell-shaped curve in the economic boom and bust cycle, the bell-shaped curve in the real estate market. These are the pictures of human action at work. These patterns are not going to be ruined, and people's behavior in the market is not going to be altered by someone promoting tactics.

Back in the old days, there was not a great incentive for people to take a trader under their wing or to teach their methods. I remember literally begging some successful traders to teach me and take me under their wing, and they had no interest. Today, however, there has been a revolution; there has been a dramatic explosion of interest on the part of the individual who wants to be his or her own self-directed market player. The crowds are so big now that there is enough incentive for people who know what they are doing in the markets to lend themselves out for a fee.

A lot of people ask, "Oliver, why do you do this?" It's a variety of reasons. I have a passion for it. I do it very well. I feel I have helped to build this industry for the past 13 years. At the same time, it is very financially rewarding. When I first began, I taught people two-on-two or one-on-one. Today, my seminars have 150 people paying upwards of three, four, five thousand dollars a pop to learn what I do.

Pristine was built and founded by my partner Greg Capra and I; we were professional traders, meaning that we earned our livelihood from the markets. We are real traders first, businessmen second. People feel that difference not only in our services but in our seminars as well. People come from all over the world to watch us practice what we preach.

You still spend the majority of your day trading?

Yes, absolutely. It is critical. We're dispensing stock market advice, guidance, and education. We've got to be in there with our sleeves rolled up; plus, it continues to be a good portion of our daily bread as well.

What about transaction costs? People often view trading as prohibitively costly because of commissions.

Transaction costs are a nonissue today. My first trade was 1,000 shares of Intel about 15 years ago—cost me almost $2,000. Today the same thousand shares would cost me $10. The issue is whether you're overtrading, not whether your commissions are too high. If someone tells me that they are losing money because of commissions, I know it's a person who does not know how to trade. If I could make money by short-term trading and pay rates that are $100 or more per trade, then $10 per trade is certainly very reasonable, even $15 or $20.

Is it enough for traders to master one trading style, or should people be proficient in all time frames?

The true professional trader knows how to handle him- or herself in the four dominant time frames. There are going to be times when you are only operating in one, but when that time frame becomes inappropriate to focus on exclusively, what are you going to do? Lose money? No, you have to be able to handle yourself when the weather changes. You have to know how to handle yourself when it rains, when it shines, when it's cloudy, when it's cold, when it's hot—in all of the time frames. That is what makes you a true professional.

Most people only know how to make money when the rising tide is

Figure 11.4   Nasdaq 100 Trust (AMEX: QQQ), January 2000–April 2001
Source: Prophet Financial Systems, Inc. (www.ProphetFinance.com).

raising all boats. In that case, you don't have to know anything—you buy every dip, and then you pray. That's what I call the ostrich approach. You buy a stock today, you take a nap, and you hope everything is okay when you wake up—it takes no skill. But when that market environment stops, when the drummer stops beating, when the sun dies down, what are you going to do? If you cannot handle yourself in the next phase or in a different time frame or in a different environment, you are not a professional, and ultimately the market is going to take every single thing you got during the lucky times.

What about long-term investors? Is technical analysis useful only in short-term time frames?

A lot of people have funds that they want to allocate to a longer-term approach. They would use the same patterns and techniques that we teach for other time frames. For instance, they may want to play the market through the Qs [see Figure 11.4]. They would look for buy setups on the monthly chart or the weekly chart of the Qs. Let's go back to the weekly chart of the Qs with a 20-period moving average. [Velez demands that all traders include a 20-period simple moving average (SMA) on their charts. On a weekly chart of QQQ, a 20-period SMA would take a rolling average of the past 20 weeks' closing prices. Velez explains the 20-period SMA, or "20," as follows: "Think of the 20-period moving average as a leash and the stock as a dog. The leash is only so long, which means that the dog can only go so far without the leash stopping it, in either direction. If a stock is way away from its 20, the dog has been freed from the leash. The odds suggest that, at least for the short term, there is going to be a multipoint snap back toward the 20. Stocks cannot remain far away from their 20s for extended periods of time."]

In the beginning of 2001, the Q dropped significantly below the 20. Then we had a three-week snap right back toward the 20. That's an opportunity to short. Then the Qs drop for many weeks, a phenomenal nearly 50 percent collapse. Again, notice how far the Qs are from the 20—the dog has run too far, the leash is very taut, and it is going to be snapped back toward the 20. Your proper entry is the next time the Qs take out a prior bar's high. Over a two-week period, the Qs snapped back again toward the 20, as it ran up to $50 or so. This will happen over and over and over again.

If you look at the first third of 2000, there is a four–red bar drop into April, and then an explosion to the upside. In the beginning of August, there is a five-bar run up, and then a collapse. I've found, by looking at thousands of charts, that oftentimes—not all the time—after three to five consecutive bars in the same direction at a fairly steep angle, the stock has pretty much run its course in that direction for the short-term, and the opposite direction is close at hand.

I like to hold things for several weeks and am not concerned with a day or two. I would use a weekly time frame to look for these setups. If you want to hold things for several months and not worry about a week or two, then focus on the monthly chart. If a person says, "Oliver, I don't like pain. I don't like any fluttering. I don't like to deal with even a day to the downside," then they are going to focus on the daily chart. If a person says, "I don't like any pain. I don't even like a moment of pain. I want to buy it, and I want instant gratification, or I get out," then they are going to take the same patterns and focus on the five-minute chart or the 15-minute chart.

What about mastering different market conditions? Have most traders been able to make the transition from the irrationally bullish market to the brutal bear market?

A lot of traders have not been able to deal with the down market. It's very difficult for novice market players—especially ones that played in one of the most bullish markets in history—to make the flip, to switch mentally to thinking in reverse. During certain parts of 1998, almost all of 1999, and the beginning of 2000, all you had to do was pull up a four-letter symbol, buy it, wait 10 minutes, and you were up. It was the easiest period in the world, and it won't come for decades again—maybe in certain sectors, but not in the market as a whole.

This current down market was actually easier if you could make the mental shift to thinking in reverse. All you had to do during the last three to six months was pull up any Nasdaq stock's four-letter symbol, sell it short, wait 10 or 15 minutes, and collect your money. Or you could wait several days and collect your money or wait several weeks and collect your money. The down market was just as easy. The hard part was making the mental shift to do the reverse. People kept throwing more money into predicting bottom after bottom after bottom, and a lot of people did not make it. This downtrend in the market has destroyed a great many people who thought that they would be involved in the market for a long time.

But similar things happen all the time; it's a function of the market. The market wipes people out who shouldn't be there—the people who are there by luck, the people who were confusing a bull market for brains. They are called the weak hands, and the market will back its truck up, knock them off, and then take off. It happens over and over and over again. There's the sifting process that the market goes through where a pile of people jump on, the market sifts out those who shouldn't be there, and what is left is a small group of people who survived. Then we do it again. Another bunch of people come on board. We sift.

Our business has always grown very dramatically. We have been in business for seven years now, and we have always had phenomenal growth. But the growth spurt really skyrocketed when the market started to have trouble in a more dramatic way, because for the first time, people stopped feeling smart all by themselves. For the first time in a long time people said, "Maybe I do need some guidance. Maybe I should go see someone who knows how to do this, and perhaps I can learn something." During the bull market, people said, "Why should I pay for anything? I'm making a ton of money."

Your web site content is offered in dozens of languages. Where is trading popular besides the United States? Do international traders operate differently?

A lot people think that America is home to the kings and queens of day trading, and that is certainly not the case. Korea has by far a more active day trading–oriented market. About 5 percent to 6 percent of our market can be attributed to day traders; 66 percent of the Korean market is day trading in nature. Everyone in Korea day trades, from grandmothers to young adolescents; it's really quite amazing. They are very sophisticated in their short-term approaches to the market. They are also far more advanced from an Internet and technology perspective. They have more high-speed Internet access in homes than we do in America; I believe somewhere close to 80 percent of the entire population is on the Internet.

We have found that the Asian community mentality lends itself quite nicely to a short-term approach in the market. We have found the same mentality prevalent in Latin America. I believe it is due to a way of life that is slightly less stable. For instance, in Latin American countries, change is so common that they can't bank on anything long-term. They cannot look beyond a few years or beyond this president. Businesspeople cannot afford to invest enormous amounts of money because if the government changes from this month to the next, they have wasted their money. Because of this lifestyle, this more unstable approach to life, these countries tend to be trader-oriented.

No matter where you go today, people are watching what the Nasdaq is doing. The Nikkei popped in 1989, and over a 12-year period declined 66 percent. The Nasdaq popped in March 2000, and it took a year to drop 66 percent—one year to do what the Nikkei did in 12 years. This drop seems not to have deadened the interest in places all over the world. Internationally, people want to trade the U.S. market more than they want to trade their domestic market. It is our mission to bring the United States to them.

Does the individual investor have all the necessary tools to take advantage of your teachings? Is it a loser's game to go up against Wall Street professionals?

A new breed of market player has emerged, and that new breed is the individual. I believe that the future of the markets belongs to the individual and no longer to the professional. The light is dimming very rapidly for the professional. The line of demarcation that has historically separated the two groups—the individual retail investor from the professional institution—is rapidly disappearing.

We have had a 26-year decline in commission rates. May Day 1975 marked the end of control of commissions, and we have done nothing but decline for 26 years, making it cheaper for anybody to access the markets, and certainly making short-term market play more viable. [On May Day 1975, Congress ended the practice of fixed minimum brokerage commissions, thereby paving the way for a discount brokerage revolution.] In addition to a 26-year decline in commission rates, we have had a worldwide collapse in interest rates, making equity participation an absolute necessity if you plan to stay ahead of the inflation monster. In the beginning of the 1980s, interest rates were around 20 percent. Today, the interest rate on a 30-year Japanese bond is zero. Lend your money to the Japanese government, and you'll get back the same amount of money 30 years later. It is not that extreme here in the United States, but we have certainly dropped to levels that make equity participation an absolute necessity.

In addition to the drop in commission rates and the worldwide collapse in interest rates, we have had phenomenal technological advancements. Almost every intelligent person has a PC in his or her home or has access to one at work. The advent of the Internet has significantly narrowed the gap between the *source* of information and the ultimate *recipient*. The gap, which has historically been controlled by the power structure on Wall Street, is almost zero today. For instance, if you were to know that on Friday Microsoft is going to announce that they are bankrupt, you would make a fortune because of the gap between the knowledge—the source of information that you get today—and the final recipients on Friday. That gap is the key to massive wealth, and it has always been on Wall Street. The Internet has narrowed the gap dramatically so that virtually everybody gets information at the same time. That has helped to level the playing field.

We have had a 26-year decline in commission rates, a worldwide collapse in interest rates, phenomenal technological advancement, the advent of the Internet, and new order-handling rules that favor the individual. Because of these new order-handling rules, no one can skip my order, no one can trade through my order. My order can be posted for the whole world to see side-by-side Goldman Sachs and Merrill Lynch. Because of all this, a revolution has emerged, and a new breed of individuals is joining the ranks every single day. Even though we have had one of the worst bear markets in history, it has not stopped or even put a dent in this revolution. We are only in the infant stage.

I see a day when there will not be multiple exchanges; there is going to be one worldwide electronic exchange that is open 24 hours a day. There will be a uniform direct-access platform that is preloaded on every single computer that gives everybody direct access to this electronic exchange. People will be able to transact through their television sets, through their remote control. In fact, trading systems for the television are in development today. In the upper left-hand corner, you will always have your open positions ticking 24 hours a day, and with one click you can change the channel, and with another click you can buy and sell securities.

Short-term trading is going to become just as normal as going to the corner store and picking up a loaf of bread and a quart of milk. I see it happening; all of the things I have mentioned are making it more viable. And the power structure on Wall Street needs it. The average spread on a Nasdaq stock has dropped over 70 percent, and when you narrow the spread—which is the source of wealth on Wall Street—what must you do to keep the same amount of money? You have got to increase volume. How do you increase volume? By saying, "Come on in, the water's warm." Making it easy. Dropping rates. Lowering the barrier and spreading the message all over the world that equity participation is a necessity. That is the only way to keep the game going.

We are on the brink of a huge revolution. Those who get prepared today, those who get the right education and the right tools under their belt, stand to be titans of the new game. That is the message I deliver.

Chapter 12

BREAKING THE RULES
The Motley Fools: David Gardner, Jeff Fischer,
and Brian Lund

Internet Alias	Investment Style
David: TMFDavidG Jeff: TMF Jeff Brian: TMF Tardior	Long-term

Year of Birth	Location
David: 1966; Jeff: 1969; Brian: 1970	Alexandria, VA

Education
David: English, University of North Carolina Jeff: management and finance, Northern Illinois Brian: Latin and Greek, University of Minnesota

Web Site (Free)
The Motley Fool: www.fool.com

A month before the XFL—the "x-treme" football league founded by the World Wrestling Federation—was x-tinguished after just a single season of play in 2001, David Gardner, cofounder of The Motley Fool, foresaw the demise. No one actually liked the league, but although most critics focused on second-rate players, soap-opera storylines destroying the purity of the American sport, ridiculous rules, and cheerleader-focused cameramen, Gardner actually lambasted the XFL for being too dull! In his opinion, the WWF didn't just need to change some of the rules; it had to completely break, obliterate, and destroy *all* the rules. Some of his suggestions: allow holding, eliminate pass interference penalties, and measure *actual* progress by the ball carrier, not forward progress as in the NFL: "In our league, we measure *actual* progress.

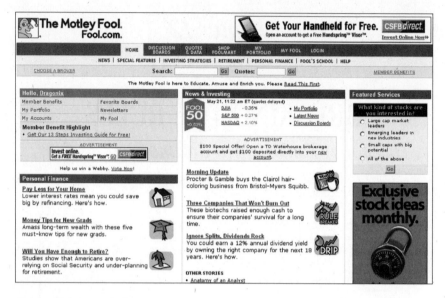

Figure 12.1   www.fool.com
Source: The Motley Fool.

We don't care if a guy breaks the goal line if he winds up on his duff back at the five-yard line. That is not a touchdown, and the ball is placed on the five-yard line. If three defenders want to pick up a running back and run him back 15 yards, let them, mark the ball there, give them credit." Icing on the cake was Gardner's proposed league slogan: "The NFL is for wussies."

If there's one thing that Gardner and his brother Tom know a lot about, it's breaking rules. When the duo decided to start their multimedia investing kingdom, The Motley Fool, nearly a decade ago, they left the suit-wearing, stodgy Street in the dust, donned their famous jester caps and a smile, and went to work. The Fool has been a textbook case in successful marketing; even those who have never read one of the Gardner's books or visited The Motley Fool web site (see Figure 12.1) are aware of their empowering, do-it-yourself, do-it-better-than-the-pros message. In an investment management class at Wharton, we even studied an academic paper about one of The Motley Fool's online portfolios. The Motley Fool is all about community and communication and taking hold of your financial life. The Gardner brothers embody each of those tenets. In other words, they were a natural fit for this book.

Overall Return -- total % Gained (Lost)						
	Day	Week	Month	Year To Date	Since Inception (8/5/1994)	Annualized
Rule Breaker	0.52%	8.17%	7.97%	30.62%	506.59%	30.42%
S&P 500	0.27%	3.72%	3.40%	(2.15%)	181.84%	16.49%
S&P 500 (DA)	0.26%	3.53%	3.23%	(2.04%)	196.10%	17.34%
NASDAQ	0.24%	4.34%	3.91%	(11.00%)	205.32%	17.88%

Figure 12.2 Rule Breaker portfolio returns as of May 2001
Source: The Motley Fool (www.fool.com).

The Motley Fool site, with message boards, columns, and market commentary, is mostly free—with a few for-pay newsletters and investment guides advertised throughout. Aside from the vibrant discussions nested deep within the site's message boards, the most intriguing parts of the site are the nearly half-dozen investing strategies and portfolios updated online, and the most interesting of those is the Rule Breaker portfolio. Rule Breakers—like David Gardner's proposed XFL and even The Motley Fool itself—look to revolutionize old industries and define new ones. When Rule Breakers grow up, they hope to be Rule Makers, firmly entrenched within their domains of expertise.

To be honest, the Rule Breaker strategy at first sounded to us a bit cliché; who wouldn't want to find great emerging companies in great emerging industries? But The Motley Fool caught many of the best-known highfliers of the past decade well before they were the best-known highfliers. So, they must be doing something right; creating investment returns like those listed in Figure 12.2 requires disciplined strategy and wide-open minds. The Fools were remarkably humble during our conversations, a feat that must have been difficult. Since 1994 The Motley Fool Rule Breaker portfolio has trounced the averages buying for the long-term.

We talked with three members of the Rule Breaker team, which makes portfolio decisions and writes online commentary three times weekly. Our first day, and the first interview that follows, was spent with Jeff Fischer and Brian Lund, who gave us a great overview of what it takes to gain a place in The Motley Fool's famous portfolio. The next day we were able to grab hold of David Gardner himself and discuss all aspects of being fools and breaking rules.

**David and Tom Gardner are obviously well-known and important fig-
ures within the world of investing. But what about you two and other
Motley Fool writers? None of your bios and backgrounds particularly
scream expertise in finance and investing, especially Brian—a Latin
major?**

Jeff: That's the spirit of the Internet and The Motley Fool as well. Everyone on the Internet has a voice, so you're very much a part of a communal learning process. Even The Motley Fool writers are not there to
be listened to; they're there to contribute to discussions and act as
sounding boards. That's been The Fool's appeal from the start in my
opinion.

Brian: People can take what they want from me or not; it's an ongoing
discussion as far as we're concerned. And to compare large things with
small, I'll point out that Ben Graham was a Classics scholar in school,
too. He spent his declining years reading Greek.

**Even though you see yourselves only as sounding boards, it must be dif-
ficult for the general public to resist following your every move, especially when you're performing so well. You even have a disclaimer on
the site not to mimic the Rule Breaker portfolio. Do you have trouble
convincing people to make their own decisions?**

Brian: All we can do is say over and over again, "We're thinking aloud;
we want you to think aloud with us." We tell people that it's a mistake
to mimic us blindly—a recipe for disaster. If they don't listen, that's their
business.

Jeff: We know there is a good deal of interest in what we buy and sell—
we can tell from e-mails and the message boards and the way stocks react after we announce our transactions. But you're making your own decisions; it's up to you.

**Principle number one for the Rule Breaker portfolio is to take a lot of
risk to get a lot of reward. Is that a bit too simple and too naive?**

Brian: That is an oversimplification. If you're looking for safety in your
portfolio, then you should be in an index fund. That's the default first
step for any investor, and for many people the final step. If you want to
go beyond that, if you want to look for better-than-market-average re-

turns, you're going to have to take risk. So, with risk comes reward, but also the potential for loss.

Jeff: We say quite frequently and transparently that we expect at least half of our investments to fail, and that's the nature of the way the Rule Breaker invests. It's the highest-risk portfolio that we have on the site. We expect at least half to fail, but with the few companies that do succeed, we expect to more than make up for those failures, and that so far has proven true.

Take us through the Rule Breaking criteria. What do you look for in a company?

Brian: First and foremost, we're looking for industries that are important and emerging. We're not interested in secondary or tertiary elements of people's lives. We want industries that are changing people's entire worlds. That's criteria number one.

Jeff: Within those industries, we want to find the so-called top dog, the emerging leader that's moving with gusto. For example, a top biotech company would have strong alliances, strong partnerships, strong pipelines. That's the second criterion.

Brian: Very good use of the Greek singular—"criterion." I said "criteria" earlier, and I apologize; it's not in keeping with my training. Third is building a competitive advantage over time to sustain the company through its growth period—things like visionary leadership, lack of competition, patents.

Jeff: We then make sure that the company has very good management and smart financial backing. Most companies we buy are young, so we can look very recently at the venture capitalists who supported them. We also look at alliances—larger companies that may have invested money.

Brian: Fifth, we look for companies that have strong consumer appeal. We are not very taken with industries that sell to other industries—for example, a company developing fiber optics that is going to sell to four or five big networking companies. We're much more interested in companies that reach individuals because we think they are better able to sustain their advantages. Once we find a company that meets all of those criteria, we then move to the current condition of the stock. The first thing we look for is a relative strength of 90 or better, which is meant to be a proxy to determine if this company has gotten some kind of acceptance in the market. Has the market recognized to some degree its potential for future growth and so awarded it a generous multiple? [A stock's relative strength simply measures (on a scale from 1 to 100) its return in relation to a market index, such as the S&P 500. A relative strength of 90 would imply that the stock has been doing extremely well compared to the index.]

Jeff: The stock should have a great potential to appreciate in value—10 times in five years. We look at the company's overall addressable market and compare that to its market value. Finally, we look for a stock that a lot of people have considered to be overvalued, that has a lot of negative buzz. So, we want a company that has shaken the world, that people see, recognize, know the name, and are calling overvalued.

Where do you find those?

Jeff: We find many of them on The Motley Fool discussion boards. A community spread around the world has got to be the best possible collective research team, definitely better than Salomon Smith Barney, Merrill Lynch, or Morgan Stanley—people stuck in a New York office. People on discussion boards are all around the world, researching new ideas, working in new industries, with their fingers on the pulses of hundreds of different emerging companies. We follow the most active discussion boards, because where there is a lot of interest, there is typically a lot of promise.

Can you give an example of when the boards have come through for the Rule Breaker portfolio?

Jeff: The first example was Iomega, back in 1994 [see Figure 12.3]. It was first talked about on The Motley Fool discussion boards, and that's where Tom and David [the Gardner brothers] heard about Iomega's new Zip drive that was still six months from launch. It sounded promising; the stock started to rise; and The Fool bought into it. The portfolio ended up making over 1,000 percent on half of its investment and 700 percent on the other half, holding two to three years.

Brian: A lot of the up-and-coming technology companies first appear for us on the message boards: At Home, 3DFX . . .

Jeff: Celera.

Brian: Yes, a lot of the biotech companies. You'll find that technology normally flies under the radar of the mainstream media and will turn up first on discussion boards. But we also are not above reading the regular financial press. EBay was a company that everybody knew—you heard

Figure 12.3 Iomega (NYSE: IOM), January 1994–December 1996
Source: Prophet Financial Systems, Inc. (www.ProphetFinance.com).

about its IPO; you could see its business model at work; and people were participating in the service. I had friends telling me, "You've got to try this eBay thing." That's really the sign of a great Rule Breaker—when everybody is talking about it, knows about it, and uses it.

You mentioned that you like stocks with high relative strengths as well as stocks that many people view as overvalued. Isn't it possible that they *are* overvalued?

Jeff: Nine out of ten times they are, and that's why we have all of these criteria; they have to meet each one. If you look at our portfolio and our trades, we sidestepped the entire dot-com implosion. We didn't buy Webvan or Priceline or CBS MarketWatch or TheStreet.com—any of those stocks that went from $90 to pennies.

Why did those Internet companies not pass the Rule Breaker tests?

Brian: In most cases, we didn't see any competitive advantage. We could see it in Amazon, which had an early jump; it had a name that was well known, well recognized. But something like Pets.com had immediate competition. For Amazon, right from the get-go, it wasn't about buying books and music. It was about being the place to shop online for everything. Pets.com—you can't do much with the name Pets.com except sell pet food, and that's just not very important.

Why did most investors seem to get it wrong and buy valueless companies? Were they acting irrationally? Start with this one: Is the stock market "efficient"?

Jeff: In the short term, no. In the long term, yes.

Brian: Sounds good to me.

Despite the popped Nasdaq bubble and the market's obvious rampant speculation in technology stocks, that answer doesn't seem entirely obvious. Can you delve deeper?

Brian: As a company matures, the future cash flows on which it is valued becomes much clearer. In the short term, it's not clear how much companies will earn. You get events that drive people to think that the future is over—like when Johnson & Johnson took Propulsid off the market a year ago. The stock fell 10 percent that day. People immediately thought future cash-flow expectations were out of whack, so they sold. Then, after a while they realized that maybe it wasn't going to affect cash flow very much, and now Johnson & Johnson is back to where it was.

But that type of reaction sounds rational. Sure, the market came to the wrong answer about Johnson & Johnson, but it at least did some math. Is the market controlled by that type of careful analysis or by careless speculation?

Jeff: I think there's a pretty equal mix of people speculating and people investing in the market almost every day, and that's part of the reason volatility has increased since the early 1990s. Speculation has become much more accessible; volume is always at record levels, indicating that a lot of people are making transactions for the short term. There are two very distinct classes out there: speculators moving money in and out of markets every week and long-term investors who make transactions relatively infrequently.

Brian: But let's be clear: The big investment houses have a considerably greater amount of money than individual investors. It's not as if individual investors are out there speculating while investment houses are sitting at their desks doing real, hard value work. They're speculating, too.

Jeff: If you look at the turnover on mutual funds, it's typically about 90 percent annually, which means that nine out of ten stocks in the fund are bought and sold every year. To get back to your efficient market ques-

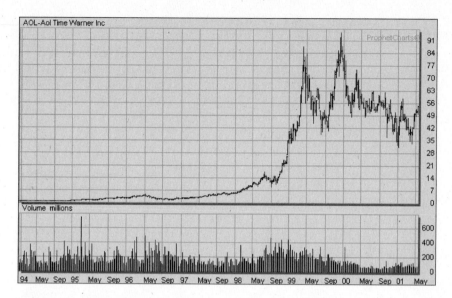

Figure 12.4   AOL Time Warner (NYSE: AOL), January 1994–May 2001
Source: Prophet Financial Systems, Inc. (www.ProphetFinance.com).

tion: Are they doing that because the market is efficient in the near term? No, they're doing it because they're speculating.

Back to Rule Makers: Where do the numbers come in? It seems we've gotten to the point of an interesting story, but companies with interesting stories don't necessarily make good investments. What about the importance of turning a profit?

Brian: Certainly we're looking for companies that can make money; that's going to come from the competitive advantage—not necessarily in the beginning, but over time if a company is able to develop pricing power and brand.

Jeff: AOL wasn't making money when we bought it in 1994 [see Figure 12.4]. In fact, a lot of people thought it would end up bankrupt; what we looked at was their competitive advantage—the best brand with the best marketing, signing up the most customers every single month. We looked at sales; we looked at gross margins; we looked at operating margins; we looked at cash flow; and we roughly estimated that once they met critical mass, they would be profitable. Everyone says AOL was an obvious investment, but in 1994 through 1997, it was not obvious. Most people thought that AOL was going to end up bankrupt.

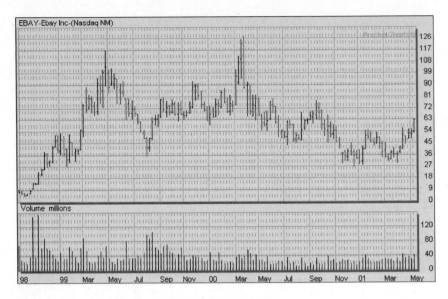

Figure 12.5 EBay (Nasdaq: EBAY), May 1998–May 2001
Source: Prophet Financial Systems, Inc. (www.ProphetFinance.com).

How often does the Rule Maker portfolio transact?

Jeff: Typically about twice per year.

Is there competition between the Rule Breaker and Rule Maker portfolio managers? It seems as if the companies in the two portfolios are completely at odds—the Breakers constantly trying to destroy the Makers.

Jeff: Our goal is for Rule Breaking companies to become Rule Makers. The best example is AOL; it went from being a breaker to definitely the rule maker in Internet media. But Rule Breakers don't necessarily emerge just to displace Rule Makers. Rule Breakers usually are innovative enough that they're creating new industries, creating demand for something new. AOL hasn't come about and displaced Rule Maker Microsoft, but it's become a Rule Maker in its own right.

Brian: You might say that AOL displaced AT&T to a certain degree—replacing long-distance communication over the telephone with long-distance communication via e-mail. Starbucks may be another consummate rule breaker. It came into a totally fragmented market and gave it unification.

Figure 12.6   Human Genome Sciences (Nasdaq: HGSI), May 1999–May 2001
Source: Prophet Financial Systems, Inc. (www.ProphetFinance.com).

Which are your favorite Rule Breakers right now?

Brian: EBay has got the mother of all sustainable advantages [see Figure 12.5]. It has a network that everybody must play in; nobody can take his ball and go to his own playground. Everybody knows that eBay is *the* place to buy and sell online. And now it's exerting pricing power by raising fees and eliminating off-site trades. It's got visionary management and the potential for very high profits.

Any others?

Jeff: I see potential for Human Genome Sciences [see Figure 12.6]. It's an eight-year-old biotech but doesn't have revenues yet. It has four drugs in trials and several coming into the pipeline. Its advantage is that it has a protein patent portfolio that is about 8,000 strong; the belief is that proteins are going to be the next emerging wave in medicine and biotechnology because proteins are a much more natural way to treat disease. You can inject proteins in a body to treat cancer, for instance, instead of injecting a toxic chemical. The treatment is much more efficient and has no side effects.

How about an investment failure? Where did the Rule Breaker criteria lead you astray?

Brian: There were several troubles with Excite@Home [see Figure 12.7]. We bought it when it was just At Home—just a broadband connectivity company. It had shared ownership of its company among many of its customers—the cable companies—and was selling to a very select group of companies; that turned out to be problematic. But where it really ran into trouble was in acquiring Excite. At Home paid a substantial amount of money to establish a media presence that it didn't need. We look for top dogs and first movers; Excite was neither of those. It was, and still is, a third-rate Internet portal. Then, of course, there was the Blue Mountain Arts acquisition, which was just ridiculous—a company with no potential for revenue. [Blue Mountain Arts is an electronic greeting card company that was acquired by Excite@Home for $780 million in cash and stock.] So, that company deteriorated from under us, but it did teach us a valuable lesson about buying companies that are at the whims of their customers.

What can investors expect from the Rule Breakers going forward? You've mentioned in columns on the site that investor expectations for future market returns are unrealistically high. Why is that? What is a reasonable expectation going forward?

Brian: They're unrealistic because they've been so good for so long. Even with this last plummet, we're looking at 15 percent annualized market average returns going back 20 years. That's abnormally high. You can't keep that up forever. If you did, the market would come to represent far too large of a percentage of GDP [gross domestic product]. In time the market is going to revert to about the share of corporate earnings in GDP, which is 3 percent or 4 percent per year; toss in a couple points for inflation and a point or two for dividends, and you're looking at 6 percent or 7 percent per year. This is something that Warren Buffett has said. A recent PaineWebber poll showed that people expect 19 percent. That's just ludicrous. You can't get that. You can't. If you're speculating, if you go put your money on black, you can get better than 19 percent, but if you're an investor, you can't get that.

Jeff: We always focus on *companies* rather than the *stock market,* and we try to teach our readers to do the same, because companies can perform well regardless of what the stock market does. So, we always try to buy companies that are going to do well no matter how the stock market performs.

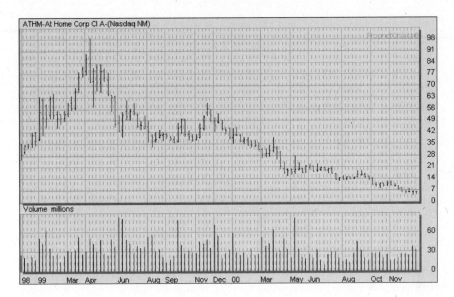

Figure 12.7   At Home (Nasdaq: ATHM), December 1998–December 2000
Source: Prophet Financial Systems, Inc. (www.ProphetFinance.com).

[The day after speaking with Brian and Jeff, we grabbed The Motley Fool cofounder David Gardner for a chat. Here is what he had to say.]

What is The Motley Fool's niche? How have you been able to build such a successful empire?

There's an obvious lack of education when it comes to the stock market and various aspects of personal finance, yet we all get asked to make important monetary decisions at different points in our lives. We realized that not only could we educate people, but we could learn a lot from them, too. The interactive nature of The Motley Fool—our discussion boards and the opportunity to learn—is an opportunity that we enjoy as well.

Talk more about The Fool as a community. Do you have any evidence that message boards can actually make people money or generate results?

The results are different things to different people. A guy came to our message boards three years ago with $80,000 in debt, and today he's out. If you talk to him, you'll find that he credits us almost completely. For someone else, it might be that he found out about a new stock or saved $500 purchasing a new car or made a better decision with his insurance. It all began with our single Motley Fool discussion board back when we were on AOL as paying customers and started our own board called The Motley Fool; we said we'd do our best to answer any questions that came our way. "We're not experts. We hope you'll answer our questions, too. Let's all work together to understand the world of money." There was a guy there who had worked in the oil industry outside of Houston for 25 years. When he disagreed with something that a Wall Street analyst said or reinterpreted a story that the media was playing one way, you would start realizing that you can learn a lot from other people. When you're running a business that benefits from the content generated by others to the tune of 10,000 messages a day, which fills four books—something no one can keep up with—you realize how many smart people there are out there and how much of a good thing it is to have them as a part of your business.

Brian Lund mentioned yesterday that investor expectations for market returns have gotten out of whack over the past 20 years. What side effects would falling expectations have on The Fool itself? How would the community that you just spoke about react to a prolonged market slowdown?

An important move for us was broadening what The Motley Fool represents, turning away from just the stock market. We love the stock market, but it's such a small percentage of one's financial life. Over the last year, while the Nasdaq has been cut in half, we all still have to make decisions about our 401K plan, insurance, mortgages.

Still, it's hard to get people excited about insurance. What do you think is most different, most controversial, about The Fool itself?

Average Americans can invest in the stock market and succeed long-term. The index fund is a default, mail-it-in approach; but for enthusiasts, we teach them how to beat the stock market. Consider Regulation Fair Disclosure, now being called into question just six months after it was passed. The big controversy is whether Wall Street analysts should be privy to news first so that they can pull out the relevant information and re-present it to the public. The idea is that the public at large is unable to interpret it. This notion that we teach—that people actually can digest that information, make sense of it, and beat the market over the long term—is extremely controversial.

One of the pleasures of working here is that we get to hear from people whose lives have directly benefited from our efforts to teach them to fish for themselves, as opposed to throwing fish out at them— which is not to say that everyone should learn investing and everyone should be trying to beat the market, because many of us don't want to spend that time or have other interests in life.

Once people take investing matters into their own hands, what do you think are the biggest mistakes that they typically make?

The first mistake most people make is that they follow too closely. They generally ask "When should I sell?" right after they buy. Whether it's because of the excitement of a quick gain or the anxiety of a loss, they tend to focus too much on the day to day. A lot of people are not aware of the tax implications of doing that.

We asked earlier what is most controversial about The Fool itself, and you responded with the simple idea that the stock market is a game that individual investors can win. But what about your actual investment strategies? What does The Fool bring to the table that's new or different?

It's hard for me to identify anything that happens in investing today that's brand new, just like it's hard to identify any significant piece of literature in the last 100 years and say that it is completely original. What we've done with the Rule Breaker portfolio that's original is synthesize other people's ideas into a coherent and useful approach to investing. The ideas of investing in the top dog of an important and emerging industry, ensuring a high relative strength, and desiring that the media is talking down the stock—each has its own forbearer. For example, the relative strength criterion comes directly from William O'Neil's work.

Great companies begin as Rule Breakers, because if they just mimic the status quo, they'll be buried or be irrelevant. They have to come along and shake things up, hoping to progress to being a Rule Maker; and in between those two stages, they get challenged by others who inevitably begin to copy them. Comparing business to evolution is helpful for me when I think about how to invest and how to think about business.

How so? Tell us more about the evolution metaphor.

Success in evolution and success in business are the same in that they both come down to adapting to changes in external conditions. I also draw the direct comparison between natural selection in biological evolution and in business, where natural selection is the selection of a company by customers. What companies pass on, their basic DNA, is their business practices, products and services, or marketing. But what happens to a lot of investors is that they don't realize that the world has changed underneath them and chopped the life from their company. They look at the financial statements of the company, and things look good, and then all of a sudden, wham, the company gets crushed be-

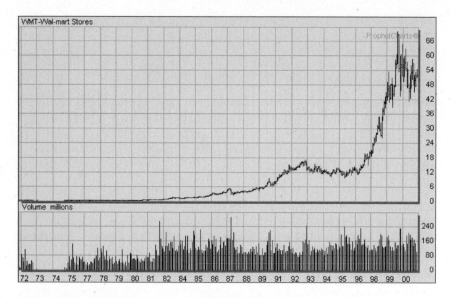

Figure 12.8   Wal-Mart Stores (NYSE: WMT), January 1972–May 2001
Source: Prophet Financial Systems, Inc. (www.ProphetFinance.com).

cause of something that was happening outside of those financial statements; maybe a Rule Breaker came along and appealed to consumers in
a completely different manner.

A typical example would be e-commerce in the last five years; the
external conditions created by the Internet forced a whole bunch of
companies to adapt, and many failed to do so completely. Borders would
be a good example. Four years ago, the bears in our Amazon discussion
board were all talking about how Borders was going to come along and
bury Amazon, yet Borders was late in getting its site up. And now, Amazon actually runs Borders' fulfillment. External circumstances change,
like when the earth goes into an ice age. The temperature changes, and
only certain species adapt. It's the same when the Internet or any revolutionary technology comes along.

**Is it always technology that drives change? Are there examples of Rule
Breakers that revolutionized industries that are more established?**

I'm glad you asked that because you're right. Technology can drive
change, but it doesn't always. Part of it is how we want to define technology; a new business practice could, in a sense, be called a technology.
Wal-Mart was certainly a Rule Breaker when it went public in the 1970s
[see Figure 12.8]. Its new technology, new way of thinking, was to offer a

huge-sized store with enormous variety at very low prices and create a one-stop shopping environment. Not only that, they took this model not to New York City, but to the small towns of America to crush all the small boutiques and mom-and-pops. Some people would define that new way of thinking as a new technology, but it obviously didn't involve biotechnology or the Internet.

Starbucks is another example of a new business practice that became a tremendously competitive weapon for the visionary who saw it and pursued it almost single-mindedly, obtaining the necessary financing and putting the model into practice so rapidly that suddenly everyone else realized it was too late.

We talked a lot with Jeff and Brian about the criteria for Rule Breaking and how difficult it can be to identify Breakers early in their corporate lives. What is your take on how a stock finds its way into your minds and into your portfolio?

Usually we do it from a direct familiarity that we have with a company's product or service. Recently, we were looking at Palm or Handspring as potential Rule Breakers; I don't think we'll be investing in either one, but that's an example of saying, "We like these things." In fact, I own one of each. And then we ask, "What does this mean? Where can it go? What can it become?" It really does start out of our own direct experience, whether it was America Online, our first selection, or Starbucks two years ago. Starbucks went public in 1992, and we were certainly aware of it, but sometimes you have to shock yourself into thinking of actually investing [see Figure 12.9].

Let me mention a short laundry list of companies that I wish I had invested in because I use their products frequently. I've had a Schwab account for 10 years now. I was the radical in my family back when I turned 18; I knew that I was a decision maker, so I moved my account to Schwab. Yet I have never bought stock in Schwab, and what a mistake that was. I've used Quicken for years. What an idiot I was not to buy Intuit stock. I've owned Dell Computers for 10 years but never bought stock. People look to me as a knowledgeable investor and look to model what we're doing at The Fool, but I always have to undercut their excitement with stories like that. It's ridiculous in retrospect that I never owned those companies because I was such a fan as a consumer.

Are there any dangers to a simple "buy what you know" strategy? Where is the line drawn between a great company and a great stock?

Certainly there are numerous examples of what appeared to be a great product and the company met with no success. The first step you have

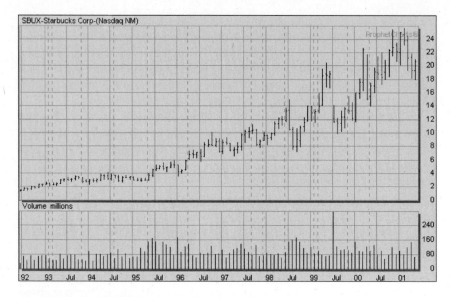

Figure 12.9   Starbucks (Nasdaq: SBUX), May 1992–May 2001
Source: Prophet Financial Systems, Inc. (www.ProphetFinance.com).

to take, beyond just being a believer in a profitable, consumer-oriented company, is to understand the competitive environment in which they live. The second thing that we encourage people to ask themselves is how the company makes money—fundamentally understanding the business model. It's one thing to be a fan of the product or service, but sometimes entirely different to see how a company tries to make money with that product or service. Boston Market, which I've written about extensively in the past, was not a fast food restaurant like McDonalds; it was a bank, and a very poor bank at that [see Figure 12.10].

A bank? Explain.

I'm going to assume that you guys had the same thoughts about Boston Market as I did, which was, "Wow, look at this new fast food chain, and gosh, they actually have healthy food!" I heard that from all my friends. I remember my brother calling me and how impressed he was. But once you actually looked at the business model, you realized it was a franchise setup; they were selling to individuals—real estate investors and entrepreneurs—the rights to open Boston Markets in neighborhoods. You could bid on your zip code in New Jersey or a county in Florida. Furthermore, they were lending the money to buy that right, so you could

Figure 12.10   Boston Chicken (OTC: BOST), May 1993–July 1999
Source: Prophet Financial Systems, Inc. (www.ProphetFinance.com).

actually not be able to afford to buy it. So, Boston Market was a bank, and management was unproven—not from the restaurant industry. They were Blockbuster Video executives.

   The secret turned out to be that actually running a Boston Market restaurant was not a profitable endeavor, and once that was discovered, suddenly all those rights that people had bought were worthless. Not only that, but they had borrowed money from the parent company to buy the rights. Boston Market was the world's hottest IPO in 1993—the stock more than doubled. By 1999 that seemed to be happening every two weeks with one speculative enterprise or another, but in 1993 it was an amazing IPO. Within six years, though, Boston Market was bankrupt. For the first several years that it was on the market, it was being piped up by Merrill Lynch and other investment banks looking at growth in sales and earnings, either not noticing or failing to point out that growth in sales and earnings was largely money coming in from franchisees buying the rights and paying interest on their loans. It's a great example of a consumer franchise that everyone knew, but a company that failed miserably. I would say we distinguished ourselves at The Motley Fool for our writing on the topic, noticing the problem well before it all came tumbling down.

Chapter 13

HELPING OUTSIDERS WITH INSIDERS

Craig Columbus

Internet Alias	Investment Style
Craig Columbus	Medium-term
Year of Birth	**Location**
1967	Scottsdale, AZ
Education	
BA, Loyola University; JD, Indiana University School of Law; MBA, Pennsylvania State University	
Web Site (Free)	
ThomsonFN Insider Trading: insider.ThomsonFN.com	

It used to be that when the going got tough for American businesses, tough managers—compensated largely with performance-based bonuses—got going. Today, those platitudes and clichés of hard work and dedication don't always hold. When the going gets tough these days, tough managers can simply cash in some chips, sell a little stock, and head off to the bank. In many cases, executives can stow away a sizable nest egg before most of the investing public has any wind of impending disaster.

Corporate insiders—top executives, board members, and midlevel managers—have inordinate wealth and risk intimately tied to a single entity. But don't feel too bad for them: While the general public tries to peer into a company's inner sanctum through windows covered with the soot of hyped-up press releases and opaque accounting numbers, insiders buy and sell regularly with clear knowledge of their firm's potential.

175

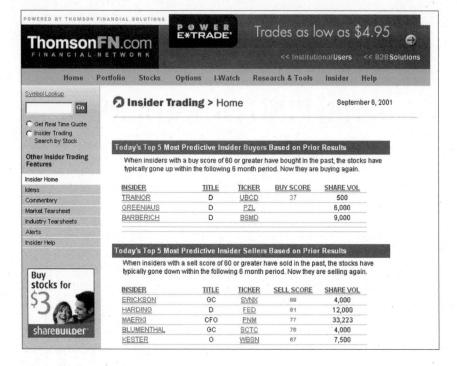

Figure 13.1   www.ThomsonFN.com
Source: ThomsonFN.

And until now, their transactions have largely been ignored or misinterpreted by the investing public.

Because stock sales by management have become widely accepted as a supplement to total compensation, it is imprudent to consider every insider sell a sign of impending disaster. Insider buying is equally mired in formalities and confusion. Yes, executives have the inside scoop on where their company is headed, but the SEC has put in place hoards of rules and regulations that monitor their transactions. By law, every insider buy and sell must be publicly reported in detail. Turning insider transaction data into valuable investment information for you and me, however, is not a simple task.

Cofounded by Craig Columbus, insiderSCORES.com, since gobbled up by Thomson Financial Network and renamed ThomsonFN Insider Trading (see Figure 13.1), has come up with a way to help the average investor make money within the insider trading ring—an arena previously reserved for the top execs who do the transacting. According to

Columbus, there is widespread misuse and misinterpretation of insider trading. We care more about how much cash Bill Gates is generating every time he sells stock than how those transactions affect our own Microsoft holdings. "People get caught up in the wealth being generated for executives; that's a whole separate social and corporate policy issue. I don't speak to that," explains Columbus. "But because they tend to focus on that, sometimes they forget the investment value of the information." There is no question that insider transactions are at least worth a look. In February 2000, the month before every major U.S. market index began its slide into bear territory, insiders seemed particularly clairvoyant. Insider selling in February reached unprecedented levels— nearly $11 billion of stock sold at the height of the market. To put that in perspective, the average dollar value of insider sells between 1997 and 2000 was $3.5 billion per month. March was another particularly heavy month for insider sellers, and then the walls came tumbling down.

After years at law school and business school, Columbus got his Wall Street start at Kidder Peabody, the financial services arm of General Electric. Like many other investors profiled in this book, he quickly became aware of the sordid underbelly of Wall Street. In 1994 bond trader Joseph Jett was accused of recording phony profits at Kidder Peabody. "It was the big scandal of early 1990s Wall Street finance. And to show you the fickle nature of Wall Street, General Electric felt like they had had enough of the investment banking business and decided they were going to divest Kidder Peabody. I had taken a job; I was just finishing the training class; I was going to get assigned back to the office here in Phoenix; and they sold the company to PaineWebber." Enough of that. Columbus left Wall Street altogether and launched insider-SCORES.com with Arizona State University professor Carr Bettis.

ThomsonFN Insider Trading is the fruit of years of research into insider trading. The site's chief focus is finding a way to make insider data useful on company- and stock-specific levels by ranking and rating each of over 30,000 active corporate insiders. The theory: Although the majority of insiders either don't try or are no good at timing their buys and sells, a very powerful few can be relied upon to signal the public about when their stock is over- or undervalued.

After reading our interview with Columbus, head over to insider.ThomsonFN.com and explore the site. Type a ticker symbol in the lookup box to see who is buying or selling at companies in which you own stock, or just browse the unusual and interesting insider trading happenings and anomalies listed directly on the site's home page— maybe you'll pick up an investment idea or two. At the very least, the next time you see Bill Gates selling Microsoft stock, you'll know if your

GATES WILLIAM H III					MICROSOFT CORP (MSFT)
	ISC SCORE	AVG RETURN 3 MO. 6 MO.		# OF DECISIONS 3 MO. 6 MO.	
BUY	---	--- ---		0 0	The stock was higher after 6 months for 0 out of the 0 buys.
SELL	21	9.41% 22.55%		52 48	The stock was lower after 6 months for 8 out of the 48 sells.

Figure 13.2   ThomsonFN Insider Trading report on Bill Gates

Note: Note the Microsoft founder's low ISC score: 21 out of 100. Gates is not particularly good at timing the market!

Source: ThomsonFN (www.ThomsonFN.com).

portfolio stands to take a hit (see Figure 13.2). (Note: It probably won't! On average, six months after each of Gates's 50 stock sales over the past 14 years, Microsoft stock was actually up 22 percent.)

Insider trading is typically associated with illegal activity—Ivan Boeski, Michael Milken, and the scams of the 1980s. How does your definition of insider trading differ from how the general public typically interprets the term?

A lot of insider trading, at least in terms of the case law that went on in the 1980s, was mostly related to tipping, like the Boeski cases in the 1980s, where somebody gave somebody else material nonpublic information. That's what most people think of when they think of insider trading. There are a number of firms that specialize in class-action lawsuits, and they typically allege the same fact pattern: some material misstatements in a public document as related to disclosure of earnings or an accounting issue. They say that the practices of the management were somehow disadvantaging shareholders. There have been some SEC enforcement actions against insiders for trading their own stock when they are in possession of material inside information. In most of those cases, the SEC requires them to disgorge profits and pay very stiff fines and penalties.

But our site doesn't even try to draw conclusions about intent; I think that's a losing proposition. I have never, in all the time we have been doing this, been willing to draw a conclusion about the motivations of individuals, about why someone was selling. That's why we try to take emotion entirely out of this process. We are simply saying that on average, here is what the odds say when this trading event has happened in the past. It's just like saying what happens to the Dow five days after the Fed cuts the discount rate and the Fed funds rate by 50 basis points. Even though I realize that people will try to make insider trading into somewhat of a sexy subject, I think there is no utility in doing that.

Before services like ThomsonFN Insider Trading, where could an individual investor discover data about insider trading?

The Internet was a huge breakthrough in that regard. Before the Internet, there were newsletters, weekly fax and mail publications, and the coverage that it would receive in the *Wall Street Journal.* But the Internet allowed you to do database or ticker searches on key individuals, which you never were able to do before. I think that's very valuable. The problem or limitation with that is that it's one thing to see that insiders are selling at a given company, but it's another thing to get a sense about what that's meant historically. For example, technical analysis: Anybody can get 10-year price charts and by very brief visual inspection get a sense for stock performance or key trends. But looking at a piece of insider trading data—rows of insider transactions—has limited investment efficacy in my mind. This is particularly true on the sell side because it's such a routine event. It may make for good anecdotal conversation, but as an investment tool, it's really not something you could use.

Clearly, however, seeing that a top executive is selling his stock can't be a good sign. It seems that, aside from making anecdotal conversation about executives getting rich, investors should probably avoid these stocks.

There are about 30,000 filings per month, and much insider trading is related to portfolio diversification and regular executive program selling. The media love insider trading as a topic because they try to read into it some kind of sinister motive, and there are great intentions of protecting the public from insider manipulation of securities. I am not saying that it doesn't happen. I'm not saying that things like Regulation Fair Disclosure are not useful in evening the playing field between what the public knows and what management and those in its closest circle of influence know. But as a practical matter, the nuts and bolts of most large-cap companies include insider trading as a large portion of executive compensation. Most savvy companies have policies that govern when executives can sell—usually around the 10-day period following earnings announcements. They are called trading windows. There are some companies where insider selling is very rare, but in many companies—particularly in technology companies—the culture actually encourages insider selling as a supplement to base salary compensation. So you have a lot of noise in the data, because it's not as event-driven as are certain other pieces of financial data. That's why a lot of it is not meaningful.

On the buy side, by the same token, almost all companies have rules that govern new insiders; when people come on to a board or join a company, they are almost always required to establish an initial position. So, some buying is related to establishing a stake in a company that reflects stature. Plus, there are some companies where management has realized that buying can be a positive public relations tool and uses it accordingly as a way to send a message to the marketplace. Particularly in bargain-hunting situations, if management feels that the company is undervalued, it can be used as a public relations tool to try to send a positive message to the market.

It sounds as if you're saying that investors can't use insider trading information . . .

I think they have to use it very selectively. There is a lot of noise in the data. When insiders file a document, there is up to a 45-day lag from the time of the original transaction until the information is made public. Any transaction that occurs in the month of January has to be reported to the Securities and Exchange Commission in Washington, D.C., by February 10. If the trade occurred on January 1, it has to be reported on February 10; and if the trade occurred on January 31, it also has to be reported on February 10. Then the SEC requires three to five days to actually process the documents before they are released to the investment public. So, you can have quite a lag. Now why is that relevant? Because a lot of times the price at which the insiders originally transacted has since changed. Information inefficiency has caused you to miss some of the powerful data points embedded in that original transaction.

All of that being said, it just requires a different set of tools to evaluate the data. Reliable data really only exist back to about 1986, but you certainly have enough to draw some conclusions and comparisons— even at the macro level, answering questions like, what is an abnormally low level of insider activity? In January 2001 the total dollar value of insider shares—the total dollar value of stock—purchased by corporate executives in the United States was $150,000,000. In February it was $144,000,000. Those were the two lowest, most bearish, levels of purchasing since September 1995. [From the beginning of January 2001 to the last day in March 2001, the S&P 500 fell over 12 percent.] So, even though there was a huge corrective phase going on in all levels of the market, the level of insider confidence was very low. And when you have 10 to 15 years of data to draw these comparisons, I think it's a meaningful macro indicator.

Beyond giving macro-level indications on the market as a whole, is it possible to use insider trading on a company-specific level? How does ThomsonFN Insider Trading make the data more useful for evaluating individual stocks?

We have built tools that show, when a specific individual insider has transacted in the past, what his or her ability has been to predict future stock performance. You are looking for somebody that is consistently right—when they buy, the stock goes up, and when they sell, the stock goes down. And just like in baseball, you want somebody that's done it a number of times. You want enough plate appearances to know that this is not some fluke event. You roll these three things into a score of 1 to 100, 100 meaning most predictive, 1 meaning least predictive. But for people who don't want to take a black-box score at face value, we show you the returns and directional accuracy: When John Smith bought in the past, the stock is higher eight out of nine times three months later. We tested every interval under the sun—one year from the time of transaction, five years from the time of transaction, but by far we found the most meaning with three and six months. Insiders are reluctant to trade too closely to any kind of material event, so I do think they have some kind of a forward-looking horizon, but with one-year or longer results, you don't get any meaningful results that you can model in a statistical sense.

Don't you think you might be mining the data a little too deep—going all the way down to the individual executive? Isn't it possible that an insider could have a high or low score purely based on dumb luck?

The way it typically works is that you see people who have bought dips effectively in their stock. That's one of the hallmarks of our higher-rated buyers. It's very good to see somebody who's done that across different market conditions and time frames. On the sell side, when you find somebody that is truly selling *all the time*, then it's almost impossible to get a very high score, because the activity will tend, on average, to balance itself out—sometimes market conditions will be in the insider's favor, but sometimes they will not.

Can you give some examples? Tell us about some insiders who are particularly good at buying their company's stock on a dip in price and who are highly rated by your system.

ZixIt Corporation [see Figure 13.3]. It's a small company, but this is a classic example. There is a guy there named Antonio Sanchez Jr.; he is actually an officer and a board member of this company [see Figure 13.4]. He is also the CEO of a company called Sanchez Oil and Gas, but he was one of the original beneficial owners of ZixIt—he owned greater

Figure 13.3   ZixIt (Nasdaq: ZIXI), November 2000–May 2001
Source: Prophet Financial Systems, Inc. (www.ProphetFinance.com).

SANCHEZ ANTONIO R JR					ZIXIT CORP (ZIXI)
	ISC SCORE	AVG RETURN 3 MO. 6 MO.		# OF DECISIONS 3 MO. 6 MO.	
BUY	100	181.73% 125.11%		9 9	The stock was higher after 6 months for 9 out of the 9 buys.
SELL	---	--- ---		0 0	The stock was lower after 6 months for 0 out of the 0 sells.

Figure 13.4   ThomsonFN Insider Trading report on Antonio Sanchez Jr. of ZixIt
Source: ThomsonFN (www.ThomsonFN.com).

than 10 percent of the shares. When this guy has bought stock in the past, it's been a very good indicator. He bought in December 2000 on a dip around $6. It was trading as high as $15 one month later. [Sanchez was rated a perfect 100 on the buy side by ThomsonFN Insider Trading. He had bought stock in ZixIt Corporation nine times between 1996 and 2001. The stock appreciated in price following every single purchase. Three months after, the stock had risen on average 182 percent. Six months after purchase, it had risen 125 percent. Amazingly, over that entire five-year period, the stock has barely doubled in price.]

And you keep scores for buys and sells completely separate?

Yes, totally separate.

How many transactions for an individual are necessary to make the results statistically significant versus simple luck? And over what time period? Any insider who started selling in mid-2000 would obviously have a high rating.

I would say that when you have somebody who has had at least three prior buys and the directional accuracy of those three is correct, it is very good. Also, when you have people that have some sense of tenure—and you still have a lot of people that have 5- or 10-year tenures in companies—that tends to be really good as well.

The actual scores on the site take into account the number of purchases, but not tenure? Is that true?

Correct. One is usually a function of the other; but yes, the site does take into account the number of purchase or sell transactions.

Do you find particular individuals who are accurate when both buying and selling?

Absolutely. Internally, those are what we call All-World Insiders. It's a small subset, but there are some people who are really good on both sides of the trade [see Figure 13.5].

Which insiders tend to be the most accurate with their buys and sells? The CEO, the vice presidents, members of the board . . . ?

As a general rule, the higher you go on the chain toward the chairman and CEO level, the more predictive. The problem is that because scrutiny of those top executives has gotten so much tighter over the last few years, predictive capability may be losing some steam. I still think that, internally, the president, CFO, general counsel, and officer are the four most predictive—more than, say, a vice president. Outside directors can also be good because they tend to have fewer constraints on buying and selling.

How important is the amount of shares that are traded relative to the total stake of the executive who is trading?

Obviously, trades that represent an impact—a material impact—on the underlying total holdings tend to be more significant.

What would be a material impact?

I think a 30 percent to 40 percent impact is material. The thing that makes it hard to completely understand, though, is that you may have

Insider	Role	Co. Name	Ticker	Market Cap. ('000)	Buy Score	Sell Score	Av. 6-mo Ret. Buys	Av. 6-mo Ret. Sells	# Buys	# Sells
TAGUE, JOHN P	CB	AMTRAN INC	AMTR	116,350	98	95	54.98%	-16.34%	13	6
WORMS, VINCENT	CB	SANGSTAT MEDICAL CORP	SANG	188,591	98	95	30.10%	-23.91%	10	7
SANDERSON, BILL M	D	WESTERN GAS RESOURCES INC	WGR	1,163,952	98	100	41.81%	-18.66%	13	12
GONGAWARE, DONALD F	O, D	CONSECO INC	CNC	5,813,214	98	98	33.88%	-27.55%	12	6
KESSINGER, RON D	OS	TRIAD GUARANTY INC	TGIC	402,111	94	97	22.07%	-35.87%	6	4
SCARIZ, DON T	CFO	EMS TECHNOLOGIES INC	ELMG	132,835	92	100	92.73%	-21.44%	4	10
GOLDMAN, ALFRED E	O	A G EDWARDS INC	AGE	3,186,255	91	89	24.77%	-10.32%	5	10
SIMPSON, JACK W	O	SCIENTIFIC ATLANTA INC	SFA	10,177,531	89	81	28.36%	-13.81%	4	4
COLVILLE, GLENN CHRISTOPHER	O	CONSOLIDATED GRAPHICS INC TX	CGX	163,473	88	84	76.37%	-12.95%	8	5
COOK, ELIZABETH C	O, D	WILD OATS MARKETS INC	OATS	189,805	88	85	60.91%	-23.13%	4	5
DAVIS, ARTHUR D	D	STANDARD MOTOR PRODUCTS INC	SMP	124,823	82	100	21.29%	-15.95%	4	15
TABAS, LEE EVAN	D	ROYAL BANCSHARES OF PENNSYLVANIA INC	RBPAA	148,133	82	99	21.34%	-10.32%	4	9
CALL, HARRY M	P	GOODY S FAMILY CLOTHING INC	GDYS	130,112	80	97	24.92%	-36.09%	5	6

Figure 13.5 All-World Insiders

Note: The buy scores and sell scores provided are based on ThomsonFN's proprietary ranking system (from 1 to 100). A negative number for average six-month sell returns indicates that the company's stock declined six months after the insider sold stock. The "role" column indicates the insider's position within the company. CB indicates Chairman of the Board; D: Director; O: Officer; OS: Officer of a Subsidiary Company; CFO: Chief Financial Officer; P: President. "# Buys" and "# Sells" indicate the total number of each type of transaction made by the insider throughout his or her tenure at the company.

Source: ThomsonFN Insider Trading research department.

insiders, using Bill Gates as a good example, who hold very few actual shares. Most of them are in options on shares, in trusts, or in all kinds of different vehicles. So the fact that an insider has reduced holdings by 30 percent to 40 percent may be meaningless because he or she is sitting on series after series of stock options. On the buy side, however, when you see somebody make a purchase that significantly increases their holdings, it is worth noting. Decreases in holdings are not a reliable indicator for just the reason I explained.

Do insiders predict movement particularly well in small-cap or large-cap companies? In certain sectors?

Absolutely. In small-cap companies, insider trading tends to be most powerful. The biggest reason is simply institutional neglect. It is far easier for insiders to signal events that have gone undetected by the professional analyst community. In other words, the goodwill that their buys reflect is not reflected in the stock price. The spotlight hasn't shone brightly enough on these companies for enough people on the Street to develop an interest.

On an industry basis: oil and gas. Insiders have always had a pretty good record of buying and selling some of the more commodity-based securities. Even in technology, the most cyclical areas of technology were traditionally things like semiconductor and semiconductor equipment, and insider trading was better in those areas as a predictor than, say, in networking or software. So I think the cyclical component is very interesting—where you can use insider trading as an early barometer of bigger cycle changes.

You mentioned that selling stock is generally accepted within technology companies. Top executives such as Bill Gates of Microsoft sell stock on a fairly regular basis and never buy. Is there a way to use insider trading to help you understand what Microsoft and big-cap companies like it are going to do in the future?

It has become more difficult with tech stocks, particularly when they were going through a hypergrowth phase and there was no shareholder backlash against insider selling. There has always been selling in technology stocks. It has been a hallmark of their operating procedures, and a big part of their compensation. But there is no doubt that the pace of the selling was incredibly brisk in February 2000 and throughout the rest of the year. One thing we have been looking at very closely is that there has to be a price at which insiders are unwilling to part with shares, and we are seeing that in technology now in mid-2001. Even in some of the larger-cap companies, the level of selling is off considerably.

Buying is not the only bullish indicator. A stock that is trending higher and nobody is parting with shares—that's a very good sign. In other words, lack of selling is a proxy for buying.

How do generic corporate share repurchases fit into this picture?

Some good studies say that when there is a share repurchase program— and you are able to prove that it's not just the announcement of the program, but that they are actually following through and executing the program—and insiders are buying the stock in tandem, it's a powerful indicator.

Do you think that an individual buying on the inside is more meaningful than corporate repurchases are?

Generally, yes.

Is it ever the case that insider buying or selling itself moves the stock, instead of the insider's knowing something about the company's future?

It's probably not enough of a liquidity event to move the stock.

From an information or signaling perspective as well, however, do stocks move simply because of this perceived signal given by management, whether or not management had intentions of timing the transaction? Has the public turned the insiders' ability to predict their stock's movement into a self-fulfilling prophecy?

Yes. I do think that's true, mostly in the smaller companies. I do think that insider buying provides a justification or a catalyst for some institutional and some individual buying.

Talk more about the laws that govern insider trading. Your site mentions something called the short-term profit rule. What is that?

The short-term profit rule was designed to prevent insiders from flipping their own securities: Once you purchase a stock, you can't sell it at a profit until six months later. But it also works in reverse. When you sell shares, you can't buy them back at lower prices until six months later. So in the current market conditions, where everything is beaten down, it has been somewhat of a limiting factor on insider buying because a lot of executives sold toward the end of last year. This sell-off has really accelerated since the start of the new year, and they are prohibited from buying their shares back at obviously much discounted prices. Executives can't act on purely market-driven reactions because of certain legal prohibitions that come into play.

Are there other rules that insiders must follow—certain times when they are restricted from buying or selling? What other asymmetries and anomalies exist in the world of insider transactions?

When there are merger discussions going on, executives are supposed to refrain from trading. Top executives involved in merger discussions should refrain from trading entirely. One of the things that has been really interesting is that you can actually use the absence of insider trading as a technique to confirm the possibility of merger or takeover discussions. [The following is an example of when a lack of insider trading activity served as an indicator that a merger was in the works. Straight from the firm's director of research Lon Gerber: "In May 2000 we explored the possibility of M&A activity at J. P. Morgan. Merger activity was prevalent following the 1999 reform of the Glass-Steagall Act. At the time, J. P. Morgan executives completely refrained from trading during the prior four months. This lack of activity supported the hypothesis that the company may indeed be in acquisition talks. The lack of trading was also significant in another regard: It marked a deviation from historical trading patterns. Historically, J. P. Morgan insiders have traded noteworthy amounts during the months of January and February, and this deviation from historical patterns lent further evidence that trading restrictions were in place due to M&A discussions. This proved to be true, as J. P. Morgan and Chase Manhattan Bank subsequently merged later in the year."]

Also, many companies—private banks in particular—are promoting kinds of hedging and derivative instruments where executives can, without actually selling shares, essentially diversify some of their risk. They are very complex instruments—things like zero-cost collars. Where insiders are using derivative-based hedges to protect downside risk in their holdings, it's been a decent indicator of short-term weakness in the underlying securities.

How can the public assess those transactions? Are they reported?

They are reported on the filings if you know what you're looking for. There are two sides to an insider trading filing. The first side contains the basic information—whether it was a purchase or a sale. The back of the document contains anything related to either options or derivative instruments. Both sides of the form are important. Typically those kinds of hedging and derivative instruments are supposed to be explained by a footnote, and depending on the diligence of the person preparing the filing, sometimes you get extensive footnotes, and sometimes you get very little.

How do stock options factor into the analysis on ThomsonFN Insider Trading?

We display them. We show when somebody was selling stock related to the exercise of options. We did a lot of research asking if sales related to stock options are more or less meaningful than sales of shares. The answer is no. There is no difference in predictive value between sales related to stock options and sales that are from common holdings.

Can insiders make transactions without letting the public know?

The short answer is no, but some of those collars and hedging instruments can make it difficult to understand the nature of the underlying transaction because some of them are so complex.

So how does all this come together into an investing strategy? What's the best way for the individual investor to use ThomsonFN Insider Trading? You say on the site that people should not use the service on its own as a trading tool . . .

I wouldn't; I don't think that's a sound strategy. I think that insider trading can be used with certain other technical factors like relative strength and momentum. If you have a discipline, fundamental or technical, insider trading is something that is always good to check as another variable. I would never say it's an exclusive trading tool, but I think it's a very good thing to at least check before making any kind of an investment decision.

Is that how you use the site for your own portfolio?

For anyone's portfolio I think it's very good as a check, a verification, a backstop. But the funny thing is, I think you can actually do it in reverse too. I think analyzing insider trades is a very good way to generate ideas that you can then confirm with fundamental or technical research. In that regard, you've got these event-driven flags that say, "Wait a minute; somebody that has had a historical track record of picking a stock successfully is buying." It causes you to go out and do some research, and you observe the catalysts—catalysts that may move a stock forward, such as a new management team, improved industry conditions, or an acquisition. It is also helpful with industry confirmation if you are looking to make a sector fund investment. Whenever you have industry confirmation, particularly as I said in cyclical stocks, it can be a very powerful forward indicator.

What other specific trading tips would you recommend? Personally or as a firm, do you favor any other key indicators?

Whenever there is buying and the relative strength of the company is positive, say 80 or higher, it's phenomenally good. Insiders buying even though the stock is still going up is very promising. It doesn't happen a lot, but at the company level when it does, it's a really good sign.

One reason that insider trading tends to be very helpful is that it's highly uncorrelated with other fundamental and technical variables. If you try to introduce an earnings variable into a multifactor model, it's typically highly correlated with other factors you are already examining.

Do these strategies of combining high relative strength with strong insider buying work a high percentage of the time? When might that formula backfire?

Frequently. It could just be an initial purchase, right? You could see a 2,000-share purchase at General Electric, but then you actually go do some research, and you see that this is an initial statement of ownership. Here you have somebody retiring from the board, somebody joining the board, and you see a purchase. It can be misleading.

Do you make any type of predictions about future performance, either for specific stocks or for the market as a whole, on ThomsonFN Insider Trading?

On the site, we say what All-Star Insider sentiment is. This is trying to track in real time what the best of the best are trading and what that can tell me about the state of the market. That's been a very good macro indicator, as you can see right now. It's been very bearish for this quarter, and it was very bearish for most of 2000, too.

At this point in most of our interviews, the question ringing in our heads is always, why start insiderSCORES in the first place? Why couldn't you have used this information for yourselves as opposed to giving it away to the world?

That's a great question. Actually Carr Bettis [the brain and chief statistician behind insiderSCORES] has started a hedge fund that uses some of these techniques. It went live in 2000.

Switching gears a bit: You guys also operate a web site called asiaSCORES.com . . .

There is a whole set of regulatory rules for Asia, which are actually very favorable for outside shareholders. For instance, the filing requirements are much stricter. You don't have that lag, so you as a shareholder can act when the price is relatively close to where the executives themselves are trading. You've got a much smaller subset of insiders in Asia—very few. It's not like America, where you have all sorts of corporate executives. You have fewer people, but the people that are predictive are incredibly predictive. So, we were tracking Hong Kong, and we had intended to add Singapore.

Is that something you are still working on?

No, it's not something Thomson is exploring.

But you believe that the data from asiaSCORES.com are actually more useful than those from your U.S. offering?

In some settings, yes.

Is there a way for individual investors to get Asian insider trading information on their own?

Some of the Hong Kong newspapers have web sites. The *South China Morning Post* is the big one, and they report the trades. But it's like back in the old days, right?

Do you expect that the rules in the United States will change to make insider data more useful—specifically in terms of the timing lag associated with reporting transactions?

There has always been a very vibrant debate as to why in the era of electronic filing we couldn't have a more real-time process. Most of these filings are still done in paper form, which is unheard of. If you required electronic filing in this new era of database technology, you really could have much more rapid dissemination of the information.

What is the argument against that?

Personal privacy, as a general matter. Theoretically, anybody should be able to fill these out on their kitchen table, through their accountant or lawyer. If you required everything to be done electronically, you would have to do them through a corporate secretary.

What does the future hold for ThomsonFN Insider Trading? You've mentioned in the past that you may actually begin to follow and rate Wall Street analysts.

I think it's the brightest part of the business because with Regulation Fair Disclosure, there is very little that can be given by management to security analysts. So you see the dispersion of estimates being much tighter. The number of preannouncements is going way up, so it becomes even more important for analysts to talk to suppliers, customers, and lower-level employees. Management is no longer spoon-feeding the analysts. The situation is rewarding the best and making it even more important to separate the good analysts from the bad.

A number of the investors we've spoken to have trashed and bashed Wall Street analysts in general. Do you feel that analyst forecasts are still a useful tool, at least for some of the population?

We've got some good research on this, and if you saw the results, you would be amazed at how little forecasting visibility analysts actually have. One month from the report date, on average, analyst forecasts are off by about 40 percent. I can show you the results down to one week, one month, three months, six months, or one year into the future on the top 3,000 companies. But all that being said, I think the pendulum has actually swung maybe too far in terms of criticism of analysts. It's in the best interests of analysts to try to make as accurate a forecast as possible because a large portion of their compensation is tied to their estimate accuracy. I think the lack of estimate accuracy has more to do with the difficulty in forecasting business cycles than it does the lack of independence of analysts from their investment banking arms.

It's a fascinating topic. Regulation Fair Disclosure is having such a sweeping effect on the way people are doing business; the general public doesn't realize the implications yet. Among professional investors, however, it's a very profound change.

What are those changes? Why is it so profound?

Having everybody acting off of the same pool of information certainly leads to a tighter consensus, a more watered-down set of opinions. Right now a lot of companies are trying to test the boundaries of Reg FD. What can and can't they say? Even during road shows or investment presentations, they are having to be a lot more careful about what they say. That's making it tough for people on Wall Street who are trying to make a forward-looking forecast.

Overall, is Regulation Fair Disclosure a positive or a negative for Wall Street?

The jury is still out at this point.

Is it a definite positive for the individual investor?

That's the ultimate irony—the jury is still out.

Chapter 14

THE INTELLIGENT SPECULATOR
Teresa Lo

Internet Alias		Investment Style	
SheSaid		Day trader	
Year of Birth		**Location**	
1964		Vancouver, British Columbia	
Education			
BA, economics and psychology, University of British Columbia			
Web Site (Free/Pay)			
trendVUE: www.trendvue.com			

Teresa Lo isn't terribly thrilled with humanity. She spent the first dozen years of her life in the Canadian brokerage business, seeing more than her fair share of scams, scandals, and greed. "There was a certain glint, a certain bewildered look in people's eyes when they talked about the mania of the day," laments Lo about the speculative bubbles that she witnessed in the gold, sugar, and real estate markets. "In retrospect," she says, "it was the look of pure greed." Lo was able to avoid the tempting call of avarice by being an outsider. She was a Chinese girl trying to make it in Canada. She was a female studying science in college, another oddity of the time. She was a woman in the brokerage business, a man's business. Eventually, Lo ended up working as a trader because "it didn't matter whether you were green or blue or brown or a girl or a guy." All that mattered was making money, and as it turned out, Lo was very good at making money.

Of course, it took several years and many costly mistakes before Lo stumbled upon a profitable methodology. Her most profound discovery over the years: "No stocks ever again." Lo despises stocks. They're too

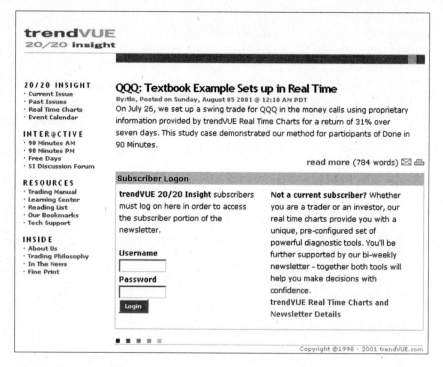

Figure 14.1   www.trendVUE.com
Source: trendVUE.

volatile. They're irrational. They're impossible to predict. She tossed conventional wisdom to the wind (along with the high-flying and glitzy stock-trader lifestyle) and launched a mission to find the perfect trading security. She eventually settled on the S&P and Nasdaq index futures. Today, all Lo does is trade those two securities. Daily, she studies their trends and hones her ability to time their movements. "Trading is boring," admits Lo. "But if you are trading for thrills, the odds of becoming successful are low. Instead of spending hours doing research and picking stocks, I spend my time perfecting trading skills and techniques. In the end, you still have to trade the stock you pick, right? And is making consistent profit boring?"

Lo boasts a fervent trading discipline that is difficult to teach, but she tries nonetheless. She launched IntelligentSpeculator.com in 1998 and replaced it with trendVUE.com (see Figure 14.1) in 2001 in an attempt to help traders avoid the mistakes she made early in her career. Unfortunately, Lo is convinced that the only way to learn is the hard way. "You have to be spanked a few times," says Lo. "You develop a new appreciation for the market after you get wiped out." Even so, it can't hurt to track Lo's analysis and advice. She contributes regularly to a forum on the Silicon Investor message board, which you can access from her web site. At Silicon Investor and other sites that she frequents, you can interact directly with Lo and pick her brain on a wide range of topics. She also writes regular market commentary that is available for daily delivery via e-mail. Occasionally, Lo even leads trendVUE Live, a for-fee multiple-day training session in which she lays out the bulk of her strategy and applies it to the markets in real time.

The core of Lo's approach is deceptively simple. This clip from her web site sums up her trading thesis:

> The most important concept in trading is that the trend is your friend—until the end, when it bends. It is very important to understand this concept. . . . In an uptrend, buy every retracement (dip). In a downtrend, sell every retracement (rally). When the trend ends, the trader will be wrong once at the turn. Proceed to use test of top or test of bottom techniques to capitalize on a trend change area. Since every retracement is potentially the last one before a test, the trader must first mark out these areas of support and resistance and then watch price action closely.

These are the tenets that Lo follows each trading day. They have nothing to do with finding the right stock or the hot play. They are strictly trading rules, so she requires only one or perhaps two securities to trade. In addition, she trades for only 90 minutes each day. She doesn't want to fight the tape. When the volume is substantial—the first 90 minutes of the trading day—she plays the game. After that, Lo takes care of her kids, fixes up her web site, and enjoys her life. She claims to make consistently 10 percent per month on a fixed $100,000 trading account. She doesn't compound her returns, and she admits flat out that she could not duplicate her performance with a larger sum of money. Instead, she takes her winnings and puts them in a safe investment vehicle. It's not hard to see why Lo considers herself the Intelligent Speculator.

You tried banking for a while after college but decided it wasn't for you. Where did you head next?

I went to work for the executive vice president of a brokerage firm called Yorktown Securities. This was in 1986 or 1987; the deals then were going from 20 cents to eight bucks in two weeks—all these tulips popping all over the place. I saw some of the things that the clients were doing, the brokers telling lies, and the promoters telling bigger lies, and I thought, "This is a horrible business." Then, one day my boss said to me, "We need you to go dig up a bunch of stuff from deep storage. You just talk to this RCMP officer, and we'll take it from there." [The RCMP is the Royal Canadian Mounted Police, the national Canadian police force.] It turns out that I was supposed to help the RCMP dig up records from the firm in an investigation into the collapse of a deal called International Telex. I spent the next weeks digging through storage for every check, trading slip—every this and that—to help the RCMP put back together the whole scam that had gone down. Basically, I learned about what happened in a real scam, and I thought, "This is really terrible. These brokers sucked all these people in." Then I thought, "How can they be sucked in?" The things that the brokers were saying were obviously fraudulent.

It wasn't until I toiled in a couple of other places and I got to meet clients and brokers that I realized that the guy on the other side of the phone had a weakness. The client wants to make some easy money fast. He wants to turn a few thousand into a large sum, which we all know is too good to be true. But he wants to believe, and, of course, he'll find a broker who will tell him what he wants to hear. So, I finally figured out the other side of the equation, and then I wound up working for 12 years at Canada's largest independent brokerage firm, whose job, really, was to crank out penny deals and over-the-counter bulletin board deals, and I learned a lot about corporate finance and how to make stocks go. But I was a girl, and I wasn't really accepted. So I went to trade, because it didn't matter whether you were green or blue or brown or a girl or a guy. If you could make money, well, that's great. Along the way, I was a broker for about six months, and that was nasty. That's when I really learned the kind of greed that the clients have in them and how they think. I got a lot of insight into the way both sides think and the psychology behind this greed and fear and supply and demand.

Tell us more about the International Telex scam you helped piece together.

It was the usual thing. You take a stock that has very few publicly traded shares, and then you create demand. The insiders can sell their stock that's supposedly locked up seven ways to Sunday. It's no different for Amazon.com or any of those IPOs, except that some of them might not include illegal activity, but the mechanics are the same. You need to have a small float at the beginning, and you have to create demand. In the states, where you have CNBC blasting all this stuff over the TV, it's pretty easy to see how a lot of these Internet deals got so inflated. It wasn't because of a new era; it was because the stock's capital structure was simply so tight.

So, who's the bad guy?

Everybody is feeding off of each other. The public wants to believe that they can have a huge return for almost nothing, and, of course, when you have people willing to believe this, you're going to find people who will tell them what they want to hear. So, they're all bad.

You fell into technical analysis after hanging around some practitioners for several years, and you eventually began to trade your own account full-time. Let's explore the basics of your trading strategy. You don't trade stocks . . .

Not anymore. I used to.

You believe that stocks are too volatile for profitable trading. Isn't volatility the trader's friend?

If you were long something, and you woke up the next day and it was half-price, wouldn't that be a pretty bad way to start the day?

True, but what about day trading? If you're not going to hold overnight, can't you use the volatility to your advantage?

I think that for day trading there is too much noise in stock charts. Look at a chart of a stock—say Juniper or whatever, because that's the latest, greatest craze that everybody's been trading for the past couple weeks. If you look at a five-minute chart, in the morning it goes wham, wham, wham, up, down, up, down; there's no sense or rhyme or reason. Everybody's got their tickets in, and somehow the market makers fill them all badly. Then it pauses for a while, and it's in this triangular shape where everyone's stuck. Then it makes a fake out to the upside or the downside, and then it drifts around, and then it finally goes. But most of the direction happens before the open—it either opened way up or way down, and the range for the rest of the day is a lot smaller than the overnight gap.

You prefer to focus on futures. How does trading futures differ from trading stocks?

They seem to be much smoother because the floor traders trade with their own capital. They don't trade with your orders, and there are so many of them fighting it out in the pit against each other—I think it's a much fairer scheme. And, of course, you don't need an uptick to short.

Two characteristics of your trading seem unusual. First, you trade only the S&P and Nasdaq futures. Second, you trade only for 90 minutes a day. It sounds like an ideal life. Why only 90 minutes?

If you pull up a chart when the market opens—say a five-minute chart—and you take a look at the volume, it mostly dies off after the first hour. Usually, when there is no volume, the spreads are larger, and the market is prone to false moves. I want to be in the market when it's moving with speed. When it's forceful, the market is very liquid. I can get in, I can get out. I don't have to worry about being stuck.

Do you think that you could make money during the rest of the day, and you just quit because you want to have the free time? Or do you have to quit in order to preserve capital?

A lot of times the market will make a move at lunchtime. I have a rule: If it's trading below yesterday's low and the low of the first hour, there is a good probability that today is going to be a big down day, so I will stay with it to see if something happens at lunch. Or if today is trading higher than yesterday's high and the high of the first hour, there's a good probability that today is going to be a gangbuster day to the upside. Then I trade with it, too. But otherwise, I do my 90 minutes in Vancouver. I've been getting up at ungodly hours for half of my life. Now, I've got two kids and I've got to get one to school. The other one is a couple of months old. So why bother? If there's no easy money to be made, I'm not interested. I've been trading too long to try to make the hard money. That's why I trade for only 90 minutes.

On your web site you use the term *net donators*. Who are the net donators in the market?

I think there are a lot of people who just trade and then go off to work. They trade for the first hour, and then they go off to work. They have real jobs. They trade for years and never make any money. Those guys are forever donating to people like me.

In the sense that this is a zero-sum game, those are the people you are taking advantage of?

Someone has to lose if I'm winning.

Tell us how you win. What's the thesis behind your trading strategy?

I have a model of market mechanics. When a security goes up, along the way it has little pauses. At the high end, it starts to churn a bit, and then after that, it either continues going up or starts to go down. On the way down, it has little pauses. And it keeps going down, and then when it can't go down anymore, it will churn and churn. After that, it either goes down more or starts going up again. That's the basic principle of market mechanics. Basically, if it's in an uptrend, every time it pauses and pulls back, I buy. If it's in a downtrend, every time it pauses and bounces, I sell. If it's churning in a trading range, I just stay out. And that's all there ever was.

How do you decide when to get in?

We want to know that the car is going at 100 miles per hour. We're not trying to anticipate something new. If you're riding in a car and the car is going 100 miles per hour in one direction, you can be reasonably sure that five or ten seconds from now, it's not going to be moving in reverse. What I'm looking for is a move in the market that's strongly directional—going fast—and on any pause, I get on. Then I'll take it as far as it can go.

[For an example of Lo's trading strategies at work, see Figure 14.2 and the following text, which were plucked from one of her four-day grueling online training sessions: "On this one-minute NQ chart, we know that it is moving at high speed without the use of any indicators because there are a ton of down bars in a row, and only a few up bars in between. When you see this, you basically set sell stops one or two ticks under each bar that is contratrend. In this example, this is a high-speed downtrend, so we set sell stops just underneath the lows of each up bar, so long as the bounce does not last for more than four to six bars."]

Why is the market analogous to a speeding car? Why can't stocks change direction in an instant?

Well, they can. But they never do turn around in one instant. That's what they call momentum.

Why do you think momentum exists in the market?

Momentum exists because people are like the herd. If it starts to go up, they get greedy, and they all want to pile in. And when the last guy who wants to buy has bought, then that's the top. Then when it's falling, everybody wants to sell and get out and save themselves. And when the last guy has sold, there's no more pressure to sell. And so it can start going up again. Does that sound too easy?

It sounds very easy.

The difference between the average retail trader and me is that the retail traders arrive on the scene of 20 different stocks every day that they've never seen before. They don't know the lay of the land. They don't know the corporate fundamentals. They've never seen the thing trade. They don't know the rhythms of the traders of these stocks. They arrive stone

Figure 14.2   One-minute chart of Nasdaq futures created in TradeStation.

Source: Intelligent Speculator (www.intelligentspeculator.com). Copyright © 1991–2001 TradeStation Technologies, Inc. Tradestation® is a registered trademark of TradeStation Technologies, Inc. TradeStation does not endorse or recommend the use of any particular trading strategy.

cold. Whereas I trade the same thing every day. I watch the same thing wiggle every single day of my life, so I get used to its rhythms. That's why I am able to do it. You need a good fundamental framework from which to work, and you also need to have some experience watching the market. Many people are into real-time scanning of stocks, and I think, "What are you going to do? Find something that's got four letters in the symbol and trade it without knowing what it is?" Come on. That's crazy. But that's what they're into. They're putting all their hopes into scanning for the next winner rather than making themselves a winner by being a good trader.

Any other reasons why so many day traders fail?

It's like going to the casino and playing poker. The hand that you get you can't really control, but you can control how you play it to some degree. Certainly, how much you bet is completely within your control. If you have a crappy hand, you fold quickly. Eventually, luck will bring you some good hands. That's just the probability. As long as you don't blow your reins out and bet too much on a bad hand, the odds are that you will be there when the good hands show up. When they do show up, you can bet aggressively, and you'll win. People don't understand this concept, and they try to see too much into these things. Or they are impatient— they think the market should be going ka-ching ka-ching.

There are people who refuse to put in stops. It leads them to have catastrophic losses that they cannot rebound from, and there are people who simply don't understand the game. It's a game about probability. It's a game where if you have a weak hand, you fold. If you have a bad trade, admit defeat, and admit it immediately. You can always get back in if you have money. If you don't, you're done. You won't be there when your supposed luck comes.

Have there ever been months when you lost money consistently?

No. I don't have losing streaks, and I don't have winning streaks, either. You win, you win, you lose, you lose, you win. . . . It just grinds out.

Are there ever days when everything you think is wrong?

No. Never happens. We've been on the air live for three years, and I don't think I've ever made one major bad call. You know why? I just do what the chart tells me. If it's going down, we follow it. If it's going up, we follow it.

Where does traditional technical analysis fit into all of this?

In trading, you have to get it out of your mind that any technique has to do with prediction. First of all, you can't predict anything, and, of course, the past doesn't mean a thing. But if you know where you are right now, right here, that's all you need to know. If you know the market is going forward at 100 miles per hour, you know that 10 minutes from now, it will not be going in reverse. It may decelerate, it may accelerate, but the odds are very low that it's going to turn on the head of a pin. You find ways, somehow, to get on board that speeding train—that's all you need to do. The key is to wait until the conditions happen.

What is the worst trade you have ever made?

I used to trade gold, and there is a mob psychology in gold all the time.

On two separate occasions over two years, there were these great market rallies in gold. I got on this fantastic run, but I had never tried pyramiding, which you read about in all these books. I bought a decent position, and then I bought some more, and I bought some more. When you pyramid and add on to the next position, you should only add on half as much, and then the next time you should only add a quarter as much. I kept on adding the same amount each time, and before I knew it, my average cost was very close to the market. I remember that we were going into a holiday on Monday, and on Friday I was watching CNBC, and they bring on John Murphy, who predicts where it's going to go next. And I said to myself, "Oh, it's the top!" It happens every time—it's a Friday afternoon, and they talk about whichever thing has gone up the most, and they bring out the technical analyst to say how much higher it can go. That's usually the top. But the worst part was that Monday was a holiday, but gold still traded in London, and it had a huge reversal. Of course, I could not get out of my position on that Monday because the market was closed. So, on Tuesday, I got out. But because my trailing cost was so close to the market, and I was margined to the eyeballs, I was wiped out. It was terrible.

How much did you lose?

I lost my whole account—and I was maybe 24 years old. I probably lost $100,000, and that was all the money I had to my name at the time. There was smoke coming out of my ears, and I was doing the calculation, and I was on my knees praying that I wouldn't owe the firm any money after everything had cleared. When it was done, the amount of money in my account was zero. I didn't care that I had lost all of my money; I was just happy that I didn't owe. For the next six months—because I had been a banker before—I got a job with this big mortgage company to underwrite residential mortgages. Then I had to get a second job. I would work from 6:00 A.M. until 1:00 P.M., and then I'd be doing all my paperwork for the mortgage brokering. Then, at 6:00 P.M. I had my third job, which was working at Tony Romas—the rib joint—packing takeout until midnight. I did that for six months until I got 50 grand back, and I went back and I started trading again. That's how I learned about leverage the hard way; you could be totally right, and on the smallest setback in the stock, you're wiped out.

We've heard that from a lot of traders who lost money when they started out. Is that an important part of the learning process?

Probably, because then you're under no illusion whatsoever that you're God.

Figure 14.3 Intel (Nasdaq: INTC), May 2000–May 2001
Source: Prophet Financial Systems, Inc. (www.ProphetFinance.com).

Is there any way to avoid that?

I don't think so. You have to be spanked a few times. You develop a new appreciation for the market after you get wiped out.

What can a long-term investor learn from what you do?

They can use the charts the same way. There's no difference. A test is a test. A retracement is a retracement. The only difference is the time frame. I do my analysis exactly the same on a one-minute chart as I do on a monthly chart. Back in the summer when Intel failed on a test at $80, I said, "If it fails here, the moving average is 45 bucks below. That's a long way to the first measured target." People responded, "No, that could never happen." And I said, "Never say never. If it passes, then it will hit this first target." And my gosh, it sure did—in one month. It was awful [see Figure 14.3].

How much of your capital do you put at risk on a single trade?

My trading account is around $100,000. I will use all of it if I want to; it doesn't matter because the rest of my money is elsewhere. I've determined that $100,000 is the amount that I can risk on a single trade. I only ever have one position on in one market. I will go in all at once; I leave all at once; and I always trade the same number of contracts.

Do you have any stories from your chat rooms or from your web site? Any trading folklore?

No. Because the subject itself—even though it seems to be all-encompassing—is actually so easy.

Chapter 15

LOOKING OUT FOR
THE LITTLE GUY

Scott Clawson

Internet Alias		Investment Style	
Jamzie		Medium-term, long-term	
Year of Birth		**Location**	
1968		Hoboken, NJ	
Education			
BSE, computer science, Princeton University			
Web Site (Free)			
Jamzie.com: www.jamzie.com			

Scott Clawson knew Yahoo! was an appealing buy back in late 1996. Although the company was merely a search engine, Clawson knew that the future held great things for the pioneering Internet company. Like most of us, however, Clawson wanted a second opinion. As a computer programmer at a hedge fund, Clawson figured that he could get expert commentary from the professional traders in his midst. Rather than concur with his analysis, however, the traders he spoke with urged Clawson to steer clear of the dot-com, citing a lack of future growth opportunities. Clawson took their advice and kept away from Yahoo!

But as the weeks passed, Yahoo! continued to rise, eventually doubling from the price at which Clawson first pondered buying. Tossing the expert opinions aside, Clawson bought a chunk of Yahoo! shares. The rest, of course, is history. When Clawson eventually sold his position in Yahoo!, he had registered a 600 percent gain.

True, nearly every technology company blossomed during the great

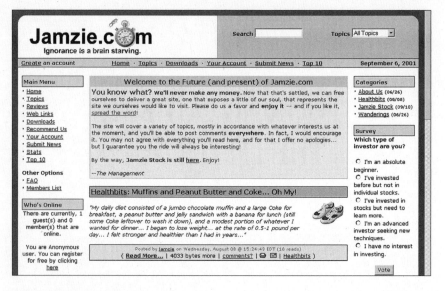

Figure 15.1   www.jamzie.com
Source: Jamzie.com.

bull run of the late 1990s. But Clawson had a knack for picking the cream of the crop. He racked up enormous gains with his positions in Broadcom, Qualcomm, and Research in Motion. More important, Clawson's methodology was rooted in traditional tenets of "buy what you know." He wasn't playing momentum. He wasn't day trading. He was using a list of seasoned criteria to handpick the greatest firms in the world.

In fact, every company that Clawson recommends must pass with flying colors when run through the Jamzie Stock checklist. "Can this company take over the world?" asks criterion number two. "Percentage earnings growth must exceed percentage revenue growth," demands item six. Then there's the all-important Jamzie Stock Total Quality Theory. Essentially, Clawson has upped Peter Lynch's ante several times over. "A company's commitment to quality will be apparent in everything it does and vice versa," heralds the Total Quality Theory. The point is that everything about a company should scream 100 percent customer satisfaction and 100 percent quality standards. Clawson perceives a high correlation between stock returns and corporate commitment to quality.

The biggest hole in Clawson's approach is a lack of timing or valuation measures. There is no question that his criteria help pinpoint the globe's top companies, but who's to say that the market hasn't already factored in this greatness and then some? Yahoo! was a great company in late 1996, and it was a stellar stock pick, too. But Yahoo! was a great company—many would say a better company—in late 1999. It's stock, however, was not a prudent buy.

Nonetheless, Clawson's investment lessons are insightful and often quite lucrative. A newly redesigned Jamzie.com (see Figure 15.1) features beefed-up community interaction, including surveys, story submissions by readers, and the ability to post comments and reactions to Clawson's in-depth articles and stock picks. Not bad for what is essentially a one-man-show that is entirely free of charge.

Clawson never forgets the professionals that scared him away from Yahoo! in late 1996. He's reluctant to follow the guidance of mainstream Wall Street, whether the advice originates from analysts, newspapers, or television programs. He has all the facts that he needs right around him. The great companies aren't hard to find because they're making sure that the whole world knows they are great. "There is a difference between being a professional and being an expert," Clawson warns, hinting at the mass of market pundits and pros.

You graduated from Princeton University in 1981 and eventually found yourself in a programming job at the Associated Press. Talk about what you did after leaving the Associated Press in 1996.

I found a programming job with a hedge fund based in Dallas, Texas, called HBK Investments. There I immersed myself in the financial world. I was working on programming financial systems right on the trading floor. I don't know how familiar you are with hedge funds, but the concept is similar to a mutual fund except that hedge funds are typically private funds. They have a small number of clients, all of whom are incredibly wealthy. Investment strategy–wise they tend to invest in arbitrage opportunities, trying to exploit inefficiencies in the market and doing a considerable amount of heavy numerical analysis to find those opportunities. The programs and systems that I was writing were operating in support of those types of activities.

The fund was focusing mostly on stocks or . . .

Mostly stocks, but it wasn't purely a buy-and-hold situation. For example, they might compare futures on the S&P 500 index with buying all the underlying 500 stocks in the index, and they might find that futures have some kind of excessive premium. So they might go long one and go short the other, and the idea is to eliminate their risk in the market and end up pocketing the excessive premium day after day after day. These are things that an individual investor wouldn't find practical to do for a number of reasons, but for an institutional company like HBK it makes perfect sense, and the key ingredient in being able to do that is to have the software to support it.

Were you enjoying the financial aspect of the markets at that point, or were you mostly interested in the technology side?

I found what they were doing mathematically interesting. I was also enjoying the financial side. I found that I went into this somewhat naive—I thought that these traders would be brilliant financial people, and that in the world of the stock market they would be right on top of what's a good investment and what's not. The partners in the firm were very bright people, but they were not particularly good stock pickers, which surprised me. Actually, nobody in the firm was a good stock picker; that's not what they do. That was an eye-opener for me—that you could have a successful institutional business that is involved intimately with the stock market that is doing all this analysis with all this software and still be missing something in terms of picking good stocks. That surprised me and really piqued my interest. I was finding that in my own individual portfolio I was out-performing the fund. It was a great confidence booster.

What kind of stocks were you trading, and how were you picking those stocks?

Around that time, Yahoo! was first going public. I looked at it, and I evaluated it in much the same way that Jamzie Stock advocates evaluating stocks. I decided that it was a great opportunity. But one of the partners in the hedge fund convinced me not to buy it.

How did he do that?

It was basically the message, "Hey, Yahoo! is a search engine. What are they going to do with that?" That was the entire analysis. In contrast, what I was seeing was that Yahoo! was a search engine but that it wasn't always going to be just a search engine; they had a great brand, a huge audience, and great growth, and they were in a very strong position to keep expanding. The partner didn't see any of that. It was basically him seeing just the search engine business and me seeing other things down the road. But at the time, I believed the partner because, well, he is a partner in a hedge fund, and he must be right. It turns out that he wasn't right, and six months later I decided I would ignore his advice and buy Yahoo! I missed out on doubling my money because I listened to the partner. But it was a happy ending. I ended up buying it anyway. I stuck

Figure 15.2 Yahoo (Nasdaq: YHOO), April 1996–December 1998
Source: Prophet Financial Systems, Inc. (www.ProphetFinance.com).

to my own convictions, and it did very well for me. Over the next year and a half it was up 600 percent [see Figure 15.2].

How did you resist selling through 500 and 600 percent?

I looked at the stock from time to time and I asked myself, "Would I buy it today?" I asked myself, "Are the reasons that I originally bought it still in place? Are they still valid?" And the answer each time was, yes.

Did Yahoo! fail to meet any of your criteria before you sold it?

I've always felt that Yahoo! was a great company. I still hold some today. But if I find a better opportunity than the stock I am currently holding and I have no cash available, I'm willing to sell the existing stake and buy the new one. That's what happened to me with Yahoo! I saw something else that I wanted to put the money into, and I eventually sold Yahoo! to do that.

You started Jamzie.com because you saw your relatives and friends mired in bad investing advice. Where does that misinformation come from?

It comes from a lot of places. One would be the news, anything from CNBC to some of the printed news that comes by way of the Internet, newspapers, or magazines. There is a focus on the short term, and there almost always is a manic hysteria that is built up, whether negative or positive. I understand why they do it—the media wants to generate excitement in one way or another because that is how they sell their product. But it doesn't serve an investor well. Most individual investors will read an article or see something on TV, and they will take it as fact. If they are saying that the market is terrible and you have to dump all your stocks, that is what they'll do. And then if the next day they say, "Oh, the market is great; now you have to buy all stocks," that is what they'll do. It's not serving their best interest as an individual investor.

Another source would be the big brokerage houses, particularly the old guard like Merrill Lynch, or the Morgan Stanleys of the world. There is this vague public relations campaign in which the firms are trying to convince individuals that they are helpless without the assistance of a big old guard broker, and I completely disagree with that. I've seen commercials on TV that will show some fictitious character, some individual investor, and he will be saying, "I bought so and so and lost all my money. Gee, I should have listened to Merrill Lynch or whoever." I have a very different message for people, and it's a more empowering message.

That message seems to have struck a chord with investors. Jamzie.com has over 70,000 registered users. Can you talk a bit about your user base and about the types of people who are reading the newsletter?

On one end of the spectrum, we have people who don't even have investments right now, but they want to and don't know how to proceed. On the absolute opposite end of the spectrum, we have a number of professional investors, people on Wall Street, that read Jamzie Stock—they read it more to see our stock picks, particularly in technology companies. They read it to look at some of the techniques and criteria that we use.

Let's dig in to the Jamzie Stock formula. Take us through your stock criteria and why your 11 points are important.

The points are a work in progress, and right now we are up to 12. At their core our criteria involve solid fundamental analysis. Inspirationally, some of the things that Peter Lynch wrote about in the early 1990s are involved, but we have actually expanded beyond what he was talking about into a few additional areas. Let's start out with the first criterion: Buy what you know. Understand the company's business. That's something Peter Lynch advocated, and it has become a mantra over the years. I don't know that people always put a lot of thought behind it, though.

It's just become something nice to say. You really need to build up a familiarity with what you are about to invest in. If you're buying a car or vacuum cleaner or anything at all in the material world, if you make a good purchase, chances are that you didn't randomly walk into a store and buy the first thing you saw or buy the thing with the slickest marketing. Chances are you went to *Consumer Reports*, you talked to your friends, you went and actually took a look at some products, you sat down in the car and took it for a test drive, and you checked out the vacuum cleaner and the specs; you really dug in, did some homework, and made an informed choice. It's no different with stocks. You want to go in as an informed investor and know everything you can about that company. Furthermore, it has to make sense to you.

Can you give us a few examples in which Jamzie went out and did some down-and-dirty research?

I do a lot of mail order. I buy a lot of computer equipment for around the house and for my home office. Because of that, almost every day we have something being shipped to us. Even without trying to, I've ended up inadvertently keeping tabs on the different shipping companies out there, and I've noticed that they are not all the same. It's not just about how quickly you get delivery. Some shipping companies have a history that every package we receive is banged up, like somebody drop-kicked it. With other companies, every single shipment is absolutely pristine. Brand-spanking-new. Federal Express has a beautiful tracking system; you can do it by web or by phone. The people that I have spoken with at FedEx are polite and professional and courteous. I've gotten everything that was supposed to be sent overnight exactly on time. I've invested in FedEx on two different occasions, held for about a year each time, and doubled my money each time [see Figure 15.3]. There really is a correlation between the way the company is run and ultimately the way the stock behaves.

How long do you think it takes for those correlations to play out? Do you have to hold a stock for over a year to see that happen?

It's definitely not day-trader material, and it's not even a month. You've got to go a minimum of several months. At the end of 1999 and early 2000, I took a look at all of my stock transactions from 1999 and compared how I had performed with the stocks I was currently holding with what I would have done if I had continued to hold the old stocks an additional year. I discovered that in almost every case I would have been better off holding those stocks another year. That taught me that the methodology I use apparently is giving me information that is two years

Figure 15.3   FedEx Corporation (NYSE: FDX), January 1996–May 2001
Source: Prophet Financial Systems, Inc. (www.ProphetFinance.com).

ahead of the market. In one year you'll have some success, no doubt, but two years is better. It's definitely a long-term investing plan.

Have you changed your strategy since then in terms of buying and holding?

I tend to buy something because it's a great company, and I intend to hold it forever. But that's never the way that it actually works out, especially for a more technology-oriented company. The market will change; the product landscape will change; or maybe the company will have a change in management for better or for worse.

Continue with the Jamzie Stock investment criteria. Try to give examples of companies that embody each principle.

Criterion 2: Can this company take over the world? "The world" doesn't mean that they are literally going to own everything on earth; it means the world of the space that they are doing business in. For example: Research in Motion [see Figure 15.4]. They make two-way pagers that handle e-mail—kind of a neat product. I discovered the company in June 1999 when I read that Intel made an investment in them, and I started to do research. At the time, nobody was really talk-

Figure 15.4   Research in Motion (Nasdaq: RIMM), June 1999–December 2000
Source: Prophet Financial Systems, Inc. (www.ProphetFinance.com).

ing about this little tiny company. But I dug in, and what was fascinating about them was that they really had no competition in the space. You have executives and technical personnel who travel a lot, and these people would benefit from having access to their e-mail remotely. The only game in town at the time was Research in Motion. I read that Michael Dell got one and was starting to carry it around, and every review of the product that I read was very positive. They marketed their service with a flat rate per month. The consumer in a lot of cases feels comfortable with a flat-rate price because it's predictable—they know what they are going to pay.

I ended up taking a stake in Research in Motion, and it went from $15 a share in late 1999 to $175 a share in April 2000. It went down after that when everything went down with the market crash, and I ended up selling my stake in Research in Motion at $50 a share. That was a mistake. I should have held on to it, but mistakes happen. Their world is the world of handheld products doing e-mail, and they are the big fish in that pond. Also, the company's business fit a foreseeable trend—Criterion 3. People seem to be getting more and more mobile over time. Your grandparents probably hardly traveled at all. Even my father lived his entire life in the same county in New Jersey. But people today move around. A product like the Research in Motion pager really fits that kind of trend.

Now we get into a few quantitative criteria: Criterion 4 is a debt-to-equity ratio of less than one—ideally zero. The debt-to-equity ratio is the long-term debt of the company divided by its equity value. You don't want to invest in a company that has a lot of debt—it's like they have a lead weight tied to their legs. A company that is heavily in debt has to make payments on that debt. In an extreme case they may end up paying 30 percent, 40 percent, or 50 percent of their profits out just to service their debt. If they have a competitor of equal size who is not in debt, that competitor has double the money to put into things like marketing or research that will add value to their product. So, the company that is heavily in debt is at a tremendous competitive disadvantage; in practice, most companies that get deeply in debt are led to an unfortunate end. They either go out of business completely, lose most of their market share, lose their dominance, or are acquired. That's exactly what happened in a lot of these leveraged buyouts from the 1980s.

Criterion 5 is a profit margin greater than 10 percent—ideally 20 percent or more. You don't want a company that's got an entirely commoditized product, competing on nothing but price. A company in a commoditized business will tend to have a low profit margin. A company that has a more unique product or higher-quality product or that in any way has differentiated itself will tend to have the power to demand higher prices for the product. You will see that reflected in a higher profit margin. Intel has a great brand and a great reputation among consumers. They have got some real competition now from AMD [Advanced Micro Devices], but until very recently, Intel was the only game in town if you wanted a good processor. I'm going to guess that they are in the 30 percent to 50 percent range profit margin–wise.

Next: Does percentage earnings growth exceed percentage revenue growth? In the long term for a company, percentage earnings growth will end up being about the same as percentage revenue growth. You would really like to find a company where the earnings growth exceeds the revenue growth. This is a bit of an oversimplification, but what that's telling you is that a company is becoming more efficient. Maybe a company has revenue growth of 20 percent, but their earnings grew 30 percent. How can that be? One way is that they found a way to trim expenses. Another way is because they are scaling up to higher-volume manufacturing or because they are getting some efficiency to scale in their marketing. They are able to sell more products at a lower unit price. An efficient company is a mark of good management.

Talk about some of your favorite managers.

One person I admire is Jeff Bezos [CEO of Amazon.com]. I don't necessarily admire his money management, although his strategy of growing
big at the expense of profit was both novel and daring. I don't know if I
agree with that, but I do agree with the way he is completely committed
to the customer. I'll give you a small example that I think is indicative
of what he is all about. I buy a fair amount of stuff from Amazon.com. I
received a shipment of a couple of books recently, and at the bottom of
the box was an envelope with a letter from him and a little 10-pack of
self-stick one-cent stamps. The letter basically said, "I'm always trying
to think of ways to make our customers' lives more convenient, and I've
been having a hard time finding ways recently. Now, in a small way, I've
found something that can help." He mentioned that on January 7 the
U.S. Postal Service had raised rates from 33 to 34 cents for a first class
stamp. He included the one-cent stamps in the package to make the customer's life just a little snitch easier because now they could cover the
postage with the old stamps that they might have had lying around and
wouldn't need to make a trip to the post office.

**We met Bezos when he gave a lecture at Wharton, and we've always ad-
mired his customer focus, too. What are the rest of the Jamzie Stock criteria?**

Criterion 7 is that actual earnings almost always exceed estimates. Analysts will doctor their numbers for the earnings estimates, and a lot of
times they will take whatever number the company offers to them and
justify it. So, in a lot of cases, these numbers are coming from the company itself. That doesn't make the earnings number particularly reliable, but you want reliability as an investor. If you have a cynical mind
and believe that earnings estimates are all doctored, what does it say
about a company if they themselves come up with their estimate and
then fail to deliver? To me that says that the company has got poor management, and we don't want to invest in a company that is poorly managed.

   You want to find an investment where, with maximum likelihood,
your assumptions about the company are correct. If you see a company
that always meets their estimates, that gives some credibility toward the
next estimate down the line. If this company had results that were a
penny higher than estimates for the last three quarters, guess what their
earnings will probably be this coming quarter?

   The Criterion 8 is that earnings this year must exceed those of last
year. That's pretty simple. We all buy stocks that we want to see increase

in value. I believe that over a long period of time, the stock price will tend to approximate the earnings growth of a company.

Criterion 9 is that ideally, earnings have increased every year, preferably every quarter, since the company was founded. That's something we call perfect earnings growth. You want to see a company that has been growing by leaps and bounds every single year and will keep doing so as long as you hold it.

Criterion 10 may be the cornerstone of all our criteria: The company must demonstrate a commitment to quality in accordance to the Jamzie Stock Total Quality Theory. This means that the company's commitment to quality will be apparent in everything it does and vice versa. If a company exhibits a very poor commitment to quality in one area, it's likely that they will have a poor commitment in a lot of areas. Conversely, if a company shows very conscientious attention to maintaining a high standard in some things, chances are that it comes from the top. That's a management imperative that's been enforced throughout the entire corporation. The Total Quality Theory gives you a proxy for evaluating the entire company given a limited set of data points or a limited window. The ultimate would be to actually be inside the company and be able to walk around and interview all the managers and employees and play with all the products, but you can't always do that. So what do you do as an investor? The formatting of the annual report—is it clean and professional? Or does it have misspellings or garish graphics? What does the web site look like? Is it well designed? Does it give information that's genuinely useful? Is it fast loading; is it bug free; do the links work? What do their marketing brochures look like? What do their ads and promotions look like? Are they compelling? Do they state a good case? Do they make you want to evaluate the product further? Call their technical support line. See if you get a human being on the line. See how long you wait on hold. See if they are courteous to you. See if they genuinely try to help you or just blow you off. The more data points that you set, the more confidence you have in the overall quality of the company.

Criterion 11: Is the company devoted to its customers? Microsoft has a deep sense of customer focus. I worked at Microsoft as an intern in 1990, so I've seen how it operates from the inside. I've attended a party at Bill Gates' house. I've even had the pleasure of arguing with Bill Gates personally about a technical issue. He won, by the way. I've seen them inside; I've seen them outside. I've got some products of theirs that I genuinely love. The thing that Microsoft has done over the years that has been extremely smart is to listen to their customers. Customers would complain about a product, and they would fix the prod-

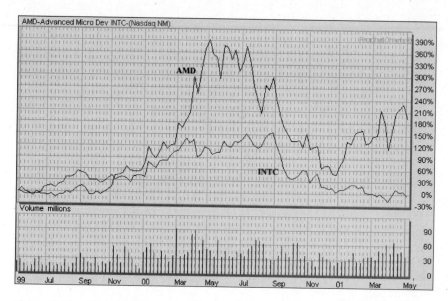

Figure 15.5 Advanced Micro Devices (NYSE: AMD) and Intel Corporation (Nasdaq: INTC), May 1999–May 2001

Source: Prophet Financial Systems, Inc. (www.ProphetFinance.com).

uct. If the needs of the market changed fundamentally, Microsoft would do their best to change with those needs. We unveiled this criterion in an article about Intel that was critical of Intel, specifically Intel in the last year or two. It basically said that Advanced Micro Devices, AMD, is now a credible competitor to Intel [see Figure 15.5]. AMD has existed for a long time and has been kind of playing second fiddle to Intel. They never had a credible product to compete with Intel. But, in the last year or two, AMD has gotten much better. They have had a change in management for the better. Intel, too, has had a change in management; Andrew Grove stepped down as CEO, and you can't say exclusively that that's why Intel has gotten into trouble, but it is an interesting coincidence. The fact is that today Intel is not as dominant as it was a couple of years ago, and it has to do with customer focus.

We have one more: Does the company's strategic vision make sense? Do their actions support this vision? The company strategy is like a puzzle. Do the pieces fit? Assuming that you are looking at a company that does have a coherent vision and a coherent strategy, then that gives you a foundation to look at these different business transactions and understand if their actions support their words.

Figure 15.6   GoTo.com (Nasdaq: GOTO), May 1999–May 2001
Source: Prophet Financial Systems, Inc. (www.ProphetFinance.com).

What stocks pass the Jamzie test these days? Go out on a limb and pick three stocks that you think will do well over the next three years.

I think Broadcom will keep doing well. And Qualcomm. I owned Qualcomm, and I made eight times my money on that stock. It was a fantastic investment for me in 1999. Then we sold it, and I am glad that we sold because the stock collapsed. However, I think they are going to come back. They are in a great position because they are right at the forefront of the next generation of cell phone technology. A third company is more risky, but I am going to go out on a limb: GoTo.com [see Figure 15.6]. In the short term, in the next 12 months, GoTo stock may or may not do well. But I think three years out they will have done very well. They have a great business model.

That's an odd choice. How does GoTo.com fit your investment criteria?

GoTo is a pay-per-placement search engine. It's basically an ongoing auction with everybody that wants a listing in the search engine. The higher you bid, the higher your listing appears in the results. Jamzie Stock is in there. We bid on the word "stock." Any time someone types in "stock" as a key word, we come up. GoTo was the pioneer of this concept, and it's by far the largest and highest quality pay-per-click search engine. It is in the advertisers' best interests to bid only on keywords that are relevant—an accurate description of their sites. That translates into a very accurate search engine. Yahoo! has differentiated itself by having a hand-edited directory with some of those same benefits of relevancy, but it's incredibly labor-intensive. In the GoTo model, advertisers do most of the work.

We've read about the concept of zero gravity in past issues of Jamzie Stock—companies that can avoid expensive fixed costs by selling nothing more than an idea or information. Would GoTo fall in the category of a zero-gravity company?

It's pretty close. They do still have a little involvement. They try to enforce relevancy by having a human editor review bids to ensure that they are not entirely off-the-wall. They also have payment processing, which means that they have to pay fees to outside parties—credit card companies, for example—but it's pretty close to zero gravity. It's low gravity.

What about the valuation of companies? How does an investor determine a good price to buy and a good price to sell? You've talked some about the rise and fall of stocks like Yahoo! and Research in Motion, but it seems that these companies fit the Jamzie Stock criteria at all points throughout both their zigs and their zags.

Research in Motion had a ludicrous valuation.

But the fundamentals and most of your criteria were still in place.

Yes.

Then how does an investor know what a company is worth?

When it comes to valuation, there is only one thing that determines the correct price of a stock, and that's supply and demand. That's it. There are different types of analysis you can use to come up with a price, but every different analysis will come up with a different so-called correct price. The fact is that the correct price is the price the market is willing to pay. The market is a great big stock auction.

Research in Motion has changed over the last 12 months—it's now a stronger company than it was a year ago, yet it's trading at lower levels than it was a year ago. That's because of investor psychology and the resulting change in the dynamics of supply and demand. The shorter your time horizon, the more susceptible you are to doing everything right and getting creamed regardless because the market turned against you—2000 was a perfect example of that. Now, as to Research in Motion and Yahoo! specifically: The answer is that if you looked at them and did your analysis and believed that these were the companies to be holding, there would have been no reason to sell Research in Motion. If a substantial portion of your analysis of Yahoo! relied on their making tremendous amounts of ad revenue, you might have changed your mind and sold Yahoo! at some point in 2000 when it became clear that Internet advertising was in trouble. If your analysis of Yahoo! focused more on the aspect of the tremendous reach it has, their dominant market position, and the way that they can effortlessly expand into new areas, then you might not have sold. A lot of your sell decisions depend on what made you buy the stock in the first place. If you were one of those people who were holding Yahoo!, you would have lost out in 2000. You would have lost a lot of money.

There is no guarantee that you are going to make money. All of our investment criteria try to maximize the probability. It's a bit like the people that count cards playing blackjack, except that I would hope that our methodology gives you a more meaningful adantage. At the end of the day, however, you can still lose. You are trying to put yourself in the most favorable risk-reward scenario.

Chapter 16

THE DOCTOR WILL
SEE YOU NOW
Ed Yardeni

Internet Alias	Investment Style
Dr. Ed	Macro strategist
Year of Birth	**Location**
1950	Long Island, NY
Education	
BA, economics and politics, Cornell University; MS, international relations, Yale University; PhD, economics, Yale University	
Web Site (Free/Pay)	
Dr. Ed Yardeni's Economics Network: www.yardeni.com	

"It's like the field of dreams—build it and they will come," says Ed Yardeni, chief investment strategist of Deutsche Banc Alex. Brown, about the motivations for launching his eponymous web site. Yardeni's intuition about the success of his web site was right on the money—his virtual home base has become one of the most popular investment destinations on the Internet. But that's not terribly surprising. The fact is, Dr. Ed Yardeni is usually right, and his macroeconomic savvy has made him one of the most influential people on Wall Street.

Predicting the success of his web site is one of Yardeni's least impressive accomplishments. Just months after the crash of 1987, Yardeni predicted that the Dow would hit 5,000 by 1993. His bold call earned him the status of lunatic in the eyes of many of his less contrarian Wall Street colleagues. His call was only slightly loony—the Dow hit 5,000 by 1995. In early November 1995, with the Dow sitting modestly under 5,000, Yardeni forecasted another double to Dow 10,000 by the year 2000. Right again. Year 2000 was more than just Dow 10,000 for Yardeni; it was also Y2K, the year that computer glitches had the potential to drag the world's economies into a frightful recession.

In 1997 Yardeni started worrying about the impact of a Y2K computer bug that could prevent computers around the globe from recognizing the millennial rollover. Again, Wall Street panned Yardeni for his contrarian style. The investment community didn't have the Y2K issue on its radar screen, and many thought that Yardeni was a nutcase for believing that a technical glitch could bring the world to its knees. When dawn broke on January 1, 2000, without hellfire and brimstone, it might have been easy to rebuke Yardeni for going overboard with his prophecies of Y2K gloom and doom. But consider the following quote from a January 5, 2000, *Business Week Online* article: "Yardeni should be heralded as a hero. After proving his skill as a consistently bullish market strategist during the '90s, he was seemingly wrong about Y2K. Or was he? More likely, his dire predictions about what could have happened might have helped head off a difficult if not disastrous situation."

If you're getting the feel for the life of an investment strategist, you can probably take a stab at Yardeni's next macro prediction for the market. That's right—Dow 15,000 by 2005. Besides his enviable track record as a stock market oracle, Yardeni has plenty of qualifications to back up his gallant predictions. He boasts an impressive academic background: an undergraduate degree in economics and politics from Cornell University and a master's degree in international relations and a doctorate in economics from Yale University. He's worked as an economist at various firms on Wall Street and presently calmly comments on the chaos of Wall Street from his perch as chief investment strategist at Deutsche Banc Alex. Brown.

Luckily for investors all around the globe, Yardeni likes to think of himself as somewhat of a Wall Street rock star. "There's a show business side of me that figures if I'm doing work that I'm proud of, the bigger the audience, the better," says Yardeni of his willingness to share his investment views on Yardeni.com (see Figure 16.1). The site is truly an admirable effort at bringing the entire world of economics and finance together in one convenient spot. The first page alone has hundreds of links, ranging from news reports to think tanks to economic history to slide shows to real estate to fiscal policy. Despite the massive amount of content, Yardeni.com is a breeze to navigate, thanks to Yardeni's no-frills approach to the web.

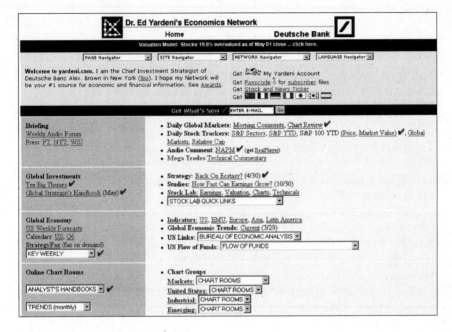

Figure 16.1   www.yardeni.com

Source: Dr. Ed Yardeni's Economics Network.

The best part of Yardeni.com, of course, is Dr. Ed. The good doctor makes all of his research and commentary available free to the public, although in some cases you'll have to settle for time-delayed information. Deutsche Banc clients have real-time access to certain portions of Yardeni's analysis, but public visitors must wait a few weeks to read the content free of charge. Because much of Yardeni's outlook is oriented toward the medium-term and long-term, the delay isn't particularly costly. Yardeni also publishes a free weekly e-mail newsletter that provides a brief glance at his current stance on the market.

Yardeni is one of the smartest and most influential people on Wall Street. His words can move markets, and, thankfully, investors can track his every move via Yardeni.com. In the following interview Yardeni tells about markets past and future, profoundly frames the entire global economy, and offers some noteworthy investment themes for the coming decade.

You spend much of your time studying trends and issues at a very macro level. How closely correlated are macro issues and the stock market? How much time should the individual investor devote to macro issues versus stock-specific analysis?

There are no rules when it comes to investing because the rules change all the time. There are times when the macroeconomic environment is paramount, and there are other times when it is more useful to focus on the fundamentals of the individual company. For example, when technology stocks were going straight up, most institutional investors I talked with basically had the attitude, "Don't bother me with the big picture, I'm making too much money in these stocks." There was a lot of momentum investing going on in technology. Today, the concerns are, How bad is the outlook for the economy? How bad is the outlook for corporate profits? When will we hit bottom on the fundamentals? It's not that there isn't any easy answer; there is *no* answer. The rules are constantly changing. That's what makes investing so much fun.

You said that investors are curious about a bottom. How, in general, do you determine when the market has hit a bottom?

There are all kinds of styles when it comes to investing in the stock market. There are lots of people who don't bother at all with fundamentals and focus solely on so-called technicals. They try to assess the mood, the sentiment, the emotions that are driving the market. From that perspective, it seems to me that a bottom will probably be made when people stop asking, "Is this the bottom?" There are too many bottom pickers right now, and I have an unhappy feeling that the bottom will be made when people who are now asking the question are sold out and are no longer interested in the question, because they don't want to play the game again for a while.

From a fundamental standpoint, which is what I'm supposed to be doing for a living, the conceptual model is actually pretty easy. Implementing it is very difficult. The math of the market is PE times E. The earnings are the E, and the PE is the price-earnings multiple, the multiple at which earnings are valued in the market. PE times E equals P, the price. What earnings should we use in that equation? How do we forecast them? My view is that the market discounts 12-month forward earnings. I consider consensus earnings; in other words, what are Wall Street's analysts collectively predicting that earnings will be for the

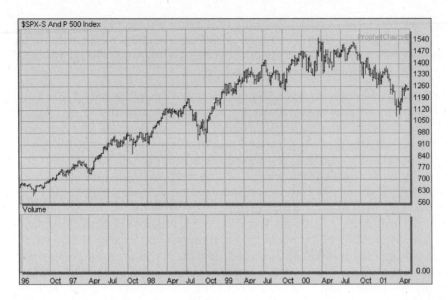

Figure 16.2   S&P 500 index, May 1996–May 2001
Source: Prophet Financial Systems, Inc. (www.ProphetFinance.com).

market, for sectors, for industries, and for individual companies over the next 12 months? I try to assess whether those expectations are on the money. I try to assess the extent to which they might change up or down. Once I have my own view, I then apply what I think is the right valuation multiple, and that's my simple model for trying to establish where I think the market could be heading.

In a sense, I'm predicting what analysts will collectively be predicting earnings to be over the next 12 months. Of course, we have that data right now, but the question is, at the end of this year, what will analysts think earnings will do in 2002? Right now, they're looking for about $64 per share. [Yardeni is referring to pro forma earnings for the S&P 500.] I think that by the end of the year they'll be lowering that to about $60 per share [see Figure 16.2].

How do you make that determination?

It's really a judgment call—hopefully an informed judgment call based on my assessment of the outlook for the economy, for sales, for profit margins, for individual sectors. It's more of a judgmental model than anything formal or scientific. Putting all that together, I conclude that analysts are too optimistic. Their expectations are going to go lower.

Back to PE times E. Is it possible that a new paradigm has emerged in which PE levels should be adjusted upward from historical norms, or in which PE is no longer a valuable metric? Are PE ratios always going to be the standard for valuing companies?

A stock price or a market index price is equal to its PE times E. The only question is how quantitatively you actually measure those. Some people use trailing earnings, which I don't think means much of anything because that's history, and it's not relevant. What matters is forward earnings—what investors collectively think will happen over the next relevant investment period, which tends to be a 12-month period. If you've got an absolutely accurate reading of what's happening to E, you still have to work with the other variable.

Until 2001, I had been the chief economist of the firm [Deutsche Banc Alex. Brown]. Now I'm the chief investment strategist, and when I volunteered to take on this job, I thought it was actually going to be easier. All I have to do is forecast two variables instead of lots of variables—just PE and E. On the other hand, the number of combinations of PE and E that one can come up with is basically infinite. That's where the challenge is; even if you've got a good sense of E, you still need a prediction of where the market is heading in terms of PE, and there's a lot of psychology there. There are obviously some fundamentals like interest rates and inflation that matter, but once you get to individual stocks, it's really tricky. You can use history to a certain extent, but history will only take you so far.

Despite the importance of assessing "big picture" issues, investors are obsessed with the day-to-day gyrations of the market. Why is the market so volatile? Who controls the ebbs and flows of the market?

It's an efficient market. It's a huge market. I walk on our trading desk almost daily, and there is no Wizard of Oz; there is no man behind the curtain controlling this market. Sometimes the market almost feels like it is out of control. I think one of the reasons we have more volatility in the market is that the market has become more democratic and less controlled by Wall Street. There are now lots of individual investors in the market, and it's a good thing. It's a real positive to see that we're getting what I call populous capitalism—more people actively participating in the stock market. That can also lead to the delusion of the crowd, which is what we experienced in 1999. It can also lead to more volatility. It means that the market may have a lot of participants who aren't paying as much attention to the old-fashioned fundamentals of earnings and valuation. If there are a lot of investors chasing stocks up and selling them as they go down, markets are prone to excessive volatility.

That's not to say that Wall Street hasn't contributed to the volatility, because in 1999 and early 2000 a lot of analysts clearly chased stocks up by delivering a fundamental forecast that justified why stock prices made sense where they were. Now, many of them are being berated by investors for jumping in and basically telling the crowd what they wanted to hear. At the end of the day, Wall Street is driven by the famous emotions of fear and greed, and the individual investor has got to be very disciplined to avoid getting sucked up in these emotional mood swings. He or she must try to be somewhat contrary.

Do you think that individual investors should have faith in the commentary from analysts like yourself and other pros?

I think the lesson of 1999 and 2000 should be: Be a conservative investor. Don't chase the hype. Don't get sucked in. I think most investors have day jobs that are keeping them fairly busy. It is very difficult for individual investors to do it on their own. I think professionally managed approaches to investing make more sense. But individual investors should probably stay away from the most volatile sectors or the most hyped-up sectors. We on Wall Street have the most unfortunate tendency to sell the public lots of mutual funds that focus on the hype of the day. There were a lot of Internet mutual funds that came out right at the top. Investors should try to avoid that. It's very hard because you hear about your uncle getting rich. And you never liked the uncle. So you figure, if he's getting rich, why can't I get rich? It's difficult, but I think investors should look at the stock market increasingly as an important place for their retirement assets and recognize that they are going to need those retirement assets, so they have to be investing conservatively.

You're suggesting that investors resist the urge to jump on the momentum train. Is there an economic rationale for momentum in the market?

Again, there are no rules. The rules change, and it's very important to realize when the rules have changed. But there certainly can be fundamental momentum in earnings. We did see some very good earnings momentum in technology in the 1990s. Recently, we've seen some great earnings momentum in energy and electric utilities. So, there can be some good, fundamental logic for momentum investing. However, sometimes the market's momentum can blow out of proportion the underlying momentum in the fundamentals; and when it does, you will typically see the PE ratio getting well above historical norms. That's when we get ourselves into trouble, when the market starts to believe in its own magic.

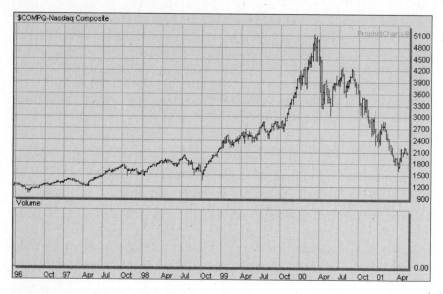

Figure 16.3 Nasdaq composite, May 1996–May 2001
Source: Prophet Financial Systems, Inc. (www.ProphetFinance.com).

Obviously, the great bull market of the late 1990s and the subsequent bust are an example of momentum going haywire. Why did the Nasdaq rise so high and fall so hard?

With the benefit of hindsight, which is always 20/20, it was just a classic bubble. While we're all well aware of the history of bubbles, and we all know how badly they can end, it's hard to resist the siren song of bubble magic. I think even rational folks may contribute to bubbles because they don't have to put all of their life savings into a bubble. They may just put a little bit. But if a lot of rational people chip in a little bit of their savings—because they don't want to miss out—it can feed on itself.

It was a Nasdaq bubble, and there were a lot of factors that all converged at the same time to make it happen [see Figure 16.3]. We did have some very good fundamentals and earnings performance for technology in the 1990s, particularly companies that were in the PC industry, either manufacturing PCs or processors or software. Many were able to get extraordinary profit growth partly because, for a very short period of time, they developed a monopoly position in the marketplace. Microsoft, Intel, and Dell had extraordinary market shares in their businesses. That convinced investors that maybe there were other companies that could do the same thing. They found Cisco, Lucent, Sun, and Oracle. But the very success of those companies created an enormous amount of jealousy in the industry. These companies were making so much money, and people started asking, "Why can't we do the same thing by coming up with same, similar, or different technologies to compete with them?" Technology is a very competitive market, so success plants its own seeds of destruction because it attracts so much competition.

One of the greatest mistakes that investors are prone to make on a recurring basis is forgetting about competition. They're swept into the successful "stock du jour," not recognizing that there are lots of other investors that instead of investing in that particular stock are looking to put money in a competitor that may take some market share away from your winner. Again, in a competitive market place, success breeds jealousy, breeds competitors. That is one of the biggest failings of investors who get swept up in these manias.

To a lot of younger investors, the whole crash seemed like a tragedy, something that they had never seen before. Was the situation considerably different from other bubbles in the past?

On the happy side, the bursting of the technology bubble is not comparable to the bursting of the tulip bubble. When the tulip bubble burst, at the end of the day, they were just pretty flowers. Technology is an industry that is very creative; they will come up with something new. In the interim, nobody is saying, "We've got too many PCs here, let's throw 'em out." We're all using these technologies every day to make us more productive, more competitive, to improve our lives. So, I think there are some substantial differences between the fundamental impact of the bursting of this bubble and some previous bubbles. At the same time, there are also some obvious similarities.

Many people justified the tech bubble with the phrase *New Economy*. Although the tech stock bubble ultimately burst, some remnants of that New Economy concept must remain today. Is there any truth to the idea of a New Economy?

This is a cosmic issue: "What is truth?" I like to believe that I was one of the originators, if not the originator, of the New Economy concept. Back in the late 1980s I wrote several pieces, one of them called "The New Wave Manifesto," which argued that we had a new wave economy. I was one of the first promoters of the idea that in the 1990s we would have a secular rebound in productivity, and we would continue as a result to have lower inflation. I didn't use the term *New Economy*. That term was really invented by *Business Week* in the second half of the 1990s, when they joined the bandwagon and a lot of investors jumped on the phrase. The spin they put on it—new, improved, better, bullish, prosperity forever—was the definition that a lot of investors embraced.

Now the term is no longer being used so readily; it has been discredited. But I still use it because I've always had a different view of what the New Economy means. It's my view in reading and assessing human history that there are two kinds of eras: There are wars, and there is peace. I have to admit that I didn't read the novel, but I don't know that anybody could really dispute this point of mine, that there are wars and there is peace. As an economist, I view wars as trade barriers. During wartime situations, power is concentrated with governments, which is where it should be, because we want our government to win the war. War is a trade barrier because you can't trade with your enemies, and it's hard to trade with your friends. Because power is concentrated with government, the consequence for the economy is that markets are very subsidized, protected, and corrupted, and they are certainly not competitive. So wartimes tend to be very inflationary as a result. I would say the end of the Cold War was the end of the longest modern war: World War II and the Cold War.

In peace times markets become globalized. You can trade with people who have been your enemies, and it is easier to trade with your friends. Markets also become much more competitive because power starts to shift away from the government to the marketplace because real power is in selling your goods and services to everyone around the world. That is only going to happen if your government gives up some of its power by negotiating free trade agreements with other governments. So markets become very competitive.

When I say we have a new economy, I do believe that we are in a new era, a new era of peace. I do believe we have a new globally competitive economy, and that we do therefore have a new paradigm, which is actually a very old paradigm, called competition. The only thing really new about this economy is that it's never been this competitive, and competition is inherently a different market. A competitive market is inherently different from a monopolized, protected, corrupted market. More specifically, in competitive markets, it's very difficult to raise prices. In a competitive market, the winners are those who actually lower prices, cut costs, increase productivity, and offer consumers better products and better services at lower prices.

I think that the New Economy still exists, maybe with a vengeance now, because pricing has become even tougher in this new competitive economy. I think that the New Economy is one where inflation is basically dead. Up until recently, the perception of the New Economy was that we had this happy combination of strong growth based on productivity and technology with very low inflation. A deflating economy with falling prices, weak profits, and weak employment would in many ways also be a fairly new economy, but a lot less happy than the one we enjoyed in the 1990s.

The key to keeping prosperity going and making this all happy is for governments to shift power to the consumer so that there is enough demand to meet all the supply that we now seem to have all around the world. That requires that the Japanese government give more power to their consumer through tax cuts and deregulation and that the Chinese, as they enter the World Trade Organization, give more power to their consumers. If that doesn't happen fast enough in this horse race between trying to keep supply and demand running neck and neck, and we find that demand falls behind, it could be a very deflationary scenario for a lot of us.

How do global demographic trends affect the horse race?

The demographic outlook is quite troubling. The Chinese census was released recently, and they are up to 1.3 billion people. They have this extraordinary dynamic there; they are now going through the agricultural revolution that the United States went through in the early 1900s. Agriculture is becoming more productive. They need fewer people on the farm. More of the population is moving to the cities—20 to 40 million people a year moving to the cities. The Chinese leadership has determined that the only way to get these people employed is to find them manufacturing jobs selling to the rest of the world, which is why China wants to join the World Trade Organization. Again, this does not have to be an unhappy story. It would be very happy if Chinese manufacturing booms and wages do well and the United States can sell them a lot of what we make. Then the world will be fairly prosperous. But we're talking about some extraordinary numbers in terms of how many people are in China and how many need to be employed as they migrate from one sector to the other.

Do these macro trends point to any promising investment opportunities in the coming years?

Absolutely. Again, there are no rules. There are no guarantees. There are always "rules," but they happen to change, which means that they're really not rules—they're guidelines. Looking back over the past few decades, it seems as though there are always one or two simple themes that you can ride for an entire decade, and do fairly well. In the 1980s we were lowering tax rates for consumers. It was a good time. There was a lot of stimulus toward the consumer, and as a result, retailers did well.

Consumer staples did quite well. In the 1990s there was tech, tech, and tech, with a little bit of telecom sprinkled in. What is it going to be in the decade ahead? My bet would be energy, electric utilities, power—these will do quite well as investment concepts.

With my outlook that inflation is dead and that there will be more deflation coming out of Asia, I kind of like the idea of owning bonds, especially government bonds. We keep paying them off, paying down the debt. So, government bonds may have lower to go. I wouldn't be surprised if the bond yield settled somewhere around 4 percent for most of the decade.

One factor that seems to sway the market considerably is sentiment about the Federal Reserve. Why do people seem to have such an obsession with the Fed? Is the attention warranted?

It's disturbing that the Fed has become so important and that there's almost a cult around the Fed chairman [Alan Greenspan]. One of these days, he may actually lose his magic. We talked before about whether there is some man behind the curtain—I don't think there is one in the stock market. On the other hand, there's the widespread view that the man behind the curtain that's running everything is the Fed chairman, and he basically has done a good job so far. But I think this tremendous focus on one individual is not healthy. It would be better if we had more confidence in the institution. It would be better if the Fed had established routine ways of dealing with the economy that we could depend on through thick and thin, and it wasn't so personality-related.

The risk here is that some powerful historical forces have been unleashed that even the Fed may find difficulty responding to. The competitive challenge of China is not something that monetary policy can do very much about. There is a need for good economic leadership, not just coming out of the Fed, but also out of the administration, and also out of the collection of global political leaders. By doing such a good job, the Fed has taken the pressure off of political and fiscal leaders. We may need a group that's had some experience, and, unfortunately, they will not have had any because the Fed has been a one-man show that everybody so far has enjoyed quite a bit.

It often seems like the stock market is fairly indifferent to the banter of politics.

A good politician will make us believe that politicians don't matter. A bad politician can make politics matter a lot. Bill Clinton was very much a positive for the market because he turned out to be a free trader who supported deregulation. He turned out to be very promarket, which was viewed positively by the stock market. However, it would be folly for anyone to say that the bull market in the Clinton years was Clinton's doing. Politicians do matter, and they matter in a very positive way if they're so good that people come to conclude that politics doesn't matter.

You cited the tulip bulb bubble and other historical manias as an analogue for what transpired during the late 1990s. What historical time period will most closely mirror the first decade of the twenty-first century?

The 1800s in America. America was the world's fastest-growing emerging economy in the 1800s. There were a lot of booms and a lot of busts, and there were wars, and there were panics, and there were manias. There were good times, there were bad times, there was overconsumption, there was overinvestment, and great prosperity. Fortunes lost, fortunes made. But overall there was great progress.

China now is potentially the world's emerging economy. And in some ways, I think the United States is still an emerging economy. The tech revolution has been somewhat discredited here, and the New Economy has been discredited. But the tech revolution, in many ways, is just starting in the United States. I think you have two emerging economies in different stages, and how they dance together will be extremely important to how financial markets and global economies perform. I think you have two potentially huge economic superpowers here: without a doubt the United States and, increasingly, China. Their interaction is going to be of key importance. Any way you look at the history of a major emerging economy like the United States in the 1800s shows that you get higher highs and hopefully higher lows, so you make progress. But there will be lows.

We've touched on a slew of international issues. Do you recommend that investors set aside a portion of their assets for international opportunities, or is it enough simply to consider how international trends affect domestic securities?

There is a tendency for strategists to say, "Yes, you should definitely have something overseas." You can invest in a lot of American companies, however, and get plenty of international exposure that way. If you invest in the Dow, you have yourself 20 percent, maybe 30 percent, exposure to the rest of the world. For most of us, that may be good enough. We have seen that overseas investments in emerging markets have been very faddish, and the risk that most investors face is that they'll be investing just as the fad is near the top. Things change a lot around the world.

I'd be more inclined for the average investor to invest in the blue chips that you know and have some confidence in. On the other hand, there was a time when Xerox was a blue chip, and look where it is now. Or Lucent—look how quickly it's had a reversal of fortune. So, blue-chip investing isn't necessarily a guarantee, either. You've got to own some government bonds. You've got to have some cash. You've got to pay off some of your mortgage. I think stocks for the rest of the decade and beyond will probably get you a return of 7 percent to 10 percent, in line with the historical trend of earnings. That's not great, but if you can put it in a 401(k) on a tax-deferred basis, it will compound very nicely.

You've spoken about China and Japan—some big economies. But it seems that economic and market catalysts can emerge from very small countries, as happened at the outset of the Asian crisis in 1997. Is that true? Is it important to pay attention to every little detail in the global economy?

The average individual can't possibly do that. I do it, but it's pretty hard—a lot of moving parts. What I try to do is have a worldview that I believe in. I try to have a big picture of some of the major trends that are influencing our economy and our financial markets. These don't have to be sophisticated, complex views. My view at the beginning of the 1990s was, "Hey, we just won the Cold War. This is a big deal. This is bullish." It was that simple. Now my worldview focuses on the impact of a billion people in China becoming a significant part of global trade. What impact is that going to have?

You think China is the most important factor to consider in the next few years?

I really do. I recognize that there has been hype about China since Marco Polo. I recognize that nobody has ever made money in China. I recognize that it is a politically volatile area that can go from being open to being shut down very rapidly. So, there are risks in making China my dominant theme for the world for the rest of the decade and beyond. But that's why anybody who is interested in the theme should read my work, because I'll be trying to stay on top of it and constantly assessing whether that view still makes sense.

Chapter 17

PROFESSIONAL SCALPER
Jay Yu

Internet Alias	Investment Style
Jay	Day trader
Year of Birth	**Location**
1971	Rockville, MD

Education
BS, business and speech communications, University of Maryland

Web Site (Pay)
The UndergroundTrader: www.undergroundtrader.com

The pure day trader—a scalper grabbing ticks and teenies who thinks five minutes is a long-term outlook—isn't the most beloved breed of investor. More than a few bankers at top Wall Street firms have cringed when we mentioned that we were including some in this book. The 2001 Online Trading Expo, the day trading industry's premiere annual gathering in New York City, had its share of moneymaking come-ons and pseudo–stock market "scientists" pitching their wares. A few systems even claimed to be able to tell you exactly when to buy or sell a certain stock—don't bother trying to understand why—with a money-back guarantee. Jay Yu's UndergroundTrader booth—despite the black T-shirts with warrioresque hatchet-in-crosshairs logos—was one bastion for calm and cool trading. What we liked about Yu was his ability to tell us why his strategies work and to give us valid insight into real dynamics of the stock market.

Yu, operator and head trader at UndergroundTrader, isn't running a scam (see Figure 17.1). He doesn't buy stocks, pump them up, and sell into the momentum. In fact, he doesn't trade at all. He's itching to get

Figure 17.1   www.undergroundtrader.com
Source: The Underground Trader.

back in the game, but as long as he's making calls in the Underground-Trader Trading Pit, he refuses to give even the perception of any conflict of interest. Yu has a knack for timing buys and sells, as if his blood pumps the pulse of the market. Traders can follow his stock-specific calls in the real-time chat room or use his predictions to help shape trading strategies in broader sectors.

As with most other real-time trading alert services, you have to pay $250 per month (or try a free two-week trial) for access to the Trading Pit, where Yu makes 10 to 20 calls per day and explains the premises for the calls in the down time. Yu is a scalper—he likes to play on the idea of momentum in the market and tries to catch minirallies and mini-breakdowns in stock prices. That's the approach in a nutshell, but believe us, it gets much more complicated.

The success stories that have come out of UndergroundTrader show that making money as a trader is possible with well-tuned strategies.

Just don't get too reckless: "Top Cat—he's doing rather well," says Yu about one of his disciples, appropriately anonymous with his "Top Cat" nom de plume. "I got very upset at him one day because he shorted Network Appliance, and he overleveraged his account big time. Luckily, Goldman Sachs downgraded Network Appliance the next day. So, he got 12 points on a large number of shares. While people in the Trading Pit were patting him on the back, however, I was ripping into him after hours—publicly humiliating him, telling him that what he did was a stupid move. Dumb. Plain stupid. Nothing to be proud about. To go 100 percent of your account leveraged in one stock trade is just madness. Don't ever do that crap again. As it turns out, Top Cat is a minister. . . . You get all walks of life."

Before you get started, you need to know the lingo, so if you've never dipped your toes into the world of Nasdaq Level 2, see Figure 17.2 for a quick introduction. Day trading is not for everyone— and possibly not for anyone—but we think that even the long-term investor can benefit from hearing what Yu has to say.

Your first foray into the market was an internship at Prudential. How did you go from such a traditional firm to the fast-paced day-trading world?

When I was 20, I started to get interested in the stock market, and I took an internship at Prudential Securities. The broker I interned with was more interested in evergreen money, sticking people into funds and getting big accounts. So, I'd go off on my own, read the S&P pages, put together my own little research reports—fundamentals, PEs [price-earnings ratios], revenue growth, and things like that. As an investor, that's what you're taught to believe in. That was initially my attitude, but I didn't have much luck with it. One of the problems was that my temperament was more of someone who was always checking the quotes throughout the day. If a stock took a half-point swing up, I'd be wondering if there was news. I didn't realize until later that stocks don't need to have news to move. Stocks move in ranges throughout the day, be it from program trading, institutional buying, or institutional selling. You have your natural wiggles throughout the day. That's when I began my journey, trying to figure out why stocks move like this; was there a method to the madness? I started thinking, if I get in at the lows of the day and get out at the highs of the day, maybe that would be better.

Through the years, I've developed a system of trading that is based

Most investors can get along just fine by looking at Level 1 Nasdaq quotes on a stock—data provided by any and every online broker or financial portal on the web. Typical Level 1 information includes the price of the last trade on the stock, the change in the stock's price for the day, and the "inside" bid and ask prices. The inside bid is the highest price someone is willing to pay for the stock, and the inside ask is the lowest price for which someone will sell the stock at any given moment. In a sense, the inside bid is the best measure of a stock's value because when an investor needs to sell stock immediately and inputs an order to sell at the market price, the inside bid is typically the price at which the trade will be executed. For most investors, Level 1 data provide more than enough information—perhaps even too much information because the bid and ask prices on liquid issues typically straddle the last trade price by a few pennies on either side.

Day traders need to look deeper into the market, and Level 2 data add multiple dimensions by displaying the open orders of all market makers and electronic communication networks (ECNs), which are computer systems on which buyers of stock are matched with sellers. Some of the more well known ECNs are Island, Instinet, Archipelago, Attain, and Bloomberg. Most traders and institutions use ECNs to bypass Nasdaq market makers and trade directly with other parties privately and anonymously. The typical trader can access ECNs by signing up with a direct-access broker. Our favorite is Charles Schwab subsidiary CyberTrader (www.cybertrader.com).

In simple terms, Nasdaq Level 2 quotes are a conglomerate of all the order information from these ECNs and other market makers. Level 2 data include "outside" bid and ask prices. To be more precise, Level 2 displays the "inside" bid and ask prices from the many market makers and ECNs that make a market in a stock. A trader or anyone with access to Level 2 can see many prices at which investors are willing to buy stock and many prices at which other investors are willing to sell. Moreover, Level 2 data list the size of the share lots so that traders can dynamically see the strength or weakness of any stock.

If day trading is a game, a trader's opponents are the market makers and other traders. Level 2 is the arena where the game is played.

Figure 17.2   A Brief Introduction to Nasdaq Level 2

on seeing a trend. You can see certain patterns play out. As you continue to watch your stocks, you get to feel the personality of the stock. Now, with UndergroundTrader I train traders throughout the day on my system, which is composed of three-minute moving average charts, one-minute stochastic charts, and three-minute stochastic charts on the Nasdaq futures. [Stochastics indicators oscillate between 0 and 100.

They compare a stock's current price to its price range over a specified period of time. A stock's moving average is its average price over a specified period of time. This indicator is used to spot trends and tends to flatten out dramatic fluctuations in stock prices.]

Chat rooms get a bad rap—at best, pure hype, and at worst, dirty scams. Talk about your initial experience with traders communicating on the Internet and about how UndergroundTrader was born.

The chat room that I was initially trading at . . . I don't want to mention the particular chat room, but we had a major disagreement because the moderator was basically promoting a lot of these cheap, low-volume stocks that would get a pop and then tank. They weren't following any methods, and a lot of people were getting taken to the cleaners. Eventually we had a major falling out. When you realize that the moderator is sending the sheep to the slaughter, you can't deal with it anymore. So, I decided to go ahead and give a one-time online trading course. I called it Underground Trading Training. I gave a little training class on the Internet for 25 people for two weeks, basically ripping apart all the myths and the B.S. that people thought was day trading. Back then, people thought you could jump into any stock that was running. People just went by feel, and it was a complete hit-or-miss kind of thing. That's when I went ahead and gathered my first group of hardcore disciples, so to speak.

After the two-week training seminar, I kept the chat room open as a free room. Basically, the students were allowed to sit in, talk to each other, share trades, and speak the language. Even today, you have traders saying, "It's going to the moon" or "It looks strong." Back then I told the chat room, don't even talk about that; don't even mention that the stock is going to go three points, because it's all B.S. You don't predict, you react. What I want to know is, does it look like it's a pump breakout or a consolidation breakout? Oversold, overbought? Is there an ax market maker? Is it fading the trend? And it was amazing to see people actually speaking the language, actually able to understand the methods. I kept the free room open, and I would post my trades. I would e-mail my trade reports to the students just to show them that it could be done, to show them that the methods work. Dell, Cisco—you can be playing these stocks and be scalping them for money on a consistent basis. I'm a high believer in osmosis. When you're hanging out with a group of people that are good in any specific field, it rubs off on you.

Since I'm running a chat room—so there is no conflict of interest—I cannot trade. I wanted to get the chat room running and try to teach as many people as possible before going back to trading. Bottom line: Not everybody can hack it in this game. Most people can't hack it. But the people who really want to learn and get on a solid footing when they come to UndergroundTrader are amazed at the information.

You threw out a bunch of interesting terms and trading concepts there. We'll get back to those shortly. More important, though, if trading can be systematically taught, why do most who try it fail? What do you think is the biggest mistake of the people who can't hack it?

It's very simple. It's a lack of focus, lack of discipline, and lack of management. When people jump into this game, they think they can jump into any stock that's moving. A lot of times they'll hang out at these free chat rooms, where there's a lot of hype. People think that if you pile into a stock, you're going to be able to make money as a day trader. The reality is, you're not. We tell traders who come to the Pit to pick one stock and watch it all day. It's a boring thing to do because the majority of the volume is going to come in on the open—first 30 minutes—and then the postopen—the next 45 minutes to an hour—and then the volume is going to slip. You'll get a lot of wiggles and head fakes, and then you'll see the volume coming back after dead zone at 2:00 P.M. or 2:30 P.M., and then in the last hour. When people don't have focus, they jump into anything that moves. And the problem is that they're the low man on the totem pole—they're the last in.

The lack of focus is the first thing, and then a lack of technique and methods. Traders are told that there are two kind of markets—trend markets and oscillation markets. Trend markets basically go in one direction: either up or down. They maintain that direction in the morning session and the afternoon session. Oscillation markets oscillate throughout the day. Swing traders tend to do better in trend markets. Scalpers do better in oscillation markets. As far as methods are concerned, traders in the Pit are initially told that there is one tool that is required to gain a foothold in this game, and that's the one-minute stochastic chart. The one-minute stochastic chart is going to show you short-term when a stock is in an overbought or an oversold area. [We did not want to turn this book into a how-to guide for day traders or technical analysts, so we've resisted including complex charts later in this interview. Figure 17.3 was chosen arbitrarily to demonstrate what a one-minute stochastic chart (in the lower pane) would look like. Stochastic values represent the position of the stock on a percentile basis versus its range over previous periods (in this case, each period represents one minute) and are used to determine when a stock is overbought and oversold (has risen or fallen too quickly). Yu explains his strategies for using stochastic indicators throughout this interview.]

We tell traders when they come in that they've got to focus on one

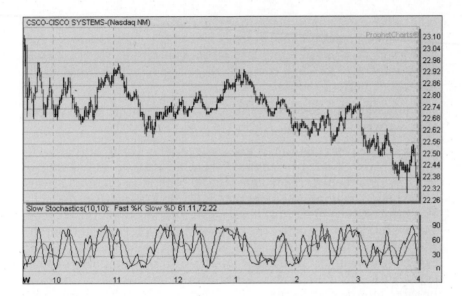

Figure 17.3 One-minute stochastic chart (lower panel) for Cisco (Nasdaq: CSCO) on an arbitrarily chosen day.

Note: Of the two lines in the chart, Yu would use the smoother one to determine overbought and oversold conditions in the stock.

Source: Prophet Financial Systems, Inc. (www.ProphetFinance.com).

stock. Watch the noodles—that's our nickname for the Nasdaq futures—and see what happens to the stochastics. [Yu uses the same type of stochastic indicator for the Nasdaq futures to determine overbought and oversold conditions in the market. In this case, though, he normally uses a three-minute chart rather than a one-minute chart.] Watch your three-minute moving averages chart and the five- and 15-period resistance and support. [The five- and 15-period support and resistance levels refer to a chart's reading five and 15 units of time in the past. For the three-minute moving average chart, Yu uses the readings from 15 and 45 minutes prior to help determine these levels.] The stock is going to oscillate in that range. Once it breaks through that range, it's called a breakout. Watch it; ingest it; let it sink in. That's what traders don't do. Right from the get-go, most of these traders jump in. They want to jump in; they want to buy stocks; they want to make money the first day. The worst thing that can happen to a trader is that they come in and they get lucky. They make money the first couple of days. It sets a very bad precedent, because then the trader's not going to want to learn. They're just going to want to jump into anything that moves. Treat this like a business; you don't expect to make money in the beginning. I know it's boring. It's supposed to be boring. That is how you develop your discipline and your focus. Trades will come to you. [As Yu later mentioned in his chat room, "Better to be bored than busted."]

So you're watching a stock. Waiting. Waiting. Waiting. When do you pull the trigger?

The basic rule is that when the stochastic oscillators slip under the 20-band and bounce back through the 20-band, it's a classic short-term buy signal. When it bounces back under the 80-band, it's a classic short signal. If you're scalping oscillations on a one-minute stochastic, the stock is eventually going to hit the 80-band, and it's going to hit the 20-band. You just have to wait and let the trade come to you. Don't jump in the trade at the 50-band. A classic scalp is when the one-minute stochastic bounces through the 20-band, coupled with a one-minute noodles bounce through the 20-band, and the three-minute noodles are rising. If the three-minute noodles are rising, there's a buy-side bias in the market—the market is uptrending. When that happens, the market makers naturally are going to up their spreads. That's when you can be paring [selling] into the buyers. You don't have to get out all at once.

As far as new traders, we tell them that once you can paper trade and get a 70 percent consistency ratio, that's when you should try the live feel of execution. So, trade 100 shares, pretend it's 1,000 shares, and try to duplicate what you did on paper. The biggest difference between paper and money is purely psychological. When money is on the line, traders tend to choke. Another problem with new traders is that not only do they want to hit the ground running and make money, but they tend to overleverage as well. We tell people to build up a comfort level. Start with 100 shares. You're not going to make money on 100 shares. The goal is to master the technique, not to make money. Your commissions alone are going to put you in the red. It doesn't matter. What you want to do is master the technique, because eventually you want to slowly increase your share load.

How long does it typically take you to teach the traders?

There are two pitfalls that traders initially fall into. Number one, they overtrade every signal and wiggle. Number two, they tell me, "You know, Jay, I've been so consistent. I'll hit seven good trades, and then on my eighth and ninth trade, I'll give it all back." Now, it's a numbers game. If you're batting 70 percent, you're using the same amount of shares, and you're using the same stop losses, the same premises—because they're all scalps—how do you give back everything in two trades? The reality is, you don't. The reality is that on the last trade, they got sloppy. They figured they were right seven times in a row—"I'm going to be right, I'm going to be right"—and they slipped. They may have taken more than the average number of shares; they definitely didn't take the normal stop loss.

The only way I can really get nailed is if I screw up the premises and the style of the trade. I'll give you an example: A scalper scalps 500 shares for a quarter point seven times. Fine, he's doing well. He's getting his little scalps. He's built up his profits. Then, he decides to swing a stock, which is fine. [Swing traders hold stocks for slightly longer periods of time than do day traders or scalpers—typically overnight to one week.] You want to swing it, that's fine. The problem is, he went in on the swing with 500 shares. You see what I'm saying? Apples to oranges. If you're going to swing, and you scalp 500 shares, you want to go into the swing with a smaller number of shares so you can use double the stop loss.

Pain is a great motivation to get your stuff right. Our ideal member is somebody who's been around the block. They've tried this game, and they're frustrated. They can't make money at it, but they want to learn. They don't want to endure any more pain. That's when I am glad to step in and give people a foothold.

Maybe there's pain because day trading doesn't work . . .

You don't believe anything, that's fine. Pull up a one-minute stochastic chart, which is divided in half—stochastic on the bottom and the big chart on top. Now I want you to pull up any stock, and I want you to go back in time today. I want you to count the 20-band bounces. And I want you to count the 80-band reversals. I want you to look at all the points, the clips, the scalps, that you could've made today. The proof is in the pudding. The stochastic indicator does work. It's beautiful seeing the lightbulb turn on with these people. When they finally get a foothold with that one tool, they want to learn. That's the evolution. You might have gotten out too early on a scalp, and you're kicking yourself. Well, that's when you move on, and you pull up a three-minute moving averages chart, and you realize, "Wait a minute, this stock is in an uptrend."

We've talked to many traders, and not many have had insight as to _why_ all of this works. Why should you buy when it breaks through the 20-band? Why should the stock go up once that happens? Why not break back down to the 10-band or whatever it may be?

They say that the markets are orderly, and to an extent that's true. Orderly buying will give you a nice solid uptrend. Orderly selling will give you a nice solid downtrend. Now, what happens is that discrepancies kick in where the futures will drop, where the futures will pop, where you get panic that comes in to disturb the orderliness of the stock. When that happens, the stock will fall. The stochastic—the only thing it's good for is to let you know short-term that the stock's price has developed a short-term panic, either buying or selling. And by utilizing the 20- and 80-bands, you can tell when that panic has set in. Buy the reversal when the panic is over; jump into that stock for the scalp when the stock returns back to its orderly trend or progression. As far as exact mechanics as to what the stochastics entail, I'm not sure. I just know that it works. It's like somebody driving a car and not knowing exactly how the car works, but he knows he can get around from point A to point B. If you take a stock, it's like a rubber band, and you stretch it out. If you take the middle of the rubber band, you pull it down, and the further down it goes, the better the possibility that it's going to snap back. That's what the stochastics are like. It's like pulling that rubber band down, and theoretically, a stock can continue down lower. However, the stochastics can't go lower than the zero-band. So, you don't enter the stock when it's on the zero-band. You enter it when it coils, when it bounces off the zero-band, and crosses through the 20-band. That's the sign that the rubber band has been released, at least to an extent where you're going to be able to get some kind of volatility on that oversold pullback.

How do you know when to sell a stock? Is there a set process for getting out of a trade?

Initially, you just want to be taking profits—in one-quarter increments. You want to be safe. Naturally, it depends on the stock, too. Cisco will pop a quarter point before it wiggles, whereas Broadcom can easily pop a half to three quarters to almost a point before it starts to wiggle. It's highly dependent on the stock.

You want to make sure that the stochastics on your stock and the one-minute futures stochastics are rising. Now you watch the three-minute futures stochastics. If the three-minute futures are rising, you want to be paring. In other words, if you're playing 1,000 shares, you want to be selling partials into each momentum tick—quarter tick, half-point tick, three quarters, whatever.

Give us an example of the ideal trade from start to finish.

Juniper, for example—the day Cisco was at a conference and John Chambers mentioned problems in the industry. This was in January, and I tell you, the rhythms and the personalities of these stocks then compared to now are unreal. On Juniper you could get two points on a sto-chastics bounce, back when Juniper was trading nicely between $110 and $140. Now Juniper is so thick that you'll get a half point, three quar-ters of a point on a stochastic oscillation. Anyway, Juniper had panicked from $115 to $109, and the futures took a dive.

Now, here's the beauty: The markets were actually up that day, and we knew they had to fall. Three-minute noodles [the Nasdaq futures] were holding above the 80-band for close to an hour and a half. I told the traders, "Noodles are going to make a full oscillation. The longer we stay compressed, above the 80-band, the stronger we're going to fall." Same thing in a weak market—the longer the noodles stay under the 20-band compressed, the greater the oscillation is going to be on the first bounce to the 80-band.

Juniper was around $116. Next thing you know, everything is tank-ing. At first I'm like, you know, I'll pat myself on the back: "See, gang, I told you. I told you we were going to fall." Everybody was out and watch-ing for an entry. All of a sudden, they realize, holy cow, something's not right here. Cisco, which would normally wiggle a half point, had just tanked a point. Juniper not only broke under $115, but also there were 29,000-share ask "cranks" pounding this thing down, pounding it down hard, like the hand of God pounding these stocks down. [According to Yu, "a crank is when you see a large size order on an ECN, on the inside, be it the inside ask or the inside bid." He explains this more later in the interview.] Juniper's dropping; it dropped under $115. Juniper tanks un-der $112, $111. I'm telling my people, "$110 is your next support. Watch out for this sucker, because Juniper's three-minute chart broke into a downtrend, absolutely, but the five period is still sitting around $114 and change." The noodles are, at this point, riding the zero-band. Juniper tanks under $110, hard. That's the last support. Juniper pulls back to about $109. We watch the noodles make a reversal, back up. The one-minute noodles picked its head back up. At that point, it was buy every-thing, buy everything central. On Juniper, for example, the five period was around $113 1/2 by that point. The fifteen period was $115, and Ju-niper's trading at $109.75. Once we saw the one-minute noodles perk up, just even peek up: Buy Juniper! Buy Juniper! $110, $110, $110! So, everybody who wanted to get a fill got a fill because the cranks were pounding this thing so hard. But the second the noodles start to turn up, the asks start to get taken in, and you get a couple of buyers coming in; our people are coming in, buying. Once the one-minute noodle starts to bounce past the 10-band, that's it. Once the one-minute noodle has gone through the 20-band, Juniper's already at $111.50. Then, at that point, I'm telling traders the five period on Juniper is $113.50, so be paring your money at $112 to $112.50. Be paring it out, be paring it out. Quite a ride! The moral of the story is that panic is a wonderful thing.

You've mentioned that each stock has its own personality. Pick a stock and tell us how it reacts differently than do the rest.

For example, take Cisco. Cisco at $30 is nothing like Cisco at $120. Basic rule of thumb is the cheaper a stock is and the bigger the float, the slower that thing is going to move. It takes a lot of volume to move Cisco even a half point. Whereas a stock like Broadcom or Juniper tends to move one point in either direction easily. You have to understand that even though that's great on the upside, you're taking the same risk on the downside. On Cisco you never have to panic, because even God needs help moving that thing, whereas you go from a Cisco to a Broadcom, and before you know it, you're down a point.

What about the open on a stock? How is trading the open different?

The three-minute moving average charts don't even have a chance to do anything on the open. The open is very momentum-based because the market makers want to figure out the ranges that the stock is going to trade in, so in essence you're not going to have market makers—unless they have major institutional order flow—hold a particular range too strong. What we look for at the open are gap fills. In other words, if Juniper gaps to $91 and pulls back to $90 on profit takers on the open, when the noodles reverse, we jump back in at $91 because it's a gap fill. Anybody who wanted to take profits took profits. Once $91 hits, it's almost as if the pullback has been erased. The sellers are out. The new buyers are in. It's a very miniature version of a cup-and-handle breakout. We call it the gap fill breakout.

If the noodles pull back on the open, we watch our basket stocks and look for any buy-side fading—when the noodles are pulling back, but the stock is holding at or near its high. When the noodles reverse, these are the stocks that are going to pop first. So, as the noodles pull back, you're going to support that bid and eat up as many shares as you can because when the noodles reverse, the other market makers are going to step right in front, the buyers are going to chase, and the traders are going to jump in. Then you get the cranks who like to come in and cross-lock and crank up these stocks. It's a snowball effect. You're only taking scalps on the open. The open can make a stock look very strong. Then after 10:00 A.M., the stock can be a tanker on the day. It happens all the time. That's why I tell people you want to be paring out. You're in? Great. Don't cheer it. Be selling; be selling into the buyers.

You want to be watching your stock. You want to be able to see whether it takes a lot of buying strength, a lot of bids coming in, to uptick that stock. Whereas, when the noodles reverse, if the bids simply evaporate, that's when you start to realize, for example, that Broadcom's got some serious sell-side bias. Or Cisco's got some serious sell-side bias. You want to be watching to see if there is perhaps an ax market maker.

Can you explain the concept of an ax market maker?

On a Level 2 screen, you've got all kinds of market makers. The way a stock normally trades is that when the futures rise, the market makers will adjust their spreads. If the futures rise, then the stock is going to uptick. If the futures fall, then the stock is going to downtick. Now, within those oscillations, you're going to have institutional orders that come in to buy or sell. So, you're going to be able to see if an ax market maker fades the oscillation. Let's say that the futures are coming down—three-minute noodles are slipping under the 80-band. Broadcom should be falling right back down with the spreads. I see cranks coming in. A crank is a large ECN bidder on the inside. I see 10,000 shares on Island on the ask. However, I'm seeing First Boston [a market maker] on the inside bid eating all the shares. Technically, since the futures are falling, Broadcom should be oscillating right back down. However, First Boston is holding the bid, and he's eating up all the sellers. It's easy for a market maker to accumulate shares without showing his symbol. However, when First Boston comes in and shows his symbol, he's trying to say, "Hey guys, look—look at me. I'm holding the stock up. I'm the ax. You can lean on me." He's accumulating shares, but he's also letting all the market makers and the traders understand that he is the ax, and he's going to support the stock. He's doing it by putting his money where his mouth is.

A beautiful example that I like to tell traders about is when you see a stock consolidating when the futures are pulling back. Let's say Broadcom's consolidating right under $75. In other words, when the futures are pulling back, Broadcom is holding solidly between $74.50 and $74.75. Now I see First Boston's sitting in here at $74.75, and he's eating up shares as the noodles pull back. He's eating, he's eating, he's eating. First Boston wants me to watch him. Rather than allowing the stock to oscillate normally back down to the lower end of the range—$74, $73.75, $73.50—he's actively buying up everybody on the bids. You've got shorts that are coming in, too. They're shorting against him until they realize First Boston's not stepping off.

When the noodles finally reverse, when the noodles finally bounce, that stock is going to break out. And you'll have an ax market maker—

once the noodles reverse, he's going to uptick. The very first people who are going to try to get out of that stock are going to be the shorts. These guys are going to be the first ones to go the other way and buy up everything at $75. Then you've got First Boston, who might keep upping his bids. Then you've got day traders who realize this is a consolidation breakout: The noodles are bouncing; I'm in. Then you've got cranks who are going to try to squeeze it right back up the other way. First Boston—every time he upticks that stock, it's going to move. It's a self-fulfilling prophecy. Every time he upticks, he's going to scare the other shorts to cover, and he's going to cause other traders to jump in so that they can lean on him.

We got most of that, but an obvious question remains: Why would there be an ax?

Let's go back to First Boston. I have an order for 100,000 shares of Broadcom. The market makers—the biggest advantage they have is order flow. If I'm a market maker and I know I've got 100,000 shares to buy, I know the stock's going to move, and I know that I can buy shares and join in on the ride. A market maker is not going to try to be transparent. He might try to go in and collect 70,000 shares. He might try to shake traders out of the stock by making it look weak, inviting in shorts. Eventually, as he gets close to filling that block, he doesn't want the mutual funds to be ticked off that they got a crappy fill. So, the times that the market makers are going to try actively to be an ax are when they're close to filling that order. They'll go ahead and try to get the remaining shares of the institutional order and cause a squeeze, so to speak, for the tail end of whatever he needs to buy. He might have gotten most of his shares averaged at $74.75, $75, but he knows that he's at the tail end of filling that institutional order, so he wants to let everybody know now that he's a heavy buyer in this stock. As he's holding against the oscillations, accumulating shares, he's actually building up more buying pressure on the other side. Once the noodles reverse, First Boston's going to keep upticking, upticking, trying to run that stock as high as he can. So, when he finally sells it to the institution, they're going to say, "Wow, he got me in at $75.50. 100,000 shares. I love you guys! I'll be back for more business!"

One of the best times to be watching an ax is on IPOs. I don't know if you were watching KPMG Consulting, KCIN, today—120 million share IPO by Morgan Stanley. Here's a pure example of utilizing an ax. KCIN opened around $21. Initially, Morgan Stanley steps on the bid and starts eating up shares. Most IPOs are junk, so you're going to have traders and market makers that come in and short the IPO right from the get-go. You've got Morgan Stanley, who needs to get rid of a hell of a lot of shares. What Morgan Stanley does is jump in at $21. You've got market makers who are already cross-locked the other way, at $20.75; you've got shorts that are coming in; you've got cranks that figure, "This IPO's got too much of a float; we're going to short it." Morgan Stanley comes in, and he sits at $21. He eats millions of shares right on the open. He ate so many shares that everybody who shorted against him got scared and went the other way. The day traders who are watching the stock realize, "Holy cow, Morgan Stanley's holding the sucker up. I'm in!" *Bang!* Market makers who want to buy the shares jump in ahead of Morgan Stanley. Once KCIN starts to rise, what does Morgan Stanley do? He keeps upping his bid. Sure, Morgan Stanley is dumping shares. He's got millions of shares to get out and into the open. But, as long as he shows himself to be the ax, he doesn't mind swallowing a million shares so that he can dump three or four million shares. Every time the stock started to show a little wiggle, Morgan Stanley jumped in on the inside bid, and he upped the bid.

To make a long story short, KCIN ran from $21 to $24.25, where it peaked out. I told people, "Get the hell out of this thing now. Morgan Stanley can't take on the world forever." On IPOs, you always watch the lead underwriter. He's the de facto ax.

What happened to KCIN when Morgan Stanley stopped playing the game?

When Morgan Stanley stepped off the bid, the stock collapsed to around $23. When the ax steps off, the stock will collapse. That's why I tell traders to always be paring, always be selling. Because the ax cannot stay the ax forever.

Just to step back a bit. You keep mentioning cranks. What exactly is a crank?

I believe the SEC has a word for that—it's called spoofing. It's not legal; it's something that I definitely tell my traders not to do. But it's a fact of life. It's a fact of this game. And they are effective, so you're going to have to live with them. A crank is when you see a large-sized order on an ECN on the inside, be it the inside ask or the inside bid. When you see 6,000, 10,000, 15,000 shares on the bid—even a Level 1 screen is going to be able to see it—it's going to knee-jerk a lot of people to jump in on the ask. Now, you have to understand that if a guy wants to buy 15,000 shares, he's not going to sit on the bid and display it. The cardinal sin in this game is to show your hand. When somebody throws 15,000 shares on the bid, they're doing it for a reason. They're doing it so that they can make you believe the perception, the illusion, that there's a heavy buyer and that you are going to be able to step in front of him—you're going to be able to step in front of this buyer and lean on him, kind of like an ax. Cranks are not absolutely stupid, either. The noodles are rising, so the stock is already trying to oscillate back up. The spreads are already being adjusted back up to match the noodles as the noodles are rising. There's buying in the market. The wind is beneath your wings, and there's a buy-side bias in the market at this point. But the crank is not looking to get hit; he's looking to accelerate the buying. He's looking to accelerate the upticks. He's looking to accelerate the panic.

Is that because he already owns the stock?

He's already got shares, so what is he trying to do? He's trying to sell into the buyers.

And who are these cranks?

They're market makers. They're professional traders. Even day traders.

Let's switch gears for a minute and talk about a few practical issues. Do you have any recommendations as to which ECN traders should use?

Absolutely. Island to Island is the fastest. No questions about it.

What makes Island different?

The beauty about Island is that you can use what is known as a sweep order. In other words, Island has its own limit book. It's almost like Nasdaq Level 2; it has all the standing orders on the bid and the ask, by price, just like Level 2. Nasdaq Level 2 is only going to show you the best or the inside Island bid and the inside Island ask. So, you always should have the Island book up. [Island's limit order book can be accessed at www.island.com.] In a panic situation, don't even fudge around with trying to hit the inside. Place a sweep order one quarter to a half point, under the bid, and get out. You know the trade is bad. You know the trade went wrong. Now, do you want to lose a finger or an arm? The only way you can get out fast is when you use an Island sweep order. You're not looking to get out on Island a half point below the bid. But, if you try to be stingy and hit the inside, someone may have already hit it, and now you just wasted precious seconds where you've got to reenter the order at a lower price. Hands down, bar none, the best fills, the best transparency, the ability to sweep—Island.

Now to the UndergroundTrader chat room: Describe your interaction with the group. How many recommendations will you make in a day?

I'll make anywhere between 10 and 20 throughout the day. The new traders should never trade the trade alerts because they don't know the stock. You have to know the premise for why I'm calling the trade alert, and you have to be able to manage it. Nothing irks me more than a new trader that jumps in on a trade alert and panics right out because he doesn't understand the premises of the trade alert. Throughout the day, I'll explain the trade alert. On trade alerts, I might get anywhere from 5 or 10 or 30 people that jump in. That's about it. The rest are just watching and waiting, and they're using the trade alert more as an alert to watch the stock. The reality is that if my call stinks, or if my signal stinks, it doesn't matter how many people jump in. My people are educated enough to say, "You know what, Jay, that call stunk; I'm getting out of the stock." I try to cater to the person who has done their homework to an extent. They've done their homework, and they want to learn.

So you do mess up every once in a while. What is an acceptable loss on a trade, and how do you recommend that people get out?

I assume that traders know the stock and that they understand the premises for the trade. One of the best analogies I've ever read: A good trader is like a good batter—he can literally count the stitches on the fastball. In other words, a good trader is going to know when the premises are whacked. As far as the amount of damage that a person is going to take, it's going to boil down to a person's skill level and experience. A good trader is going to be able to salvage something.

Let's say we're playing Broadcom, and I'm looking for a breakout through $85. Broadcom's been consolidating; 15-period support sitting at $84.50, five-period resistance sitting at $84.75. Noodles are on the ground and look like they're going to break out. I'll jump into Broadcom here. The 15-period support is strong. I could take my stop at the 15-period support, but the reality is that Broadcom usually wiggles underneath and above these 15 and five periods by a half point. So I give myself a stop a half point to three quarters under the 15 period. As long as my premises hold up, I'm going to stay in that trade. Let's say the noodles move back up. Great, Broadcom buyers come in. Broadcom is ticking now. Broadcom is ticking $85.25, $85.30, $85.50. Then, all of a sudden, the noodles tank on me. The noodles tried; they tanked. I'm still in that trade. I'm still in that trade until Broadcom breaks back down from the consolidation, which will happen around $83.50 or $83.75.

You've talked a lot about scalping one or fewer points on any given trade—mostly off of breakouts and breakdowns. Are there any other trading strategies you'd recommend?

Some people prefer to swing trade, because it's not as tenuous and there's not as much tick watching involved. Some people prefer the scalp because you're not a sitting duck in that stock. Personally, I'm a scalper. I like scalps. Sun Tzu said, "A skilled fighter puts himself in a position that's undefeatable." Well, in this market—in any market—an undefeatable position is cash.

Chapter 18

BEAUTY AND THE STREET
Karin Housley

Internet Alias	Investment Style
Chick Karin	Long-term
Year of Birth	**Location**
1964	Calgary, Alberta; Afton, MN
Education	
BA, communications, SUNY Buffalo	
Web Site (Free)	
Chicks Laying Nest Eggs: www.chickslayingnesteggs.com	

It wasn't long ago that Karin Housley thought an IPO was "one of those flying things you read about in the *National Enquirer*." Even now, after landing funding for an investment web site (see Figure 18.1), hobnobbing with the famous Motley Fools, and authoring a successful guide to investing—she couldn't quite understand why we'd be interested in interviewing an ordinary mother of four.

But two hours of talking to Housley is all it took for us to realize that her life is anything but ordinary. Housley's husband, Phil, is a veteran of the National Hockey League—a journeyman who's put together envious numbers in his 20-year career. But only a die-hard fan could have followed Phil—and Karin—through the teams and locations in which they've played and lived: Buffalo, Winnipeg, St. Louis, Calgary, New Jersey, Washington, and back to Calgary. The first time we talked to her on the phone, she was somewhere in Minnesota; sounds from her kids streaking through the room competed with ringing cell phones and Barbie phones that sounded like cell phones. There was a disaster with a

Figure 18.1   www.chickslayingnesteggs.com
Source: Chicks Laying Nest Eggs.

FedEx package she was expecting. And, oh yeah, one of her friend's husbands was traded to a different hockey team.

Before all this, Housley studied at the University of New York in Buffalo. She was the associate producer of several news programs for ABC and NBC. Then her husband got traded to Winnipeg. "I moved, and I couldn't work. So I just had babies. That was it," she says. Such is life.

Now Housley is a "Chick"—a member of the Chicks Laying Nest Eggs Investment Club—and as such, she is required to lounge around in her pajamas, take back control of her family's finances, and enjoy investing with friends. And there are pictures of all this at her site. It's the type of stuff that producers of the *Oprah Winfrey Show* dream of. Despite admittedly learning how to invest only in 1998, the Chicks have developed a careful 12-point checklist for analyzing companies. See Figure 18.2 to get the lowdown on the rules.

It sounds like simple advice, but the key is the investment club. Ten heads are a force to be reckoned with, and Karin has put together a way for women (and men—don't be shy; just pick a unisex username so as not to draw too much attention to yourself!) to get started investing with friends. ChicksLayingNestEggs.com will teach you how to start a

Step 1. Buy What You Know
How well do you know it; how often do you use it; and how much do you like it?

Step 2. K.I.S.S.
Keep it simple, sister. Can you easily explain the product's industry to your cute little niece? Can you draw it with a crayon?

Step 3. Industry
Who are its competitors? Is the industry growing faster than other industries? Do you understand it?

Step 4. Leader in Its Field
Is the company top dog in its industry? Is it the leader of the pack? (Sing it with me: Leader of the Pack . . . vrooooom, vrooooom).

Step 5. Repeat Profitability
Is this a company that has an opportunity to make a profit from its customers time after time? Will consumers use it again and again or over and over?

Step 6. Gross Margins
Are gross margins at least 50 percent?

Step 7. Net Margins
Are net margins at least 8 percent?

Step 8. Cash to Long-Term Debt
Does the company have more cash than long-term debt?

Step 9. Flow Ratio
Is the company's flow ratio better than 1.25? [The flow ratio is a concoction designed by the Motley Fools that gives a measure of a company's operating efficiency and inventory control. The calculation of the flow ratio is as follows: (Current Assets – Cash) / (Current Liabilities – Short-Term Debt).]

Step 10. Increasing Growth
Is the growth of the company (and its industry) moving in a positive direction? Are revenues (sales) increasing?

Step 11. Strong Management and History
Who are the people running the company? What have they done? Do you like what they stand for? What is the company's history?

Step 12. On Sale
Is its stock price lower than its 52-week average?

Figure 18.2 The Chicks' Dozen
Source: Chicks Laying Nest Eggs (www.chickslayingnesteggs.com).

new investment club—from forming a partnership to setting down club bylaws and operating procedures. You can set up a message board for club communication and hold meetings in a club-only chat room. That leaves just one thing: actually picking stocks. Not a problem. You can read other clubs' message boards and see what they're buying—even the

Chicks communicate openly online about their portfolio. The Daily Focus, written by a different Chick each day, highlights great companies, investment tips, and CEOs.

The first thing you'll want to do when you get to the site is "Meet the Chicks" (that's where the pajama picture is!). In the following pages you'll meet the Head Chick and hear how 10 women put Wall Street in their pajama pockets.

You were a communications and psychology major in college, and you worked in television media after leaving school. How did you become interested in investing?

I never really was interested, not even the slightest bit interested. We had this guy in Philadelphia who was handling all of our money, and I was busy moving around the country and having babies. But when the fourth one came, and we thought Phil was going to retire, I freaked. You hear all these stories of players who retire and have no idea what is going on with their money—someone could be siphoning off the top. I totally trusted this guy who was handling our money, but I was still angry with myself for being clueless. I'd call him up and try to go over the statements that I'd get every month, and he would speak way over my head. I would try to get him to strip it down to my language, but he couldn't, because that was the language he spoke, and this is what I spoke. So I read one of those books—I think it was *The Motley Fool Investment Guide*. And I thought, "This is so unbelievably awesome; I'm going to invest in the stock market!" But I didn't. I thought I was going to, but I didn't.

That's when I decided to e-mail all of my girlfriends and ask if they could help me figure this out, because I wanted to see how what the guy was doing in Philly—it was all mutual funds and annuities—would compare to investing strictly in stocks. Then I would be able to understand what he was doing with the money and how our future looked. I've got to send four kids to college. You would think that after playing 20 years in the NHL you would have money, but I was still losing sleep at night trying to figure out if we were okay. So, I got my girlfriends together, and between the 10 of us, we stripped down the language to something we could understand. That's how I got interested, and now I'm addicted.

Why was it important to discuss your questions and worries with other women?

Because women are social beings—much more so than men. Men are more private about their stock market careers and their investments, so they keep to themselves. But women need support for anything that they do; they need the help and support of other women. I read some books about Warren Buffett, and I read some books by Peter Lynch. And still, I was sitting there going, "I kind of understand it, but not really." Then I read *The Motley Fool Investment Guide,* and I wanted to do it. I really wanted to invest. But I was too scared to do it by myself.

Are there any characteristics of women that make them better stock pickers than men?

I think women are just patient. That's the greatest characteristic of any stock picker.

What about a willingness to work together that men don't exhibit?

Men are secretive about the stocks that they're going to buy until after they buy it. Why? You're not going to change the world by buying 100 shares. In contrast, women ask, "What do you think about this?" They like to get the opinions of other women. Women don't bring egos to the table. Their families and their home life are much more important than their money, and I think that's flipped when it's men. Money is very important to women, but it's not number one on our list. I think that we can put it all in perspective much more easily than men can. When the stock market has a down day, we just say, "You know what, I'm going to go to the park with the kids. Screw the market." But guys, they go to sleep with it.

   The title of our book is *Chicks Laying Nest Eggs: How Ten Ordinary Women Started an Online Investment Club and Crushed the Market— And How You Can, Too.* We were a little upset about this title, because that's not what it's all about, especially for women. For men, the only reason you want to be in the stock market is to make money. Women have fun hanging out with other women and learning about this stuff, learning about balance sheets and income statements and, more importantly, learning about how companies are run. You're sitting in the grocery store and you see Starbucks, and you think, "I'm going to go home and run Starbucks through the Chicks' Dozen." Your whole way of looking at the world is so much different that it's empowering, as much as I hate that word. It's an Oprah word. But it is empowering to know about companies and about the corporate world.

Given the advantages that women investors seem to have, why are there so many men on Wall Street?

Because there have always been men on Wall Street. It's going to be slow to change.

What are the mechanics of your investment club? How do you pick stocks? How much money does each person contribute?

We buy a stock every three months. We each invest $50 a month, so that's $500 a month, and every three months it's $1,500. So, we invest in the market four times a year, $1,500 each time. We last bought in December. January is pretty much our downtime, and we don't do a lot except keep tracking the companies. Each girl will find a company to track—if there are any news releases or if earnings come out, you post that to the message board, and that's all you're required to do for January. We do all of our meetings online. At February's meeting, every girl comes to the table with a new company that they want to research, and that can come from various areas of her life. At the March meeting, we have it narrowed down to three out of 10 companies that we really like, and then we vote. We dissect the companies during the two weeks prior to the buy; we get down and dirty, and sometimes, some of the girls are adamant about not buying one of them.

Fifty dollars per month doesn't sound very substantial. Do you tend to use the investment club for education purposes rather than as your primary investment vehicle?

I think investment clubs should be used as education, especially for women, because we're just leery. All of us were in the club, and it still took me five months to do my own investing. I was putting my $50 a month in with the club, but I was still scared to death to open my own online account. It took my mother two years. We're hesitant beings. I don't think women would do anything over $100 a month; I think that's too much. Have your own personal portfolio to see if you beat your investment club. I know I am not beating my investment club. I wish I had listened to the nine other women when it came to investing in stuff like Amazon. They vetoed Amazon.com, and I said, "Come on, it's the future." I still believe in it; there's no way I'm selling it. Collectively, they're a lot more cautious than I am. I have no qualms about being 90 percent technology, but my mother is in the club, and there is no way she is going to be that tech heavy. Even having America Online and Yahoo! was too much for her. She vetoed Yahoo! but got outnumbered.

Do you think it's important for the members of investment clubs to live in the same geographic area?

We didn't feel it was very important for us to be within miles of each other. Some people want to be able to see the other people in their club face to face more often than we do. I think that when you're starting a club, the best thing is to get online. It's so much easier when you do it online than when you do it face to face. If you're going to report on Pfizer at a face-to-face meeting, you have 10 women and 10 different reports, and you're going to start talking about the new patents or the new drugs. To sit through that 10 times over—each girl's report is 10 to 15 minutes long—by the end of all that, you're just ready to go home. Who even wants to sit there and vote? So, I think it's important when you start a club that you find a place online, get a message board, and do most of your communicating on there because studies have shown that most clubs end up dissolving after two or three years because people are tired of going to the meetings and sitting there. One of the things that saved us was getting online and getting a message board.

Are all the investment clubs on your site for females only?

No, one group of men just got a message board on the site. They said they hoped we didn't mind if they were spying on what we were doing. I think there may be some guys lurking on our site, reading the stuff and not admitting it. I don't know if they really like the chick pajamas or if they're reading the investment content, but I know there are a couple that are lurking. They would never say anything.

One of the tenets of your Chicks' Dozen is, "Keep it simple, sister." Why is that important?

We had a vote one time that came down to Amgen and General Electric—it was the only vote in which we were tied five to five [see Figure 18.3]. It was about 45 minutes online, going back and forth and back and forth: Why GE? Why Amgen? Why not Amgen? Why not GE? Jack Welch was stepping down; that was a minus. Amgen was in an industry that none of us really understood. We knew it was growing gangbusters, but we didn't really understand it. GE is a god of a company, and Amgen is still relatively new. Back and forth, back and forth. GE eventually won because Chick Susie kept throwing questions at us about Neupogen and other drugs that Amgen had come out with or had patents on, and about the new patents that were pending. And who really understood them? How do we know that it's the leader in biotech companies? What about Genentech? Susie was throwing out all of these questions, and that got a few people to break at the end because we didn't know the answers. It was just a little over our heads. So, that point of the Chicks' Dozen is just as important as gross margins being over 50 percent. "Keep it simple, sister" is just as important as the numbers.

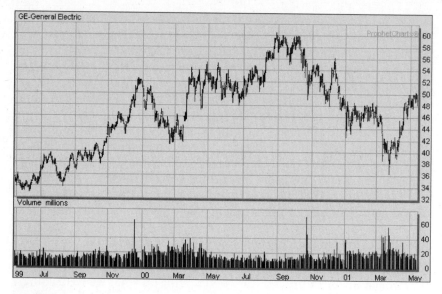

Figure 18.3 General Electric (NYSE: GE), May 1999–May 2001
Source: Prophet Financial Systems, Inc. (www.ProphetFinance.com).

When do you sell?

We have to own a company for at least two years. We buy, and then that's it. We're in for two years, unless some disaster happens, like Larry Ellison dies on his yacht in one of his sailboat races.

Have you sold any stocks yet?

No. Gap is on the block [see Figure 18.4]. We're going to discuss it at this March meeting. Chick Megan wants to sell. I still love the Gap; I just think it's going through a reorganization. This is how women are. We love the Gap. We buy our kids' clothes there. They're just going through a little problem; they'll be back on their feet. The great companies do that. You see it in all of them. They have a reorganization period, and they're back in the right direction.

You also recommend that people focus on industry-leading companies. Why?

We want our companies to be the leaders in their fields because they're the biggest and the most well known. When you're in that spot, you can grow faster than the others by scooping up smaller companies. They're

Figure 18.4   Gap (NYSE: GPS), May 1999–May 2001
Source: Prophet Financial Systems, Inc. (www.ProphetFinance.com).

the company that everybody turns to. They're not going anywhere; we can sleep owning them because they've been around a long time and deserve respect.

Where do you look to find those companies?

We look in our own houses, in our own environments, in our own lives. For example, Starbucks has been up to buy for many votes [see Figure 18.5]. I am there every single day with all of my kids; I just brought the kids there for lunch. We were at a grocery store in Minnesota, and right in the grocery store was a Starbucks. In the back of the church that we go to in Calgary is a Starbucks. Everywhere you turn—you think that they've saturated the market, but they're still growing. So we always look somewhere in our lives for a company that we know and use and want to pull through the Chicks' Dozen and see if it meets our criteria. Do we think this company is growing? Do we feel it's going to be around 10 years from now, and be even bigger than it is now? Unless you know and use it in your everyday life, there's no way that you can judge its growth. Chick Julie always brings up some sporting goods company. She's totally into that whole field, which is great. I know nothing about the company, but Julie knows everything, and I trust Julie to tell me what she thinks. Then

Figure 18.5   Starbucks (Nasdaq: SBUX), May 1999–May 2001
Source: Prophet Financial Systems, Inc. (www.ProphetFinance.com).

there's Susie, who knows everything about NHL teams and sporting arenas. Lynn used to be a nurse, so she knows all about the medical field. When you have an investment club, everybody brings his or her own areas of life to the table, so you can diversify that way.

What do you think of Wall Street professionals? Do you look at analyst recommendations before you buy?

Honestly, we do not look at anything that anybody recommends. It all comes from us. Why would anybody want to sit there and listen to a guy on the TV or in the newspaper tell you from day to day which stocks he thinks you should buy or shouldn't buy? You would go crazy trying to keep track of every single analyst telling you what's good today and what's not. There's not enough time in my day to sit there and watch. I wouldn't be comfortable listening to somebody else tell me what to buy. I'm buying a stock because I want to buy it, not because somebody else says it's the buy of the week. I don't dislike them. I just giggle at the way everybody follows everything that they say.

You can ask people, "Why did you sell your Gap stock?" And they'll say, "Because it dropped five points." Well, it's going to drop five points. Every single stock you buy is going to drop at some point or another. I don't think a lot of Americans are long-term buy and hold. They're always in for the quick return. They want to buy a stock, turn it around a week later, and make money. Then you count all of their transaction fees every single time they whip one around like that and the time that they spend—at the end of the year, was it really worth the $220 gain that they have to pay taxes on? It baffles me, but I guess some people like to do it that way. I don't know if it's a game or if it's an addiction. Life is way too short to get wrapped up in buying and selling.

What is the biggest mistake that most investors make?

I think the biggest mistake people make when investing in the stock market is not having a philosophy, because if you have a philosophy, whether it be a personal philosophy or a club philosophy, you're going to put a lot more thought into buying in the first place. I think that people need to have their own investment philosophy before they put any money in the market. It will save you a lot of heartache and questioning after the fact. The second mistake is that a lot of people panic. It's human nature. They think the whole world is caving in. I think that people have to look at the reasons that they're buying and selling, and not panic when the market turns, which is great with an investment club, because you've got nine other people.

But you still say you watch the stock market day by day?

Because I'm addicted. I find the market interesting. I really enjoy it; it's like a hobby. For 10 minutes a day, usually before I go to bed at night, I'll hop on my computer, see what happened that day, and then get off.

Do you find it frustrating when your stocks are going down?

No. You don't get frustrated. You just roll your eyes and remind yourself what your philosophy is. But I do get excited when they go up, if that was going to be your next question.

We were going to ask about your best and worst buys.

Personally, my best is Amgen, because as soon as we didn't buy it as a club, I went right out and bought it, and now it's up 450 percent in two years [see Figure 18.6]. As a club, America Online is our biggest winner, with Nokia not far behind. Our worst has been Yahoo!, and personally it's been Yahoo!, too.

Is there any way you could have avoided your Yahoo loss?

We didn't see the market going any lower. People think of the whole Internet sector like it's all one company. When you get the Pricelines and

Figure 18.6 Amgen (Nasdaq: AMGN), May 1998–May 2001
Source: Prophet Financial Systems, Inc. (www.ProphetFinance.com).

the Pets.coms, and all of those start going out of business, they think Yahoo! is the next one, but they don't even know what Yahoo!'s balance sheet and income statement look like. They just all of a sudden sell their Yahoo! stock because all the Internet companies are going out of business. It's hard to convince somebody about what's going on inside the company when they're totally clueless.

Do your husbands invest?

With a few girls, there's this little competition going on between the husband and the wife. My sister Jana and her husband Mac—he's got his portfolio, she has her portfolio, and then they have the Chicks that they're both trying to beat. The Chicks are winning.

Chapter 19

WHARTON WIZARD

Jeremy Siegel

Internet Alias	Investment Style
Jeremy Siegel	Long-term

Year of Birth	Location
1945	Philadelphia, PA

Education	
BA, mathematics and economics, Columbia University; PhD, economics, Massachusetts Institute of Technology	

Web Site (Free/Pay)	
JeremySiegel.com: www.jeremysiegel.com	

Ten days after the September 11, 2001, attacks on the Pentagon and World Trade Center, one word can describe the economic, political, and emotional mood of the United States: uncertain. Uncertainty weighs on the minds of the country's citizens and leaders as they decide on an appropriate reaction to the tragedy. Uncertainty leads tourism and consumer spending to a temporary halt, with repercussions that ripple through the economy. And uncertainty, according to Wharton finance professor Jeremy Siegel, obliterated over $1 trillion of market capitalization in the week following the attacks.

When the shock of the terrorism finally subsided and some semblance of normalcy returned to our lives, we decided to find a final interviewee for the book. Such a life-altering event with national and international implications could not go ignored in these pages—not to mention the fact that we wanted someone to make us more certain that the economy and the spirit of the American people would overcome the catastrophe.

Figure 19.1   www.JeremySiegel.com
Source: JeremySiegel.com.

We found ourselves spending a lot of time on the Internet on the day of and in the days following the tragedy, keeping tabs on the latest tales of heroism and war. The chatter on most stock-related message boards turned from profit seeking to concern for the families of the missing and deceased. The individuals on the ActiveTrader IRC chat channel (see Chapter 10) coped by discussing news and telling stories of the horror. In fact, for up-to-the-minute happenings, the distributed mass of individuals in the chat room and on message boards provided a far more effective means of information dissemination than did the television networks. Chat participants often had intelligence on the disaster a full 15 minutes before it was broadcast on CNN or rival stations.

Once the shock subsided, we discovered that numerous nervous individuals were turning to the Internet for advice on how the disaster would affect the economy and their own portfolios. One bit of e-mail we received that week stood out:

In light of the terrorist attack on the United States, the economic out-look has turned extremely pessimistic. A recession is 90 percent prob-able. The Fed must lower interest rates 50 basis points immediately. If not, the stock market is apt to drop 10 percent on reopening and con-tinue to fall after that. Downside risk of 20 percent or more is envi-sioned. Although the short-run market outlook is very pessimistic, a declining market will open up long-term opportunities.

Jeremy Siegel graduated from Columbia University in 1967 and re-ceived his doctorate in economics from the Massachusetts Institute of Technology in 1971. He's been teaching at the Wharton School of the University of Pennsylvania since 1976, and he rocketed to fame with the 1994 publication of *Stocks for the Long Run*. The book is Siegel's trea-tise on long-term, broad indexed-based investing and is lauded as one of the best investment books ever written. He now makes regular appear-ances on CNBC and CNN and is often quoted in the financial media. So when Jeremy Siegel says the Fed must lower interest rates, it is not so much a prediction as a recommendation. That's the type of respect given to this professor who studies the stock market like the Bible and whose Bloomberg machine is attached intravenously to avoid any delay in re-ceiving market information. With e-mail in hand and his best-selling book on our shelves, we knew that Siegel was our man. Nothing pro-vides credible reassurance better than a brilliant, long-term bull.

Our first experience with Siegel was as Wharton freshmen, staring through windows in the main undergraduate business school center, Steinberg-Dietrich Hall, as the eccentric professor presented a jam-packed Finance 101 class with his famous 15-minute daily market com-mentary that preceded every lesson. During our junior year, we were chosen to participate in a minilecture series with Siegel, and we finally figured out why he is such a popular professor. In three two-hour ses-sions, Siegel jumped from his statistical-market studies to up-to-the-minute information on commodities, consumer sentiment, and other various economic indicators. It was market minutiae to the nth degree, but to Siegel it was an intricate storyline more interesting than any novel. He pieced together disparate facets of finance into a meaningful picture of the stock market's mechanics.

When JeremySiegel.com (see Figure 19.1) launched in mid-2000, we rushed to register at the site. In fact, that is why we received Siegel's e-mail market commentary the week of the September 11 tragedy. The site is still a work in progress—the message boards are barren and, ac-cording to Siegel, more features are under construction—but there is no better place to follow the thoughts and theories of this market maven. Data sets, presentations, and charts from Siegel's lecture circuit are posted to the site. Most recently, efforts have focused on making every Siegel radio, television, and print appearance available at the touch of a mouse so that individual investors can track his every thought. Devoted fans can register for the site's highest level of membership and receive personal e-mail responses to questions posed to the busy professor.

Even though he is often a short-term bear, Siegel is always ready to recommend a calm, long-term approach to the markets. "Stocks for the long run," he preaches and teaches. For the first time in a long time, though, he divulges in our interview that the markets are undervalued and ready—once uncertainty subsides—to make a long-term bull run.

Do you think that the terrorist attacks of September 11, 2001, accelerated an inevitable fall in the markets? Would the markets have eventually fallen to these levels, regardless?

The economy was in a precarious situation, and the markets very likely had more adjustments to make before the attack, but clearly this made the situation worse than it would otherwise have been.

Can you talk about the market mechanics that caused the dramatic fall? Was the reaction efficient, or was it a panic?

You have to understand that whenever there is an increase in uncertainty, there is a shortening of investors' planning and investment horizons. Returns far in the future get discounted at a higher rate, and because stock prices depend on cash flows that are far into the future, those cash flows are going to be worth less. That is what sends stock prices down in times of uncertainty.

The media have been filled with stories of patriotic individual investors opening new accounts. Even Warren Buffett announced that he will not sell because of the attacks. So where is all the downward pressure coming from?

From what I understand, most small investors are basically holding firm. A lot of the institutions are selling, and there are redemptions from mutual funds. There is also some foreign selling. But mostly there are just not many buyers. You don't have many people right now that are willing to step up to the plate at these prices. If there is news that motivates sellers and not many buyers, the price must definitely go down.

What would cause a change in sentiment?

The only way to change the sentiment is to reduce the uncertainty. As long as uncertainty reigns over the market, it's very hard to get people to commit to long-run assets such as equities.

Would it be unfair to say that large-scale emotional sell-offs are a guaranteed buying opportunity?

For the long run, they tend to be a very good buying opportunity. But one has to remember that sometimes you get emotional sell-offs from markets that are considerably overvalued; even with the sell-off, the market may not get down to a fair valuation. An example of that was in April 2000 when the Nasdaq went down 500 points in one day. There was emotional selling, but the Nasdaq was too high even after that decline.

How does one make that determination between a buying opportunity and an extended downtrend? How would you characterize this week's decline?

I think stocks are good long-term values today. Long-term stockholders will do better in equities than they would have done if they bought before the attack or a year ago. I estimate that from current levels, long-run, after-inflation annual rates of return will be somewhere between 5 percent and 7 percent per year.

What is the most important factor in coming to that conclusion?

I consider that the price-earning ratio of the S&P in normal times should be in the low 20s. We have earnings now that are going to be depressed dramatically this year, but normal earnings for the S&P 500 as a whole are around $50 per share right now. That would mean that 1,000 to 1,100 would be the current fair value of the S&P 500 Index. We're now at 970, so we're below fair value.

Why should stocks converge to a predictable PE ratio? Why the low 20s?

The PE ratio of the S&P 500 has historically averaged around 15; I've done research that implies that with certain structural changes in the economy and the market, the fair value of the PE is now appreciably higher. I put the fair market PE ratio in the low 20s for the S&P.

Does a long-run convergence to a certain PE ratio help explain the core argument in *Stocks for the Long Run* that the equity market is best for those with a long planning horizon? Explain how stocks become less risky over the long run.

I've done statistical studies showing that the historical standard deviation of longer-term returns—more than 15 years in length—in the stock market happen to be less than that of the bond market and less than the return from rolling over in money markets. That is why I've come to the

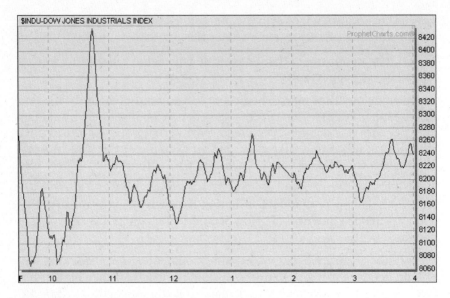

Figure 19.2   Dow Jones Industrial Average, September 21, 2001
Source: Prophet Financial Systems, Inc. (www.ProphetFinance.com).

conclusion that in the long run, stocks are far less risky than they are in the short run.

[Siegel interrupts the interview with a reaction to the markets . . .]

Wow, the stock market has turned around 300 points in about 20 minutes [see Figure 19.2]. That's quite dramatic. We'll see how long *that* rally lasts. [Siegel's disbelief that the market could sustain its intraday rally was dead-on. The Dow opened at 8,356 on September 21, 2001, hit a high of 8,438 during our interview, but subsequently tanked and closed the day at 8,235.]

It's funny that you would notice the market's gyrations during our conversation. You're well known for being glued to your Bloomberg terminal for up-to-the-minute news and market information. Is it important for the average investor to keep close tabs on the stock market?

No, it's not at all important for the average investor.

How often should average investors tune into CNBC?

They can check it as often as they would like, but the evidence is that the less often they act on the short-term movement of prices, the better off they will be. Investors tend to get scared out of the market when it is precipitously falling and prices are low. If you follow too closely, you can get wrapped up in the sentiment of the moment. There is evidence that it is usually a good time to move in the market when there is fear and trepidation. And if there is a tremendous amount of confidence or over-confidence, investors should be wary of stocks. You can really make a lot of wrong decisions if you give in to your emotions.

Given that applied finance is a relatively new discipline, what progress is left to be made? What are the most perplexing problems yet to be solved?

Finance as a rigorous discipline is fairly new. The most perplexing problem is how to integrate the behavior and psychology of individuals with the "rational man" model—which assumes the goal of maximizing expected utility—that has dominated finance theory. Integration of behavioral finance into financial models is occurring now.

Will that integration cause a significant change in thinking among practitioners and academics? For example, will we see a dramatic change in the curriculum of a Wharton class five or ten years from now?

I think it will shift what is taught. You have to understand that the field of economics, which is based on utility maximization of a rational man, has gotten economists pretty far over the past 250 years. Essentially, economics says that individuals maximize their utility, and when you get to an area of uncertainty, you're maximizing your *expected* utility. But it appears that some more psychological and behavioral characteristics might make the uncertainty model less useful than the certainty model.

To what extent do individual investors need to understand the theory of finance?

They have to understand the principles of diversification; they have to understand the principles of how a changing time frame affects their investments; and they have to understand what long-run returns are possible in the market. I think that some of the problems in year 2000 were due to investors' overly optimistic expectations about what returns were possible in the equity market.

What about understanding history? Should investors be familiar with particular boom and bust cycles?

No—just that they have occurred in the past and they will occur in the future.

Speaking of boom and bust cycles, in a recent *New York Times* article, Robert Shiller said it is possible that the Dow could be lower after inflation in 2011 than it is today. [Siegel's personal friend and occasional academic counterpoint, Robert Shiller, is a Yale professor of economics and the author of *Irrational Exuberance*.]

I don't think that is going to be the case.

What would have to happen for that to come true?

Over periods of even several years, stocks can sell at a discount or premium to their true long-run value. But 10 years out, I can't say that 10,000 is my best guess of where the stock market will be. It could be there, but the market also could be at a large premium again. I think the fair value going out—I have to do some calculations. Let me take a look at my calculator . . .

Currently, the dividend rate is about 2 percent on the Dow. If you assume that there is only going to be a 5 percent real return (and that is pessimistic) over the next 10 years, that would be a 3 percent real appreciation in the Dow index. 1.03 to the tenth power is 1.34. If we multiply that by the current level of the Dow, which is 8,391, we get 11,276. However, I think the current level is now undervalued for the long run. If you say that 1,000 is the fair value of the S&P 500 and that corresponds to 9,000 on the Dow, that would give over 12,000 for the real level on the Dow in 2011. It could be as low as 10,000; that's a real possibility. I think that 10,000 would be within the range of two standard errors, but it's not my best guess.

What national and international trends will dominate the economy over those next 10 years?

On the domestic side, the aging of the population is important. Breakthroughs in biotechnology are going to be very critical and extend life expectancy. Internationally, the whole question of globalization will dominate. Globalization is the integration of world economies so that we can all enjoy the benefits of trade and comparative advantage. My feeling is that globalization will better the lot of the world's population significantly. The events going on now [the terrorist attacks in New York City and Washington, D.C.] certainly put a hold on much of the progress that has been made toward globalization.

What opportunities might the aging of the population open up to investors?

You have to think about what kinds of goods they will buy.

Sounds easy. But is it possible to pick specific stocks? Is there such a thing as a good stock picker over the long run?

There is definitely such a thing as someone who *has* picked good stocks. Does that mean that he or she will be able to pick good stocks in the future? That's an open question.

Very few individuals have had very good investment performance that cannot be attributed in large part to luck. Unfortunately, there is also a psychological propensity in that the average individual sees somebody win three, four, five times in a row and believes he's a winner. Go to the craps table in any casino. Once someone starts winning four, five, six times, everyone thinks, "Boy, this guy's a winner!" Well, you know, the probability that he's going to lose on the next roll is no different now than it was on the very first roll he made. People think there's something to a streak of good luck; they think that someone who has done well in the past will do well in the future. I'm not saying that there are those who won't continue to perform well, but it's still an open question.

What approach should the individual investor take to tackling the markets?

I recommend that they buy my book.

Would that lead people to invest in index funds and broad-based sector funds . . . ?

I'm coming out in 2002 with a third edition of my book. There is a question that the growth in indexing may have led to some overvaluation of popularly indexed stocks. The evidence is not conclusive, but to the extent that, for instance, stocks that get added into the S&P 500 jump up in price, that would lead to lower long-run returns for the investor. I'm exploring that at the present. I have not come up with a definitive conclusion, but it does provide a caution.

If that were true, what would it mean for the investor?

If overvaluation happened more with the S&P 500 stocks than it did with the others, it would mean that you'd want to shave down the S&P relative to its market weight.

Back to the terrorist attack to conclude the interview: As registered members of JeremySiegel.com, we occasionally get e-mails from you with predictions of the Fed's actions. Could you comment on the Fed? Is the attention given to the Fed warranted? Will Alan Greenspan be the

one to save us from an impending recession brought on by the terrorist attacks?

The Fed is critically important, but many people attribute more power to the Fed's ability to control economic activity than it has. They do have the ability to withstand any banking crisis or liquidity crisis. We see them doing that right now during this crisis, and that is a very powerful policy. But their ability to stop a recession is far more limited than I think many people believe.

Why is that ability limited?

They control the short-term interest rate. They don't control long-term rates. They can't control expectations. Take a look at the crisis we're in now. Their ability to keep spending higher than it would be otherwise is very limited. Even if they lower the Fed Funds rate down to zero—and that's only very short-term—how much extra spending would that entail? Some, yes. But enough to offset the decline in demand that this terrorist attack will cause? I doubt it.

Chapter 20

THE MATHEMATICIAN MEETS THE MARKETS
Suri Duddella

Internet Alias	Investment Style
Suri Duddella	Short-term

Year of Birth	Location
1967	Arlington, VA

Education
BE, mechanical enginering, Osmania University, Hyderabad, India; MS, robotics, University of Washington

Web Site (Pay)
Sixer.com: www.sixer.com

Please, please, please have the Sixer.com web site (see Figure 20.1) open on your computer as you read through the following interview. Click on "education" at the top of the main page, and get ready to do some serious exploring—primarily under the "indicators" tab, where you'll find detailed explanations of Suri Duddella's favorite trading strategies. Technical analysis—predicting future stock movements from charts, patterns, and mathematical indicators—generally involves some complicated concepts, but Duddella, founder and operator of Sixer.com, manages to take it to an even higher level. We had plenty of trouble getting him to boil his methods down to the nuts and bolts, and we headed back to the India-born ex-robotics engineer several times for further simplifications and clarifications. In the end, though, it was worth the hard work—something Duddella insists is crucial for successful trading. By following his own technical advice, Duddella has managed to

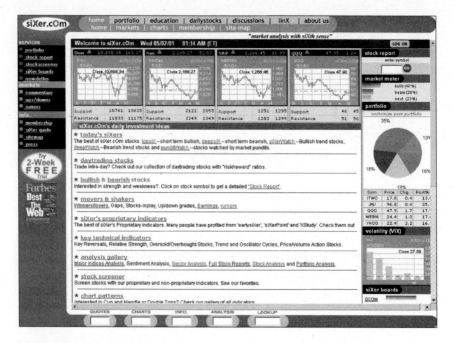

Figure 20.1   www.sixer.com
Source: Sixer.com.

rake in an average 76 percent annual return on his investments since
1996.

Duddella is your classic engineer, always looking for the most challenging project. He's worked in the robotics and automation groups at
Boeing, Ford Motors, and Anheuser Busch. But the stock market has
proven to be his ultimate contest. How he ended up here, entrenched in
the world of trading, is a serpentine story in itself: "When I was at Anheuser Busch in 1993 or 1994, we were building a local area internet application. It was there that I transitioned from robotics to the Internet.
I was offered a position at a company in Washington, D.C., that was
building an Internet security model for trading applications. When I
came to D.C. in 1995, they asked me to develop a trading application for
the utilities industry. I was around a bunch of traders who were developing trading models, and that's when I realized the true potential of
mathematical applications in the market."

Applying his analytical mind to the stock market has proven to
be Duddella's most difficult task, and keeping an enormous site like

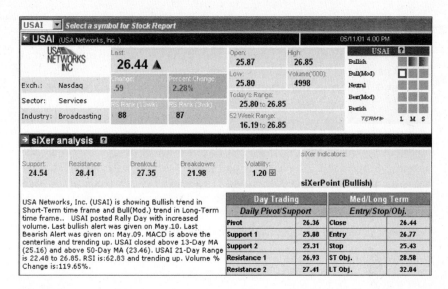

Figure 20.2   Sample Sixer.com analysis for a topSix stock—one of Duddella's bullish picks—on an arbitrarily chosen day
Source: Sixer.com (www.sixer.com).

Sixer.com updated daily is no easy undertaking. "I get up at 5:30 in the morning," Duddella tells us. "For the past few years I have developed the habit of sleeping very little. The first thing I do is look at the S&P futures. I'm quite interested in what's happening on the Nikkei, DAX, and FTSE markets, because they tend to give a signal of the general trend in U.S. markets. Our site is almost 400 pages, and we have achieved about 90 percent automation. Still, it requires a lot of maintenance and tweaking. There are the gazillion e-mails I receive every day—I have to respond to every one of them. My trading plan is devised by midnight every night for the next day, and at about 9:30 A.M., I'm deciding whether I'm going to be in the market, what I have to invest, and what are the best times to get in. It's the same journey until 4:00 P.M. At 4:00 we collect all the market data, run all the algorithms, and update the Sixer site, which takes about two hours. Then I have to go check out all the indicators and figure out a basic plan so I can prepare for the next day."

On Sixer.com, Duddella provides the topSix and deepSix—a total of 12 stocks ready for quick swings on the upside and downside listed on the main page of the site—his daily stamp of approval. Click on any of them for an in-depth technical description of why the stock is ready for a move [see Figure 20.2]. The "dailystocks" link at the top of the page will give you access to all of Sixer's stock screens, allowing you to determine which stocks are triggering both standard analytics and Sixer's proprietary technical indicators. Access to the site is well within any budget at $24.95 per quarter. As with most for-fee sites, a free trial is available.

Duddella admits that there's room for fundamental analysis in every portfolio. He makes sure that he understands the key business details of each and every stock in his basket of trading possibilities. But he insists that the technical health of a stock is just as important as a top-notch business model. "Timing is an issue that a lot of people miss," he explains. "Since 1997 I have been using my own algorithms for market analysis. In 1998 I wanted to provide the results of my passion for markets and mathematics to online investors. I formed Sixer.com to educate and empower individual investors. I also believe in 'the more you give, the more you get' . . . especially knowledge."

Sixer.com offers a wide array of traditional technical analysis tools, but you put together your own proprietary indicators as well. How do your models differ from what is already out there?

My stock selection is purely based on technical analysis. I use market indicators to find overall sectors first and then try to find stocks in those sectors. I like strong stocks that are oversold and overbought; stocks breaking out of trading ranges; stocks violating patterns, divergences, support, or resistance; and stocks giving signals from Sixer's market leading indicators. Some of the models I implement come from my understanding of advanced mathematics, such as ergodics, which studies heuristics applications and predicts the movement of waves and what happens due to certain triggers. [Vaguely, ergodic theories study systems by their averages and long-term dynamics, rather than precise moment-by-moment behavior. These theories have interesting implications when applied to the stock market, and they are the foundation of a number of Sixer's algorithms.] On the site, we provide both the popular indicators—RSI, MACD, and stochastics—plus we provide some of the indicators that we developed. You don't see them anywhere else. [MACD stands for moving average convergence/divergence, a technical indicator that describes when two smoothed moving averages cross. Duddella explains RSI and stochastics in his own words later in this interview.]

We don't want to turn this into a guide on technical analysis. Besides, your site is full of great educational information. In general, though,

how do you make the decision to buy or short a stock? Is it because all the indicators for a certain stock seem to align?

For trading, I use two different computers, and each has between six and eight windows. Each of the windows has at least two or three indicators showing me what's happening with a particular security. So, I have between 15 and 20 indicators in multiple windows. First of all, I have screening capabilities; my algorithms return to me a short list of stocks. If I am interested in finding out about Microsoft, my setup will show me how every single indicator is performing. Using my experience, I look at each indicator to figure out what's happening—how the volume is acting, how the basic MACD and RSI indicators are performing. The best indicators that I use are the divergence indicators. If a stock is reaching its high, but its RSI or MACD indicator is not reaching a high, the indicators are signaling to me some weakness in the stock.

Can you talk more about divergence indicators? You're saying that certain movements in stock prices are somewhat contradicted by the indicators themselves?

Oscillators—RSI and stochastics—are perfect examples of divergence. A stock has reached a certain high, pulled back, and again reached that high a second time. If the RSI or stochastic indicators are not also reaching the same level, then you have a divergence. That means that the stock is signaling weakness, and once it reaches the second high, it is not going to continue rising anymore.

You seem to be hinting at buying stocks that are overbought or oversold. How do you tell if a stock is overbought or oversold?

One indicator can tell you if it's overbought or oversold—the relative strength index, or RSI. If RSI is above 75, you know that the stock is overbought, and if it's below 25, you know that it's oversold.

The topSix and deepSix appear to be the crux of your site—six long plays and six short plays every trading day. Specifically, how do you pick those stocks?

We take 400 stocks and run them through our proprietary filters and algorithms, and 30 to 40 stocks come out. We cover these stocks in the SixerWatch, a listing of all bullish stocks, on the site. I have to go through those stocks every day to figure out what else is happening—for example, if a company is going to come out with earnings. If I don't expect the stock to meet earnings and it comes up in the topSix, then I probably won't post it.

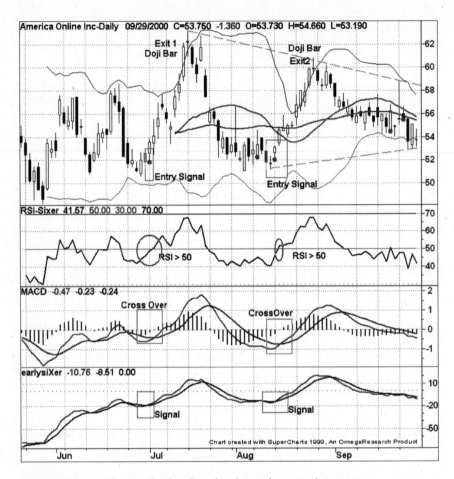

Figure 20.3 Graph created with technical analysis software TradeStation Pro

Source: TradeStation Pro (www.tradestationpro.com). Copyright © 1991–2001 TradeStation Technologies, Inc. Tradestation® is a registered trademark of TradeStation Technologies, Inc. TradeStation does not endorse or recommend the use of any particular trading strategy.

Could you take us through some trades and show us what triggered your algorithms? You've shown us a chart of America Online from May 2000 to September 2000. Can you give us an overview of what is pictured [see Figure 20.3]?

The top pane has got the stock prices in a candlestick pattern. [Candlesticks are the shaded and transparent boxes that show the stock's price movement. In this case, each candlestick represents one day. A shaded candlestick represents a down day for the stock, and a transparent candlestick represents a day when the price rose. Either end of the rectangular part of the candlestick represents the day's opening and closing prices. The prongs extend to the high and low trading prices for the day.] The two dashed diagonal lines are called the trend lines. The trend lines are the best examples of support and resistance. I also indicated Bollinger Bands. [Bollinger bands are the two serpentine lines that roughly border the stock's price movement as indicated by the candlesticks.]. The second pane, which is called "RSI-Sixer," is a relative strength indicator. The relative strength calculation is fairly standard, but I've modified it for myself. The fourth pane is what we call an earlySixer indicator, and that's where you see the crossovers. MACD is the other standard indicator.

The entry signals—labeled on the top pane where you see the dots— and the exit signals are triggered by the earlySixer indicator.

How does earlySixer trigger an entry?

If you look at the earlySixer part of the graph, you can see when the crossovers happen—that corresponds to the entry signals in the top pane.

But what exactly are those two lines that make up earlySixer?

Those are our proprietary indicators. EarlySixer is one, and the other is a signal line. Basically, when these two lines are crossing, that's when we generate an entry signal.

What does that mean, though? What does the crossing represent?

I don't want to give too much away. One line is the mathematical expression of the stock price and its prediction capability. The other line is the signal line, which takes the mathematical expression line and smoothes it by a certain factor. When these two lines are crossing, you get a signal. For example, when the signal line is crossing above, you get an entry signal. When it's crossing below, you get an exit signal.

How does RSI factor into this analysis?

A relative strength above 75 is an overbought condition, and anything below 25 is an oversold condition. RSI is the best indicator for overbought and oversold conditions. If the stock is crossing above 75, and all the other indicators are positive, it will tend to continue to go up. Once it starts going down, you know that the stock is going to fall. The same also applies when the stock is in an oversold condition. The best time to buy is when the stock is falling below 25 and then turns back.

If I were searching for a stock that already has a bullish condition, I would look for a stock for with a relative strength above 50. On the AOL chart, on the first entry, there was a signal from earlySixer; the relative strength also triggered above 50. The MACD histogram [in the third pane] is also giving a signal because it was in a negative condition that then started to come up to the positive side. Most of the technicians out there look for MACD crossover. That happened two days after my entry signal. For me, the entry signal provided by earlySixer is definitely a leading indicator of market conditions.

You're saying that your entry signals are actually more prescient than the others are?

That's how I trade, and that's how I trust. Everybody uses different indicators. Some people only trade on the patterns—they don't even look at the signals sometimes. They say, "I see a head-and-shoulders pattern, and that's how I'm going to trade."

If you look at the chart, another signal we clearly got was from the Bollinger Band itself. For example, if I entered into this AOL trade in July, the first short signal I would get is when it actually punctured, closed outside, the Bollinger Band. The Bollinger Band is calculated and graphed two standard deviations above the 10-day exponential moving average. When AOL punctured the Bollinger Band, a lot of technicians would get out at that point because they think the market will reverse the stock back to its exponential moving average.

Does a user of Sixer.com need to know what all of this means? If they visit the site and see that momentum, MACD, and the oscillators are all screaming "buy" for a particular stock, can they just buy?

An average investor needs to do quite a bit of due diligence for trading. We provide the technical health of a stock. We do not recommend that anybody go on our site and buy the stock without doing anything, but we do list the stocks that we think are going to go up and the stocks that are going to go down. Fundamentalists go and buy Dell and Cisco because they are great companies, but technical analysis adds timing. You need to know the best time to get in and the best time to get out. We provide those entry and exit points purely from a mathematical point of view.

What is your typical holding period?

The max I will own any stock is about three weeks. Most of the time, however, I will sell or cover after three to four days.

You have no qualms with holding positions overnight?

I have no problems. I'm not a day trader per se—although many times my stocks will hit my automatic sells on the negative side or positive side on the same day that I enter the trade. But I do not go and close my market positions at 4:00 P.M. because I have flexibility—I can trade until 8:00 in the evening to sell my positions. And the best thing is that right after the market closes, my algorithms tell me what is happening, and maybe tomorrow will not be a good day for the securities that I am holding. Then I can go and sell until 8:00. So I don't worry about holding positions unless I know that the market is going to tank in the next couple of days—in that case I would rather take everything out before 4:00.

Can you get good executions in after-hours trading?

I personally do not like it. The spreads are high, and the volume is thin. Even at 4:02 P.M. the spread goes from $0.25 to $0.75 on any security. I absolutely only sell—I never buy—during after-hours trading.

Does Sixer.com provide help determining when to sell?

If you click to get stock analysis, we tell you the resistance levels, projection levels, and support levels for the stock.

Is there a place for technical analysis in everyone's portfolio?

Educated and savvy investors should at least use basic indicators—not blindly go and buy Intels and Ciscos because they are the best companies. If you know that a company has negative momentum built in and the stock is going to fall, you shouldn't go and buy it just because it's cheap.

How does technical analysis differ for a short-term trader versus for a long-term investor?

If you're looking at an RSI indicator—I use the 14-day indicator because I know that the 14-day indicator works for me. But if you ask a day trader, they might laugh and say, "Well, I use a 5-minute indicator." A long-term investor might want to look at the 14-week indicator.

As you mentioned earlier, a lot of technicians also use visual patterns that can be seen in a stock's chart. Do you do any of that?

I do trade on patterns. Two of my favorite patterns are cup-and-handle and head-and-shoulders, although I've started to mistrust head-and-shoulders. I also look at triangles—which is another pattern that is absolutely phenomenal, especially when used for short-term trading.

Can you describe what triangles looks like?

Imagine this: Let's say that a stock trades between $100 and $50, a $50 range on a single day. Then the next day—I'm taking big ranges, but these could be much smaller—the range is smaller, and even smaller the next day. The stock chart follows a triangular pattern until it reaches an apex. At that point, the stock is going to get some type of reaction because all the people who have bought the stock are not going to leave it, and all the people who have sold the stock are looking for something else to buy. From there, it's going to break out, and it's going to tend to go up—in the positive direction—if it has got the volume.

Do you have a feel for Sixer.com's accuracy in terms of predicting movements of stock prices?

We have done quite a bit of analysis. We took 1,000 topSix stocks and analyzed how many stocks have hit the actual entry point. Basically, 80 percent of the stocks have hit the first entry point. That means you entered into the market. Within one week 72 percent have hit the first target price. About 12 percent to 15 percent of stocks hit the downside limits—the sell-stops on the lower side.

How high above the entry points do those initial upside targets tend to be?

They are completely mathematical calculations, and they tend to be anywhere from 5 percent to 12 percent on the upside.

What software would you recommend to the budding technical analyst?

The best software out there is TradeStation. I like it because it gives you the capability of writing your own algorithms in a basic language. It's expensive, but it's the best out there.

One last question: Why do you think you are a better trader than most people?

I don't want to say that I am a better trader. I use my intuition and knowledge. Some people out there think they can study a book or take a class and become a better trader in a matter of a month or two. That's not going to happen. That's the reason that 90 percent of traders fail. I've spent the past four or five years testing and backtesting my own algorithms to figure out the best uses for them. EarlySixer is my favorite indicator, but I've probably only followed it in the past two years. That means that it took me three or four years to find the single best indicator for me. Once an investment play is discovered, one needs to study market conditions for the entry and devise a plan for the exit. Managing money should be the top priority for a trader. I have a written plan for every trade. I use rigorous discipline to avoid both greed and fear. People need to put in a lot of research in order to be successful in the stock market . . . unless they have 100 percent great luck, which I don't.

Chapter 21

KING OF THE MARKET MERITOCRACY

Ken Kam

Internet Alias	Investment Style
Ken Kam	Medium-term, long-term
Year of Birth	**Location**
1960	Los Altos Hills, CA
Education	
BS, finance, Santa Clara University; MBA, Stanford University	
Web Site (Free)	
Marketocracy: www.marketocracy.com	

Ken Kam wants *you.* The bell has sounded; the pistol has fired; the line has been drawn in the sand. Think you're a great investor? Prove it. It's you versus the world in the Internet's highest-stakes investment simulation, where make-believe dollars blur with real investment riches. "We are looking for people who can deliver performance," says Kam, founder and CEO of Marketocracy.com (see Figure 21.1).

Kam knows a thing or two about performance. In 1993 he cofounded Firsthand Funds, a family of funds whose flagship portfolio, the Technology Value Fund, had the best five-year track record of any mutual fund as of September 1999, returning a whopping average annual return of 50.6 percent since inception. But pummeling every mutual fund in the country was not enough for Kam; he wanted to turn the entire industry on its head. Kam recognized that his prowess as a fund manager stemmed from his industry expertise and experience, not from financial savvy or accounting acumen. Prior to launching Firsthand Funds, Kam

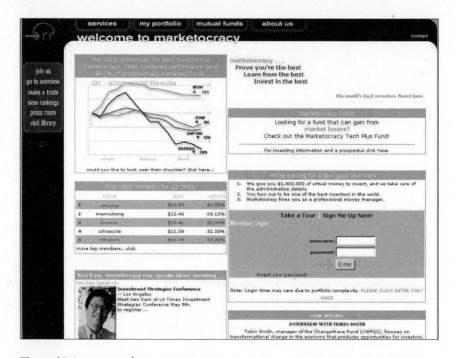

Figure 21.1   www.marketocracy.com
Source: Marketocracy.

was a founder and vice president of Novoste Puerto, a medical devices company that is now publicly traded with a market capitalization of several hundred million dollars.

Kam attributes Firsthand's outperformance to his experience as a successful entrepreneur. And experience, Kam argues, is what traditional fund managers are lacking. As the mutual fund industry currently stands, the dream of young finance students to manage other people's money can be realized only through a career devoted to number crunching and climbing the ranks from junior analyst to fund manager. This cookie-cutter recruiting approach all but guarantees that the mutual fund industry misses out on the most promising and profitable candidates for money-management positions.

To solve this paradox, Kam turned to the Internet and its ability to link investors from around the globe. In 1999 he jumped ship at Firsthand Funds and launched Marketocracy. Marketocracy invites the world's best investors—from amateurs to professionals to everything in between—to compete in an extremely realistic mutual fund management simulation, duking it out with each other, with actual fund managers, and with the stock market at large, in an effort to win what is perhaps the Internet's most remarkable grand prize. Once Marketocracy gathers sufficient performance data from a three-year investment simulation, the company will reward the winners with an invitation to become professional fund managers. Marketocracy has already set up all the legal and logistical components necessary to launch a family of funds; now all the company needs is a few talented managers. To date, the leaders of the pack hail from all over the vocational and geographic map: A programmer from Pennsylvania registered a 17.67 percent return in one quarter; a computer scientist from Maryland turned in 15.41 percent quarterly performance; and a retired U.S. Air Force officer produced a 13.37 percent return. The playing field has been flattened like a pancake. Will you be the next king of this market meritocracy?

To be sure, Kam's got the same lofty goals as most Netrepreneurs: revolutionize an industry and bring Wall Street to Main Street. It's hard to find fault in Kam's argument that the fund industry's current money-manager recruiting mechanisms are a bit out of whack, but we know for certain that Marketocracy is facing a steep uphill battle with the minds of wary investors. It's one thing to say that an amateur investor can do as well as the pros (a tenet to which we most certainly subscribe), but it's quite another to convince mutual fund investors to hand over their hard-earned money to an amateur. It is ironic that the struggle in which Marketocracy is now engaged pits the amateurs against the pros, and the winning amateurs' ultimate prize is an invitation to join the other team.

Even if you're not ready to step up to the fund-manager plate, Marketocracy offers some unique opportunities to explore—and invest in—the pulse of the market's smartest, including Kam himself. While Marketocracy waits for its elaborate simulation to play out, the company has launched three funds managed by credentialed Wall Street veterans: Kam runs Marketocracy's Medical Specialists Fund; successful hedge fund manager Paul McEntire runs the Technology Plus Fund; and *ChangeWave Investing* author Tobin Smith runs the ChangeWave Fund. Visitors to the site can pay to listen in on conversations among the site's top 100 investors and receive aggregated statistics on their weekly buys and sells as well as analysis from the market meritocracy king himself. After reading the following interview with Kam and Marketocracy chief operating officer Robin Stevens, you can judge for yourself whether the Internet will live up to Marketocracy's motto and uncover "the world's best investors."

You ran the top-performing mutual fund in the country for a while. How did you get started managing money?

Ken: When I was a second-year business school student, five of us decided that the best way to stay in touch was to start an investment club—to have money on the line so that we would be forced to call each other and have dinner once per quarter. Two of us in the investment club started to get really interested in doing the homework. I was one, and the other was Kevin Landis.

He became a product manager at a semiconductor company, while I went off after business school to start a medical device company. In the process of building that company, we did everything—basic R&D to develop the product, clinical trials to prove that it was effective, FDA [Food and Drug Administration] submissions and inspections to get approval in the United States, building a sales force to distribute the product both here and internationally—and ultimately we sold the division. When I was done with that endeavor, a number of investors who had put the early money into the company asked if I would continue managing their money. So Kevin and I formed the Firsthand Technology Value Fund. We were just at the start of this huge boom in health care and technology stocks, and in that fund we kept doing what we had always been doing in the investment club, supplemented by the experiences that we each had in industry and by the Rolodexes that we had built. That perspective is what gave us an investment advantage to interpret news and frame questions about each company so that we could seek out answers from people more informed than us. Firsthand became very successful, and last year I left to start Marketocracy.

We definitely want to talk more about your investment strategy, but let's first discuss Marketocracy itself. Where did you come up with the idea?

Ken: Most people would like to have the best money managers in the world—those with the best track records—managing their money. Yet, when you look at the statistics for the mutual fund industry, on average, roughly 80 percent of fund managers don't beat the S&P 500 index. My conclusion was that the current process that the mutual fund business uses to recruit portfolio managers does not end up finding the best money managers in the world.

Why is that? Where do fund families traditionally look for managers, and where should they be looking?

Ken: Being a successful fund manager takes firsthand experience. Compare that to the way the industry recruits portfolio managers now: They go to the top business schools, recruit maybe 400 or 500 people per year into the industry as analysts, and have them spend their whole career on Wall Street. What you get are a bunch of people who are very good observers, but who have not had significant experience outside of the mutual fund industry. What we need is a way to look at everybody else—to cast the net as widely as possible and find the people who really have investment talent. I don't think shareholders care where somebody went to business school or about anything else on a manager's résumé other than how well he or she has performed. Using the Internet, Marketocracy can give the opportunity to be a portfolio manager to a lot more people and end up selecting the best investors in the world.

We are creating a minor league for portfolio managers, and we will recruit people to the big leagues as their track records warrant. Then, if there is underperformance, these same folks will eventually be replaced with other people who have better track records from the minor leagues. You create a meritocracy, where portfolio managers have to earn their position by virtue of demonstrating performance. And they have to keep earning their position by continuing to perform.

Do you find that most fund managers are adaptive? Can they make the transition between strategies and sectors when market dynamics change?

Ken: Most fund managers—the good ones, anyway—understand what they are good at, and when market conditions change and the market stops rewarding the kinds of stocks that they are good at analyzing, the only strategy that they have is to allocate money to other people or to go to cash. Our answer to that issue is that if you have a big enough minor league—have track records for enough people—then somebody will be able to do well in any market environment. When one person's style starts to go out of favor, the style that is working and the people that exercise or implement that style best ought to get the funds.

When we started Marketocracy, we knew that we had to have at least three years' worth of data in order to select portfolio managers on the basis of a reasonably long track record. We are only about a year and a half through that process now, but in another year and a half to two years, we will have three-year track records for more than 40,000 separate virtual funds. That number is four to five times the number that Morningstar follows; it's going to give us a lot of flexibility to find the right managers in any market environment. Those are the people who we are going to hire to manage a family of funds.

What other problems do you see with the mutual fund industry as it currently stands? Most investors probably wouldn't know the first thing about actually managing a fund.

Ken: The scarce resource is the talent—the people who have the perspective to make the right judgments about where a company is going. Transactions costs, regulatory compliances, tax planning—those are all things that you can almost mechanize.

Robin: It's not very well known to the public how you become a mutual fund manager. It's shrouded in mystery to the man on the street, fraught with regulations. What we do is strip that away, because we are already an established mutual fund company; we handle all of the regulations, the administration, the mystery, and people can concentrate on delivering consistent returns.

Would it be possible for them to do it without you?

Ken: I did it without us when we started Firsthand Funds. You know how you do it on your own? First you get a million dollars and give about half of that to a lawyer to write a prospectus and register you with the SEC as an investment advisor. Once you get your fund's prospectus approved, then you have a fund with no distribution; investors can't call Schwab and buy your fund because Schwab won't carry you right away. We had to be the number one fund in the country for three years before Schwab would distribute our fund. So, for the first three years you are basically selling your fund to friends and family, hoping that you build a good enough track record to attract the brokerage community.

If Marketocracy decided to launch a manager plucked from your simulation, would Schwab carry that fund immediately?

Ken: It's not automatic, but they picked up our first two funds upon inception.

What are the mechanics of hiring and compensating Marketocracy fund managers?

Ken: The mechanics are pretty simple. We are not innovating on structure; it's going to be a straight mutual fund with a set of managers. The innovation here is how we recruit the managers.

You are saying that a star manager would be compensated as highly at Marketocracy as he or she would be at Fidelity?

Ken: Yes. We are not giving out coffee cups or T-shirts; we are giving out basis points. Based on how well the funds do and how big the funds get, portfolio managers recruited in this manner are going to be well compensated. I was president of Firsthand Funds for five and a half years, and we took that from zero to $6 billion during that time. If we are even half as successful with Marketocracy, we are going to be sending out some big paychecks.

What are typical fund manager fees for actively managed funds?

Ken: The average fund fees are about 147 basis points.

In dollar terms, how much do you think a good fund manager at Marketocracy could make?

Ken: In our models we are currently budgeting to pay 30 basis points per fund, so if you have a billion dollar fund, which is still on the smallish side, $3 million. If five people split that up, that's a lot of money.

How will you distribute the fund?

Ken: We already have the distribution channels set up. We have contracts with Schwab, Fidelity, TD Waterhouse, and about a half dozen other brokerage houses.

How many funds will Marketocracy eventually offer?

Ken: Most of the fund industry does this backwards; they decide that they are going to start a fund based on what's hot, what people want to buy, and they go look for a manager. We are doing it the other way around, finding out what kind of talent we have first, and then creating the prospectus around that.

Where does your talent currently lie? Do your top investors use varying styles?

Robin: The largest group is looking at fundamentals and has an expertise in an area about which they feel strongly. They know we are looking for fund managers, so they are looking for long-term plays.

Ken: There is a group that looks at investing from a technical perspective, and it's been interesting to see the interplay between the fundamentalists and the technicians. Over time, the technicians have been able to win the respect of the fundamental analysts.

Do you have any individuals on Marketocracy who have consistently performed better than have professionals on Wall Street?

Ken: Yes. In fact, the group as whole. If there had been a fund invested in the same things that the top 100 people in aggregate bought, that fund would have beaten 96 percent of all mutual funds. For Q1 of 2001, the top 100 people would have beaten 99.7 percent of all mutual funds.

Isn't that an unfair metric? By definition, the top 100 must be the best! If you group the top 100 traditional Wall Street mutual funds, those 100 funds would have beaten all other mutual funds as well.

Ken: If you could figure out how to get those top 100 guys to tell you what they are buying and selling every day and learn from them, then that might be as valuable. I would also tell you that if you picked the top 100 out of a group of 4,000 professional equity fund managers, you are going to get a group that is very good, but if you pick the top 100 out of 40,000 people, you are going to get a group that is on the whole much better.

Have you ever taken the top 100 from one quarter and analyzed their performance over the subsequent quarter? Do the best managers tend to remain on top?

Ken: If you had followed what the top group from Q4 2000 did throughout Q1 2001, you would have beaten over 90 percent of all equity funds.

What about performance on an individual basis? Marketocracy is, after all, focused on finding individual performers. Who are some of the top candidates to manage funds in the future?

Robin: Our number-one guy since inception is Colin Williams. His net asset value as of the end of Q1 2001 is $16.51, which means that after nine months, he has returned 65 percent. Everybody starts out at $10. He has a health care–based fund and is a junior analyst in Chicago. He has also worked in the medical industry for part of his career. Our number-three guy last quarter is an engineer at Cisco; everybody thinks that means he is a tech investor, but he is actually a serious value investor. His Q4 2000 return was 17 percent. If our 100 top guys were mixed in with the top 100 mutual funds, the new top 100 would include 63 of our guys.

You currently have three funds publicly available on your site. Tell us about those funds. How did you find the managers?

Ken: When we have three years of data, all the things that we have been discussing will enable us to build toward our ultimate goal of having the best fund family. But if you ask who the best investors are now, the answer is probably hedge fund managers. So, in the interim between now and the time we can start to recruit people to become portfolio managers, we've gone out and looked for managers with great track records who are not generally available to the public. The first two we found were Tobin Smith and Paul McEntire. Paul McEntire runs a hedge fund called Skye Investment Advisors, and on average over the last 10 years, his hedge fund has beaten the market by 10 percent per year. We created the Technology Plus Fund for him to exercise—as much as possible within the mutual fund framework—his investment style. The unique thing about the Technology Plus Fund is that it can short up to 40 percent of its assets. Here you have a manager with a great track record, previously unavailable to the public, who is now managing a mutual fund that is available through all the normal mutual fund distribution channels, and the fund enables people who want to stay invested in tech to have some protection on the downside. Since we launched the fund on the last day of December 2000, that fund has been down, but only 55 cents, or 5.5 percent, year-to-date. Compared to the Nasdaq, that's pretty good performance.

The second guy is Tobin Smith, author of *ChangeWave Investing*. He also runs a hedge fund that is generally not available to the public. His fund is a capital appreciation fund that is down 60 cents, or 6 percent, year-to-date.

Robin: They are both at the top of their listing in Bloomberg. Change-Wave is in the top quartile, and Tech Plus is in the top 10 or top 20 funds in its class on Bloomberg.

Ken: The third fund is the Medical Specialists fund, which I run. That one has done the worst this year, down about 18 percent year-to-date, which is not bad for the biotech and health care sector, but not as good as we had hoped.

What are the total assets under management at this point?

Ken: Total assets under management are about $32 million.

Let's talk about your personal investing strategies. You ran the top-performing mutual fund in the country during the late 1990s. What is your secret?

Ken: What I think can be analyzed are company fundamentals, trends in an industry, and whether a company's strategies are appropriate for its opportunities. All of these things become evident only in the stock price in the longer term. You have to force yourself to ignore short-term market volatility—learn how to take advantage of it, but not to make short-term volatility the fundamental driver of your investment decisions. A manager should be able to identify the handful of things that have to go right for a company in order to create a double in market cap within a reasonable investment horizon, say two or three years. He should then have a network of contacts in the industry to be able to put those questions to the people who are in the best position to answer them.

Can the average investor possibly replicate that strategy?

Ken: If you are going to try to replicate what we do, I would suggest that you focus on the industry in which you work. Look at your company's suppliers, look at all the people who buy your company's products, look at all of your competitors, and see if you are a good analyst of your own industry. Most people's jobs offer them much more relevant investment information on a day-to-day basis than an analyst's job does. An analyst is able to talk to top management, but top management is always going to give an optimistic spin. The people who really know what is going on are the sales reps, the people who take orders, the people scheduling the production floor. If a sales rep starts noticing that every lost sale is to the same company, then he ought to be looking at what that company is doing right.

Can you give us an example in which all aspects of this strategy successfully aligned for you into a profitable investment?

Ken: One of my best stock picks was Arterial Vascular Engineering [see Figure 21.2]. They make a device called a cardiac stent. Heart attacks are caused by clots that prevent blood flow from reaching your heart; doctors go in with a catheter that has a balloon at the end to break up the clot so that blood flow can be restored. After they take out the balloon, it's typical to put a little wire-like coil in to hold open the artery so that it won't spasm and collapse, causing a second heart attack. That wire coil is called a cardiac stent. Three years ago, the market for cardiac stents didn't exist, but it was such a huge advance in the treatment of cardiac disease that I started seeing it in the cath labs even while the devices were still in clinical trials. All the big players were making versions of cardiac stents; Arterial Vascular Engineering was one of the few pure plays. They were the smallest company and looked like the weakest of all the suppliers.

When you implant a cardiac stent in the heart, it's important that the stent be visible on a fluoroscope, because if it's not visible, doctors don't know where they are placing the stent. If it's not placed in the right area, blood can clot on it, and blood clots are what cause heart attacks

Figure 21.2   Arterial Vascular Engineering (OTC: AVEI), May 1996–December 1998
Source: Prophet Financial Systems, Inc. (www.ProphetFinance.com).

and strokes. If you can't see the stent on the fluoroscope, no doctor is going to use it. Once I identified that as being key, then it was just a matter of going to enough physicians to get a sense for who had the most visible stent on the market, and that turned out to be Arterial Vascular Engineering. This is very different from what each of the big players would have told Wall Street analysts. These companies had pictures of their stents that were crystal clear, and in all fairness, if you use the most modern equipment and you are willing to spend the money to have the machines tuned up right before every procedure, you could have made every company's stent visible on the fluoroscope. So it didn't look as if there were any competitive differences. But the reality of the situation is that most hospitals update their cath lab equipment only once every 10 years and maybe only tune their equipment once every six months. The reality was that a lot of the stents from the major manufacturers were basically invisible on the equipment that most hospitals were using, and the only way to find out which stents were visible was to ask doctors. That feedback helped me make the decision about buying Arterial Vascular Engineering, which in 1997 was one of the best-performing Nasdaq stocks.

What about the financial picture of a company? You told a great story, but aren't there a lot of companies with great stories and poor stock performance?

Ken: In 1996 Arterial Vascular Engineering's product was not yet approved in the United States. It was approved in Europe, so we could see in a fairly large market how their product actually competed against the big boys. They were the market leaders in Europe at that time, but if you looked at their income statement, it was just beginning to show sales. The price-to-sales and price-to-earnings figures would have looked outrageous compared to the S&P 500. But when you considered their potential to double sales over the next year by getting approval in the United States, it looked cheap. You can't ignore financial metrics, but you have to be able to use them within the proper context for each situation. You can't apply the same metrics uniformly across all industries.

Where do you seek out new investment ideas?

Ken: I have an open invitation for any doctor to e-mail or call me whenever they find something that works better or worse than they expected. Frankly, however, I am beginning to see a lot of ideas in other areas besides health care getting discussed on the m100 list on a level that is useful for a professional manager. [The m100 are Marketocracy's top investors who are permitted to converse privately among each other to share ideas and strategies. Marketocracy offers a for-pay service that compiles data and thoughts from these investors.] On other bulletin boards, maybe 20 percent of the discussion is reasoned analysis. The other 80 percent are scams or people expressing an emotional perspective, not an analytical one. What's different about our m100 list is that the participants have earned the right to get my attention because of their performance. They are teaching me how to look at stocks in other industries, and I find that very valuable. How you find good ideas is that you find credible teachers and you listen.

One of the things we find most interesting about Marketocracy is that since the site's inception, the market has been steadily falling. Your top investors have had to attempt to create winning portfolios under extremely difficult conditions. What is your opinion on how an investor's portfolio and strategy should change in a declining market?

Ken: When markets are more richly valued, you have to relax some of the rules; you have to search a little harder for value, so it's okay to be heavily diversified and have up to 30 positions. When the market has corrected, the best thing that you can do is go through an intensive analysis and rank your positions from one to 30, sell the bottom 10, and reinvest the money in the top 10. This allows you to recognize some tax losses, and it focuses your portfolio on your best ideas and positions you for any upturn in the market. Too many people in a down market become afraid to do anything; they don't want to sell until they break even, and that's a mistake.

Let's end with this: In your view, where are the most exciting investment opportunities over the next decade? Where should investors be putting their money?

Ken: We are on the verge of major discoveries in biotechnology. Over the next 20 years, any pharmaceutical company that hasn't changed its method of drug discovery to encompass these biotech techniques is going to be obsolete. Because a lot of these biotech companies don't look attractive using traditional financial metrics, there is a lot of volatility; but make no mistake about it—the underlying science is going to lead to some revolutionary treatments within a reasonable investment horizon. Already, the number of biologic agents that are getting approved every year is increasing. The potential to use genomic information to tailor a drug regimen for each patient's specific DNA will lead to the approval of a lot of drugs that would not otherwise have gotten approval. Companies have developed drugs that turn out to be toxic to 2 percent of the population but end up being able to help the other 98 percent. Having a test that can differentiate between the 98 percent that a drug can help and the 2 percent that it would hurt is the critical piece that we need in order to get approval and turn drug candidates from dry holes into profitable products.

GLOSSARY

This glossary is provided by Dr. Campbell R. Harvey, the J. Paul Sticht Professor of International Business at Duke University's Fuqua School of Business. Harvey developed and maintains the Hypertextual Finance Glossary, available at www.duke.edu/~charvey/Classes/wpg/glossary. htm. This Internet-based glossary serves up more than 7,200 business, finance, and investment definitions. Besides boasting the largest financial glossary on the Internet, Harvey's home page offers access to his classroom materials as well as web casts of his lectures and numerous links to Internet-based financial tools.

Given his creative and rigorous use of the Internet in all aspects of his teaching and investment activities, we couldn't resist tapping Harvey for this book's glossary. Consider the following pages a bit of brains that can shed some light on the rhetoric of those crafty bulls and bears.

10-K. Annual report required by the SEC each year. Provides a comprehensive overview of a company's state of business. Must be filed within 90 days after fiscal year-end.

10-Q. Quarterly report required by the SEC each quarter. Provides a comprehensive overview of a company's state of business.

Arbitrage. The simultaneous buying and selling of a security at two different prices in two different markets, resulting in profits without risk. Perfectly efficient markets present no arbitrage opportunities. Perfectly efficient markets seldom exist, but arbitrage opportunities are often precluded because of transactions costs.

Ask. This is the quoted ask, or the lowest price an investor will accept to sell a stock. Practically speaking, this is the quoted offer at which an investor can buy shares of stock. Also called the offer price.

Balance sheet. A summary of a company's assets, liabilities, and owners' equity. Also called the statement of financial condition.

Bid. The price that a potential buyer is willing to pay for a security. In trading, the bid-ask spread is the difference between what buyers are willing to pay and what sellers are asking for in terms of price.

Block trade. A large trading order, defined on the New York Stock Exchange as an order that consists of 10,000 shares of a given stock or at a total market value of $200,000 or more.

Breakout. A rise in a security's price above a resistance level (commonly, its previous high price) or a drop below a level of support (commonly, the former lowest price.) A breakout is taken to signify a continuing move in the same direction. Can be used by technical analysts as a buy or sell indicator.

Call option. An option contract that gives its holder the right (but not the obligation) to purchase a specified number of shares of the underlying stock at the given strike price, on or before the expiration date of the contract.

Capital structure. The makeup of the liabilities and stockholders' equity side of the balance sheet, especially the ratio of debt to equity and the mixture of short and long maturities.

Cover. The purchase of a contract to offset a previously established short position.

Covered call. A short call option position in which the writer owns the number of shares of the underlying stock represented by the option contracts. Covered calls generally limit the risk the writer takes because the stock does not have to be bought at the market price, if the holder of that option decides to exercise it.

Credit risk. The risk that an issuer of debt securities or a borrower may default on its obligations or that the payment may not be made on a negotiable instrument.

Cyclical stock. Stock that tends to rise quickly when the economy turns up and fall quickly when the economy turns down. Examples are housing, automobiles, and paper.

Debt. Money borrowed.

Debt/equity ratio. Indicator of financial leverage. Compares assets provided by creditors to assets provided by shareholders. Determined by dividing long-term debt by common stockholder equity.

Derivative security. A financial security such as an option or future whose value is derived in part from the value and characteristics of another security, the underlying asset.

Discount factor. Present value of $1 received at a stated future date.

Discounted cash flow (DCF). Future cash flows multiplied by discount factors to obtain present values.

Divergence. When two or more averages or indexes fail to show confirming trends.

ECN. Electronic communications network.

Equity. Ownership interest in a firm.

Federal Reserve System. The monetary authority of the United States, established in 1913 and governed by the Federal Reserve Board, located in Washington, D.C. The system includes 12 Federal Reserve Banks and is authorized to regulate monetary policy in the United States as well as to supervise Federal Reserve member banks, bank holding companies, international operations of U.S. banks, and U.S. operations of foreign banks.

Fixed cost. A cost that is fixed in total for a given period of time and for given production levels.

Fixed-income securities. Investments that have specific interest rates, such as bonds.

Float. Number of shares of a corporation that are outstanding and available for trading by the public, excluding insiders or restricted stock on a when-issued basis. A stock's volatility is inversely correlated to its float.

Fundamental analysis. Security analysis that seeks to detect misvalued securities through an analysis of the firm's business prospects. Research often focuses on earnings, dividend prospects, expectations for future interest rates, and risk evaluation of the firm. Antithesis of technical analysis.

Futures. A term used to designate all contracts covering the sale of financial instruments or physical commodities for future delivery on a commodity exchange.

Futures contract. A legally binding agreement to buy or sell a commodity or financial instrument in a designated future month at a price agreed upon by the buyer and seller. Futures contracts are standardized according to the quality, quantity, delivery time, and location for each commodity. A futures contract differs from an option because an option is the right to buy or sell, whereas a futures contract is the promise actually to make a transaction. A future is part of a class of securities called derivatives, so named because such securities derive their value from the worth of an underlying investment.

Gap opening. In the context of general equities, opening price that is substantially higher or lower than the previous day's closing price, usually because of some extraordinarily positive or negative news.

Gross profit margin. Gross profit divided by sales, which is equal to each sales dollar left over after paying for the cost of goods sold.

Head and shoulders. In technical analysis, a pattern that results in which a stock price reaches a peak and declines; rises above its former peak and again declines; rises a third time but not to the second peak; and then again declines. The first and third peaks are shoulders, and the second peak is the formation's head. Technical analysts generally consider a head and shoulders formation to be a very bearish indication.

Hedge fund. A fund that may employ a variety of techniques to enhance returns, such as both buying and shorting stocks according to a valuation model.

Income statement (statement of operations). A statement showing the revenues, expenses, and income (the difference between revenues and expenses) of a corporation over some period of time.

Inside market. Refers to over-the-counter trading. Best (highest) bid and best (lowest) offer, often used in the over-the-counter market.

Insiders. These are directors and senior officers of a corporation—in effect, those who have access to inside information about a company. An insider also is someone who owns more than 10 percent of the voting shares of a company.

Investment bank. Financial intermediaries who perform a variety of services, including aiding in the sale of securities, facilitating mergers and other corporate reorganizations, acting as brokers to both individual and institutional clients, and trading for their own accounts.

Leverage. The use of debt financing, or the property of rising or falling at a proportionally greater amount than comparable investments. For example, an option is said to have high leverage compared to the underlying stock because a given price change in the stock may result in a greater increase or decrease in the value of the option.

Leveraged buyout (LBO). A transaction used to take a public corporation private that is financed through debt such as bank loans and bonds. Because of the large amount of debt relative to equity in the new corporation, the bonds are typically rated below investment-grade, properly referred to as high-yield bonds or junk bonds. Investors can participate in an LBO through either the purchase of the debt (i.e., purchase of the bonds or participation in the bank loan) or the purchase of equity through an LBO fund that specializes in such investments.

Limit order. An order to buy a stock at or below a specified price or to sell a stock at or above a specified price. For instance, you could tell a broker, "Buy me 100 shares of XYZ Corp at $8 or less" or "Sell 100 shares of XYZ at $10 or better." The customer specifies a price, and the order can be executed only if the market reaches or betters that price. This conditional trading order is designed to avoid the danger of adverse, unexpected price changes.

Liquid asset. Asset that is easily and cheaply turned into cash—notably, cash itself and short-term securities.

Liquid market. A market that allows the buying or selling of large quantities of an asset at any time and at low transactions costs.

Long position. Owning or holding options (i.e., the number of contracts bought exceeds the number of contracts sold). For equities, a long position occurs when an individual owns securities. An owner of 1,000 shares of stock is said to be "long the stock." See also **Short position.**

Long-term debt. An obligation having a maturity of more than one year from the date when it was issued.

Market maker. In the context of general equities, one who maintains firm bid and offer prices in a given security by standing ready to buy or sell round lots at publicly quoted prices.

Momentum. The amount of acceleration of an economic, price, or volume movement. A trader who follows a movement strategy will purchase stocks that have recently risen in price.

Moving average. Used in charts and technical analysis, the average of security or commodity prices constructed in a period as short as a few days or as long as several years and showing trends for the latest interval. As each new variable is included in calculating the average, the last variable of the series is deleted.

Mutual fund. Pools of money that are managed by an investment company. Mutual funds offer investors a variety of goals, depending on the fund and its investment charter. Some funds, for example, seek to generate income on a regular basis. Others seek to preserve an investor's money. Still others seek to invest in companies that are growing at a rapid pace. Funds can impose a sales charge, or load, on investors when they buy or sell shares. Many funds these days are no load and impose no sales charge. Mutual funds are investment companies regulated by the Investment Company Act of 1940.

Naked option strategies. An unhedged strategy making exclusive use of either a short call strategy (selling or writing call options) or a short put strategy (selling or writing put options). By themselves, these positions are called naked strategies because they do not involve an offsetting or risk-reducing position in another option or in the underlying security.

Offer. Indicates a willingness to sell at a given price.

Option. Gives the buyer the right, but not the obligation, to buy or sell an asset at a set price on or before a given date. Investors, not companies, issue options. Buyers of call options bet that a stock will be worth more than the price set by the option (the strike price), plus the price they pay for the option itself. Buyers of put options bet that the stock's price will drop below the price set by the option. An option is part of a class of securities called derivatives, which means that these securities derive their value from the worth of an underlying investment.

Outside market. Used in the context of general equities, outside the inside market (above the lowest offering and below the highest bid).

Over-the-counter (OTC). A decentralized market (as opposed to an exchange market) where geographically dispersed dealers are linked by telephones and computer screens. The market is for securities not listed on a stock or bond exchange. The Nasdaq market is an OTC market for U.S. stocks. Antithesis of listed.

Overbought. Used in the context of general equities. Technically too high in price, and hence a technical correction is expected. Antithesis of oversold.

Oversold. Used in the context of general equities. Technically too low in price, and hence a technical correction is expected. Antithesis of overbought.

Pattern. A technical chart formation used to make market predictions by following the price movements of securities.

Pit. A specific area of the trading floor that is designed for the trading of commodities, individual futures, or option contracts.

Present value. The amount of cash today that is equivalent in value to a payment, or to a stream of payments, to be received in the future. To determine the present value, each future cash flow is multiplied by a present value factor. For example, if the opportunity cost of funds is 10 percent, the present value of $100 to be received in one year is $100 \times [1/(1 + 0.10)] = 91.

Price-earnings ratio (PE). Shows the multiple of earnings at which a stock sells. Determined by dividing current stock price by current earnings per share (adjusted for stock splits). Earnings per share for the PE ratio are determined by dividing earnings for the past 12 months by the number of common shares outstanding. A higher multiple means that investors have higher expectations for future growth and that they have bid up the stock's price.

Profit margin. Indicator of profitability; the ratio of earnings available to stockholders to net sales. Determined by dividing net income by revenue for the same 12-month period. Result is shown as a percentage.

Program trades. Orders requiring the execution of trades in a large number of different stocks at as near the same time as possible.

Put option. Gives investors the right to sell (or put) a fixed number of shares at a fixed price within a given period. An investor, for example, might wish to have the right to sell shares of a stock at a certain price by a certain time in order to protect, or hedge, an existing investment.

Range. The high and low prices, or high and low bids and offers, recorded during a specified time.

Relative strength. Movement of a stock price over the past year as compared to a market index (like the S&P 500). A value below 1.0 means that the stock shows relative weakness in price movement (underperformed the market); a value above 1.0 means that the stock shows relative strength over the one-year period. Equation for relative strength is [current stock price/year-ago stock price] divided by [current S&P 500/year-ago S&P 500]. Note that this can be a misleading indicator of performance because it does not take risk into account.

Resistance level. A price level above which it is supposedly difficult for a security or market to rise; price ceiling at which technical analysts note persistent selling of a commodity or security. Antithesis of support level.

Retracement. A price movement in the opposite direction of the previous trend.

Return on equity (ROE). Indicator of profitability; determined by dividing net income for the past 12 months by common stockholder equity (adjusted for stock splits). Result is shown as a percentage. Investors use ROE as a measure of how a company is using its money. ROE may be decomposed into return on assets (ROA) multiplied by financial leverage (total assets/total equity).

Scalp. To trade for small gains. Scalping normally involves establishing and liquidating a position quickly, usually within the same day.

Screen stocks. To analyze various stocks in search of stocks that meet predetermined criteria. For example, a simple value screen would sort all stocks by their price-to-book ratio and pick the stocks with the lowest ratios as candidates for the value portfolio.

Secondary distribution/offering. Public sale of previously issued securities held by large investors, usually corporations or institutions, as distinguished from a primary distribution, where the seller is the issuing corporation. The sale is handled off the New York Stock Exchange by a securities firm or a group of firms, and the shares are usually offered at a fixed price related to the current market price of the stock.

Sector. Used to characterize a group of securities that are similar with respect to maturity, type, rating, industry, or coupon.

Short interest. Total number of shares of a security that investors have sold short and that have not been repurchased to close out the short position. Usually, investors sell short to profit from price declines. As a result, the short interest is often an indicator of the amount of pessimism in the market about a particular security, although there are other reasons to short that are not related to pessimism. For example, hedging strategies for mergers and acquisition as well as derivative positions may involve short sales.

Short position. Occurs when a person sells stocks that he or she does not yet own. Shares must be borrowed, before the sale, to make good delivery to the buyer. Eventually, the shares must be bought back to close out the transaction. This technique is used when an investor believes that the stock price will drop.

Simple moving average. The mean, calculated at any time over a past period of fixed length.

Specialist. On an exchange, the member firm that is designated as the market maker (or dealer for a listed common stock); member of a stock exchange who maintains a "fair and orderly market" in one or more securities. Only one specialist can be designated for a given stock, but dealers may be specialists for several stocks. In contrast, there can be multiple market makers in the over-the-counter market. Major functions include executing limit orders on behalf of other exchange members for a portion of the floor broker's commission as well as buying or selling for the specialist's own account to counteract temporary imbalances in supply and demand and thus to prevent wide swings in stock prices.

Spread. The gap between bid and ask prices of a stock or other security.

Squeeze. Period when stocks or commodities futures increase in price and investors who have sold short must cover their short positions to prevent loss of large amounts of money.

Stochastics index. A computerized tool measuring overbought and oversold conditions in a stock over a certain period.

Stop order (or stop). An order to buy or sell at the market when a definite price is reached, either above (on a buy) or below (on a sell) the price that prevailed when the order was given.

Support level. A price level below which it is supposedly difficult for a security or market to fall (i.e., the price level at which a security tends to stop falling because there is more demand than supply). Can be identified on a technical basis by seeing where the stock has bottomed out in the past.

Target price. In the context of stocks, the price that an investor hopes a stock will reach in a certain time period.

Technical analysis. Security analysis that seeks to detect and interpret patterns in past security prices.

Technical analysts. Analysts who use mechanical rules to detect changes in the supply of and demand for a stock as well as to capitalize on the expected change. Also called chartists or technicians.

Teeny. 1/16 or 0.0625 of one full point in price.

Tick. Refers to the minimum change in price that a security can have, either up or down.

Trading range. The difference between the high and low prices traded during a time period.

Trendline. A technical chart line that depicts the past movement of a security and that is used in an attempt to help predict future price movements.

Treasury. U.S. Department of the Treasury, which issues all Treasury bonds, notes, and bills and oversees agencies. Also, the department within a corporation that oversees its financial operations, including the issuance of new shares.

Uptick rule. SEC rule that selling short is allowed only on an uptick.

Volatility. A measure of risk based on the standard deviation of the asset return. Volatility is a variable that appears in option pricing formulas, where it denotes the volatility of the underlying asset return from now to the expiration of the option.

Zero-sum game. A type of game wherein one player can gain only at the expense of another player.

INDEX